Our Mothers
Our Selves

Our Mothers Our Selves

Writers and Poets Celebrating Motherhood

Edited by

Karen J. Donnelly

and

J. B. Bernstein

BERGIN & GARVEY
Westport, Connecticut • London

Library of Congress Cataloging-in-Publication Data

Our mothers, our selves : writers and poets celebrating motherhood /
    edited by Karen J. Donnelly and J. B. Bernstein.
        p.   cm.
    Includes bibliographical references and index.
    ISBN 0–89789–445–6 (alk. paper)
        1. Motherhood.   2. Motherhood—Literary collections.
I. Donnelly, Karen J.   II. Bernstein, J. B.
HQ759.066   1996
306.874′3—dc20   95–36903

British Library Cataloguing in Publication Data is available.

Library of Congress Catalog Card Number: 95–36903
ISBN: 0–89789–445–6

First published in 1996

Bergin & Garvey, 88 Post Road West, Westport, CT 06881
An imprint of Greenwood Publishing Group, Inc.

Printed in the United States of America

The paper used in this book complies with the
Permanent Paper Standard issued by the National
Information Standards Organization (Z39.48–1984).

10 9 8 7 6 5 4 3 2 1

Copyright Acknowledgments

Contents

II – Beyond Reflection   81

III – Beyond the Whole   167

Introduction

Karen J. Donnelly and J. B. Bernstein

This body is your body, ashes now
and roses, but alive in my eyes, my breasts
my throat, my thighs. You run in me
a tang of salt in the creek waters of my blood,

you sing in my mind like wine. What you
did not dare in your life you dare in mine.
                    —*from* My Mother's Body *by Marge Piercy*

We are our mothers' daughters, our mothers' sons, and our mothers live inside us as we go beyond and extend the meaning of their lives. It is time to join hands and embrace the pain with the joy, to allow for differences, and to bring the celebration of motherhood into the fold of feminism. We must recognize our oneness and pass this strength on to the next generation.

This book was conceived out of love for an idea, an idea that motherhood belongs to everyone; everyone either has one or is one or has the potential to be one. But it has been an idea that has been battered, bruised, blamed, misconceived, degraded, and omitted. We feel motherhood belongs in the forefront of women's, men's, children's, yes, family issues. The experience of motherhood is different for everyone, and these differences need to be explored, admired, respected, accepted, and convened under one protective multicolored umbrella...the stories, poems, essays and pictures preening like a peacock at the height of its beauty.

The first three months of putting together this womb-book were outrageous; our idea changed from a very small seedling to a full-fledged concept, nurtured in the beginning by warm and encouraging responses and submissions from Anna Quindlen, Alicia Ostriker, Sharon Olds, Andrea Dworkin, and Marge Piercy followed by all the other exceptional artists who joined to celebrate motherhood in their own way. We received submissions from all over the world, from both genders, all lifestyles, races, religions, nationalities, and backgrounds. Our goal to make the essence of feminism a way of being in the world, of being free and in control, of sometimes sitting on the edge, yet seeking balance, began to take root.

We have arranged this anthology in three sections, trimesters if you will, to represent motherhood from three points of view: mother to child, child to mother, and to mother and child. The first section, Beyond Self, concerns the process of mothering from the mother's own vantage point; this includes the choice to be a mother or not, to conceive, adopt, abort, in addition to the emotional bonds, the regrets, the ecstasies, the separations, and the reunions.

Beyond Reflection refracts the thoughts and feelings of child toward mother: the inheritances, the rifts, the anger, the warmth, the disappointments, the acceptance, the field of dreams. Mother's eyes become the mirror that reflects her child, but the child pushes barriers and explodes in recognition of self.

In the last section, Beyond the Whole, an onlooker views motherhood from a more out-of-body experience. With one foot in and one foot out, this person can experience the process of motherhood subjectively, yet from a distance. New fathers partake of the birth experience; essayists involve themselves in the fears and joys of adoption; fiction writers mythologize and poets poeticize. A language of metaphors and similes about long-lost mothers, newborn babies, and everything in the middle creates the whole.

The birthing process of this book has been a joy for both of us; the labor pains are easily forgotten and the results will be forever etched, each piece an immortal tribute to an ongoing life force that will braid the spirit of motherhood and feminism into a new proclamation of "inclusivity."

Dedication

J.B.—This book is dedicated to my family...Marshall, Linda, David, and Nicole, my mother who died in April 1993 and my father who would have been proud...to my friends, especially Ronnie and Barbara...to my professors at Southern Connecticut State University...and of course, to my co-editor who complemented not only my skills (or lack of), and my creativity (or lack of), but also my moods and disposition.

K.D.—Without the encouragement and support of my husband, David, *Our Mothers Our Selves* would never have been born. I dedicate this book to him and to our daughters, Cathy and Colleen...to the love and strength I have always received from my parents, George and Norma Miller...to my sisters, Ellen and Jan, and their daughters, Sarah, Alicia, and Jessica. The world needs all the strong women it can get. To J.B., I say thank you. The part of this book that is mine, is yours.

We also thank our agent, Aleta Daley, who kept the faith and provided much-needed encouragement, and Matt McCaffrey, the computer magician, who knew how to do everything and did it on time and with a smile.

I – Beyond Self

My knowledge has soared above me
Beyond intelligence,
Beyond the senses;
But of this I must keep silent
And stay still where I am.

It is like a desert
To be here below,
For here,
Neither sense nor words
Can reach or penetrate.

—Hadewijch of Antwerp, a thirteenth-century Dutch mystic

The Moment the Two Worlds Meet

Sharon Olds

That's the moment I always think of—when the
slick, whole body comes out of me,
when they pull it out, not pull it but steady it
as it pushes forth, not catch it but keep their
hands under it as it pulses out,
they are the first to touch it,
and it shines, it glistens with the thick liquid on it.
That's the moment, while it's sliding, the limbs
compressed close to the body, the arms
bent like a crab's rosy legs, the
thighs closely packed plums in heavy syrup, the
legs folded like the white wings of a chicken—
that is the center of life, that moment when the
juiced bluish sphere of the baby is
sliding between the two worlds,
wet, like sex, it is *sex,*
it is my life opening back and back
as you'd strip the reed from the bud, not strip it but
watch it thrust so it peels itself and the
flower is there, severely folded, and
then it begins to open and dry
but by then the moment is over,
they wipe off the grease and wrap the child in a blanket and
hand it to you entirely in this world.

from A Street in Bronzeville

Gwendolyn Brooks

to David and Keziah Brooks

the mother

Abortions will not let you forget.
You remember the children you got that you did not get,
The damp small pulps with a little or with no hair,
The singers and workers that never handled the air.
You will never neglect or beat
Them, or silence or buy with a sweet.
You will never wind up the sucking-thumb
Or scuttle off ghosts that come.
You will never leave them, controlling your luscious sigh,
Return for a snack of them, with gobbling mother-eye.

I have heard in the voices of the wind the voices of my dim killed children.
I have contracted. I have eased
My dim dears at the breasts they could never suck.
I have said, Sweets, if I sinned, if I seized
Your luck
And your lives from your unfinished reach,
If I stole your births and your names,
Your straight baby tears and your games,
Your stilted or lovely loves, your tumults, your marriages, aches, and
  your deaths,
If I poisoned the beginnings of your breaths,
Believe that even in my deliberateness I was not deliberate.
Though why should I whine,
Whine that the crime was other than mine?—

Since anyhow you are dead.
Or rather, or instead,
You were never made.
But that too, I am afraid,
Is faulty: oh, what shall I say, how is the truth to be said?
You were born, you had body, you died.
It is just that you never giggled or planned or cried.

Believe me, I loved you all.
Believe me, I knew you, though faintly, and I loved, I loved you
All.

How to Live

Meryl Shader

I've been working on my list. Keeping track, Maria. Like you told me.

The things I like are simple, contained. I like buttered toast, when the toasting is unburnt and golden-brown, and the butter spreads evenly across the flaky scalp of bread.

I like color. Bright colors and soft, dusty colors, colors in which something has been added, or taken away. The addition of gray to green, how soft and mossy it becomes, a color to lie down upon, a color upon which to rest your cheek. Or orange with pink, the hot energy of coral, bursting and sexual and full of itself.

I like words. Fancy words, twenty-five-cent words, my father called them. I will not say that to a child, never. Henry can fall in love with anything under the sun, words and sentences like his mother, pottery like his father, or something of his own, aquatics, ethnography, geometric proofs. Anything that brings him the same joy he finds now, suddenly unearthing the mysterious curl of the telephone cord, the fiery rat-a-tat-tat of popcorn in the microwave, his giggly surprise when peek-a-boo eyes appear behind doorways or slatted hands.

For me, there's pleasure in rhythmic sentences, terse, tense stringings of word bursts that jangle the nerves and punch out their meaning. Words like little berries, words plump and pungent. Like *cacophonous,* a clattering, attention-getting word. *Onomatopoeia,* but that's unoriginal—once learned, every junior high schooler throws that around, buzzing or hissing like a fool. I like *laconic,* too—I hear that and think of my high school dates, lanky boys with sexual heebie-jeebies and not much to say.

There are wonderful food words, such as *turmeric,* aromatic and exotic, or *coriander,* as lacy and romantic as an old-fashioned name.

I liked the name *Hannah.*

And Henry. Actually, I like, love, adore everything about Henry: there are no words. There are just the obvious delights, the shape and the sound of him, the hollow wail that means tired, tired; the smile when he first sees me, the way it tugs up the corners of his mouth, dimpling a space below his eye, lighting his face. It is bliss, it is pure reward.

I like the murky slate stage his eyes are passing through, blue becoming brown, different in different lights. I like the look of him sleeping: arms spread-eagle, the width of him extended within crib walls, a papoose-like bulge of blue terrycloth. His hair, sparse and white-gold, fuzzes his scalp, a thread-bare cap that I cup with my palm; it rises, gently, and drops, as breath goes in and out.

I like Henry's striped overalls. Essence of little boyness, I say as I scoot a diaper out from under him and button him up. He grins at me, his cheeks dented and gooey, tightening a fist around the toy he makes of my finger.

Henry looks like Hart.

I like Hart's beard. Like a bird's nest, it looks softer than it touches, built from thick brown thatches and streaks of grey-white. I have woven my fingers through it countless times, noting the uneven growth from left to right, its comforting weight. It was the first thing on Hart I wanted to touch.

I like and also hate, because of what it tears inside, the way that Hart looks when he hands Henry over to me at the end of a visit. His face withers, collapsing into puckery folds of skin. From that face I know that Henry will always be all right, even if something happens to me. I know his father looks at him with my own sense of marvel and reverence. This boy of ours is an unbounded miracle, seemingly unrelated to the colicky coupling that produced him. Sunday afternoons, I collect Henry into my arms and watch Hart's face collapse, offering cups of coffee which are refused; but brittle and wary, we meet this way and compare notes: he drank so many ounces of formula, he liked sweet potatoes but refused carrots, the bruise was there on Friday, not to worry.

I appreciate this. I am grateful for whatever Hart can manage. I can drop by, sometimes; we have gotten that far. Surprise visits are allowed, a joy that I want for my boy, to know and love his father; and his studio behind the store is a destination that gives purpose to our afternoon walks.

Hart may go blank for a moment, putting aside tools, the flinty shapes he teases into clay, wedges, jars of murky glaze, as if hiding the magic he works with his hands. Nails muddy and encrusted, or soppy with wet clay, he wipes them on the lap of his apron, and then lifts his head out from under it, regaining himself, greeting Henry and then me.

His work still seems like magic to me, even now: that dark liquids, granite green or cloudy dark, once fired, bring forth cinnamon red, or spattered patterns of bluish streaks; there is no resemblance between the blaze of the finished work and the original tears of glaze that drip, sad and thick, down the cheeks of dishes Hart lines up for firing. I used to wander in, quietly seating myself on a splattered stool. I'd examine the day's work, trying to predict from the unfinished pieces what would emerge from the kiln. I was rarely right, but ever amazed. Hart would nod and smile, not speaking. I didn't penetrate his fog of concentration, didn't want to.

Now Hart cannot work with my eyes on him or his work, and he stops everything to focus on Henry, sometimes unsnapping him from the stroller and lifting him high above his head before telling me hello. Makes the whooshing sound that Henry adores, blowing air through his teeth and motoring him about the room, high above the worktables and soupy, clay-splashed surfaces, guiding our son in flight.

I do like being a mother.

I am less afraid, now.

I have met several baby Hannahs, and no longer back away from them, worrying, shooting looks of fear at their mothers, unaware of what they risk, asking so much of their girls. I liked that name, too.

An old name, it seemed a gift I could give my daughter, to greet her on this side of the womb. A symmetrical name, Hannah, two syllables, perfectly inverted, reflecting back on each other. Han–nah. Balanced, like yin and yang. And solid, grounded in history.

Hello, Hannah. We practiced saying it, danced, singing the name, waltzing ungracefully, separating the stomachs of our bodies, ungainly as bears but silly with giddy grins. Hart hummed her name above the bulge of taut skin she slept beneath, buzzing me with the surface of his lips.

But of course I did not greet her, plied from darkness and sticky membranes, and then resettled against my chest, cushioned inside my arms.

Instead, pieces dislodged and drained, discovered as cramping, bloodied splotches. Hart crying with me, bundling my body into towels, as if diapered, whisking me into the rusted station wagon. Gripping and patting my arm. Hold on, Nina, we're almost there. Oh, he tried. Steered with one hand, patting, tap-tap-tub, to calm me, keep us connected, webbed together, not alone. I left him, though, wailing for Hannah. Shrieked, even, squeezing his arms white, then quiet, steely quiet, a tight wire of control in which there was no baby.

For a time I truly believed we'd killed her with that name. Nothing that perfect, nothing so seamless as *Hannah* could survive. Our love, unseamless and imperfect, could not sustain a Hannah, could never have kept her alive.

This passed. I am not afraid to look at the Hannahs I meet, children in Henry's day care, girls introduced when we mothers stop each other on the street, smiling and peering into the other's stroller, members of the same club of baby worshippers. The Hannahs may grip my finger. I will even hold them, let them rest their hands against my neck, wrap little legs around my waist. I am not choked, now, fearful of killing them, worried that their breaths will stop, their limbs splinter and fold.

Hart said we'd have another baby.

Not Hannah, I told him. Never a Hannah.

Hart never really understood, touched cool washcloths to my temples and waited for me to heal, and then wanted a sorrowful rejoining, a careful placing of limbs, a ceremonial miming of the sweaty, heated sex that had raged through our bodies. But I could not, would not let him back into places where Hannah had swum, could not let him hammer against fragments that might still be there, howling silently, lost ghosts of summer.

After Hannah, my body shriveled and expelled. Blood, blood, I was supposed to look upon the coughing up of my insides as normal, cleansing; but I felt instead as if she were clutching, battered by a tide that eventually drained her from me, in splotches and drops. An ugly process, my own body cruel and determined.

We could use it to glaze your pots, I told Hart. Reds are hard, he'd always said, difficult and therefore prized. I reminded him of this.

He looked away. He looked at his hands.

I began to swim again. I had liked swimming. I went every day, padding vigorous, unenthused strokes through chilly water, mending, or trying to; stepping out, dripping and shivery, shaking like a wet terrier, blue-cold.

You were always a good swimmer, Hart said.

I like being praised.

I took pride in punctiliousness. I hung my suit, towel, goggles, and cap every night in a neat row that filled the bathroom with the smell of chlorine.

I'm proud of you, Hart said.

She's a good teacher, they told Hart. If she needs time off, that's all right. She can come back when she's better, we'll have a class for her. They sent flowers.

I like flowers, and everything to do with flowers. Flower paraphernalia, bud vases and ceramic bowls and wicker baskets, containers in which flowers can lean, exhale, and droop. I like flower shops, and florists, if they really know their blossoms, don't just lazily pull a few tired stems, wrap them in cellophane and a generic yellow ribbon. I like a place in town in which a young Chinese woman asks me about my mood. She listens, nods. Her husband interrupts, calling out from the back, suggesting lilies for my table, jonquils for a friend. One of the other teachers, a friend, remembered, and they ordered mine from that store. The arrangement came with two notes, one from the school, and another one, printed in Chinese with the translation penned on the back in black, acrobatic strokes. So very sorry you have sick trouble, it said.

I liked the arrangement. There were daffodils and tulips, sunny and fresh and optimistic. I put them on the front mantle.

I began to notice other people at the outdoor pool, swimmers who came or left while I was there, recognizable faces in the locker room, familiar swimsuits in lanes near mine.

I noticed one woman who walked out in a terry robe, a floral print of riotous blues and lavenders. I liked the crazy colors with which she decorated herself: polka-dotted bikini, quilted cotton bag, purple Spandex headband that lifted thick, round curls of dark hair from her eyes. She lay on the grassy area, rubbing gel into her arms and legs, leaning back to catch the last rays of afternoon sun that were blown about with the petals that decayed and dropped.

One day, a sudden windiness slapped at the surfaces of the water and sent everyone else out of the lanes and into the heated dressing rooms. I was holding onto the cement side, panting, unwrapping hair that clung like seaweed to my face and eyes, preparing for another set.

You a fish, or what? she said.

To me.

Hey, aren't you cold? She had wrapped a chartreuse-and-yellow striped towel around her middle. On her, it looked long and chic, a strapless summer thing. She was meandering back towards the locker room, squinting in the direction of the pool, the wind whipping at the bottom of the towel. I looked up at her, teeth on edge, arms pimply with goosebumps.

Do you remember?

Of course you were beautiful. That was never a question, not in your mind, I'm sure, with your careless, raucous sense of yourself. You were just being friendly.

I like friendliness. I respect it, let's say. I appreciate what friendly means, soldering humans together, easing us into acquaintanceships, making us feel less singular, less bubbled and sealed off in our own experience. I was awkward. But it was nice to be spoken to.

There was a drawl, a slowness to certain syllables. It was charming.

Her name is Maria, I told Hart. I have a new friend at the pool, I said.

I began to like swimming a lot.

I arrived before you did, slicing through my laps with knife-like efficiency, looking out for your splashy figure as I came up for air. You'd wave to me, a big hello, and I'd continue, pleased by the attention.

Soaked and exhausted, I'd spread a towel beside yours and plop down. We bought drinks from the machine, little tins of metallic apple juice. You avoided junk food, wouldn't share the candy bars I chewed with fierce hunger, but then brought apricot rolls, peach bars, delicious, with oats and grape sweetening, you instructed.

I liked you very much.

All I can say is that I really didn't know what I was doing, didn't recognize. And I had been not myself, or too deep inside myself, with sick trouble, although you did not know that.

And I'd always intended to try again, to have a baby, to make a family. Nina, you said.

Do you remember?

By then our picnics were delicious, illicit: I'd sneak in wine or champagne in an old plaid thermos, and we sat in the farthest, brushiest area away from the pool. It was decadent, summer fun, but the talking was real. Our families, where we came from, your research, friends, anything at all.

Nina, you said. You don't know how to live.

There was no one around. It was light, but late, and the splashing had stopped and only a few people at a distance, resuming street clothes and regular lives were clicking their shoes hurriedly, en route to their cars.

I was not insulted. I was curious. A bee was buzzing around in a nearby patch, and I was aware of its presence, and the fact that I might need to move away, or remain on guard.

It was not so different from kissing Hart. You smelled of suntan lotion, a coconut perfume, and I thought for a brief moment of food, something I might want to hold in my mouth.

It was a very short kiss, nothing to be observed.

You should come to my house, you said.

I liked that kiss very much.

I did not know that I was pregnant. I told that to Hart, later, as if there were some consolation in that. I don't know if it would have mattered, if knowing would have stopped me from seeing you.

Seeing you. Touching you, inhaling you, uncovering and exposing, and it was so much I hadn't counted on, such newness and silk, diaphonous beauty no longer hidden.

But you said it again. Nina, you don't know how to live.

You said there was sadness under everything. With me, there was always a holding back, a secret.

Before I knew you, I said.

Everyone has secrets, you said. Everyone has had sadnesses.

All right, I said.

Do you remember?

This is how to live, you said. You have to make lists of what you like, and review them often. That's all there is to it, you said. That's the way to live. You don't know what you like.

What do you like? I asked.

Lots of things, you said. Zydeco music. Daylight savings time. Your smile was sly. I like tits, you said.

Do you like mine? I asked.

What happened next was very nice.

I like mud, you said. You told me more about gardening, what you grew, the silty feel of dirt in your fingers, the curve of bulbs. We went out to the yard, naked, stubbed our toes in dark soil. You ran dill across my back.

I like my breasts, you know. A funny thing to admit. They're small, wide-ish, flat, not the pert globes I once wanted. I like that I like them, as if I'm finally accepting the truth of my lanky, square-hipped body.

I understand that you could not bear to be around when Henry was born, but you missed the miracle of my life. I know you were hurt, and Hart was tearing apart, but he stayed with me, cried over Henry's head in the staggering emotion of birth.

You were right, Maria. I didn't know how to live. I am trying to learn, though. I would like to learn.

I am noticing myself, as best I can with an infant who howls and sleeps and needs me when he needs me, without regard for clocks or schedules or sleepy wishes of mine.

I liked those evenings we drove off in your funny old car and parked at the base of slippery hills just outside the city.

A surprise, you told me, daring me to race you up, up, up. Insane! I said, since only an insane animal would move quickly in such muggy heat. Only mad dogs and Englishmen! You only laughed, daring me, peeling off the slimy tank top that clung to your damp back, the aqua darkening in the wettest spots. You beat me, and then stood, panting, looking down from your triumphant height. You were radiant, Maria, the last bit of sun shining behind you, you were gold and lean and strong. Sweat trickled into my eyes as I stood still, catching my breath. My eyes smarted, that's what I said when I finally reached you, but really, it was you, it was knowing what I'd reach at the end of my climb, that's what teared my eyes.

Oh, Maria.

The surprise: a sudden, shadowy pathway behind a sledge of branches, door-like, you pushed aside. And then a narrow river of sunlight, silvery rays that illuminated a bed of mossy leaves. Like a jungle clearing, you said; I was almost spooked, reverential before such old quiet, and you wanted me back, silly with lust and fun. You came up from behind, bouncing on jelly-legs, making bird sounds, hoots to distract, turn me giggly. Feathery fingers at my throat, and humid breaths, the small pinkness of tongue, first tracing, then sparrow-like and darting.

No, no, I said at first, wanting my new piousness. I had in mind a silent sit, a chance to breathe in wisdom, smelling life.

But you, your warm skin, and shiny, glistening hair. Slender wrists and tapered fingers, all the curves, big and little, echoed again and again across our bodies. Earlobe and belly, underside of breast, round nipple, heel of foot. Quickening, everything breathy and tightening, knotted, then given away. Floating, Maria, high, high up, if only briefly.

So now. I am doing what you said. I'm looking out for what I like. I am making lists. I am reminding myself of things that sweeten my view, things that make me suck in my breath, or razz my senses or settle my muscles, easing me, washing my soul.

I like the way the light looks at this time of day, warm but turning, becoming blue, then dark, ready for night.

Barbecue smells waft in from the neighborhood, and calls of kids over fences and across parks, their mothers hurrying them, wanting to see their faces across a table of white corn and chicken and watermelon chunks.

I bustle about with Henry, talking as if he understands me, as if we're really in conversation about whether or not to cook pasta tonight, whether the strawberries will really be sweet or just look that way. I tell him about the choices in the video store, what movie we might rent, or whether it's going to be a night of grading papers, correcting spelling errors with red pens and gold stars.

I like you, Maria.

You're on my list, Maria.

Sometimes, when Henry is asleep, I think I will begin some productive task, laundry, or a letter, but instead I sink against the couch, letting the give of pillows hold my back. With my lids closing, I lean into cushions, breathing slowly, my body heavy. Against the smoky frame of partial-sleep, I see you, Maria. Not saying goodbye, not telling me that I can't have you and family life with Hart. Not gasping with rage or hurt at my enormous stomach, the one you said excluded, the one that told you I wouldn't leave him behind.

In these moments, I see you again on top of the hill, glowing and proud, grinning down towards me, wiping your forehead, trying to slick back the curls that droop against your wet skin. Your arms are wide open, coaxing me, then extending out and up, as if reaching for everything, as if the horizon itself were not big enough for the sound and smell of summer. As if you could suck in your breath and hold forever the quieting heat of afternoon, the thrill of unhidden skin, the salty bliss of movement and escape.

And I'm making my way towards you, Maria. Struggling, panting, never easy with new climbs, but pushing, coming up to what you've found. Only this time it doesn't end away from the world, dappled in semi-darkness and hidden. This time, sick trouble doesn't touch us, and Hart is given his due. Henry is sleeping behind the brush, peaceful in his nap, quiet for the time it takes to hold close to another woman and feel her pulse against the damp ground.

Miscarriage

Rawdon Tomlinson

The day before, a freak blast of hail
stripped the leaves like locusts,
fashioning a garden of black juices and spikes,
pitting the melons, cracking their vines
to dried umbilical cords, knocking tomatoes green
to the ground, neatly shedding a dead dress of leaves
around the base of each tree.

Last night the cold moved in with a full moon
and blood. (Some thing knew something.)
Your body contracted like a drunk's
with the dry heaves, laboring with death—
hope and fear adrift
in the middle-of-the-ocean dark.

I rake the leaves; I rake
as our daughter walks circles under a sky
washed bruise; I rake as the painkiller drops you to sleep.
The gray-green undersides of maple leaves
are scattered like fish belly up in a lake,
their black fingers curled back brittle;
I rake them into piles the wind takes;
I rake as blackbirds of hot light
and stainless steel with blood bright as spray paint
strafe and peck the nerves to bits.
I rake into the night.

—Now the movie of glass children, each word
an incision. What you have seen you haven't seen
but know by the hole it makes in you
through which all of the whys fall,

trapped like crazy sparrows that continue
building the nest after the chicken hawk.

In your nightmare you try fitting its head back
onto its body, grasping it slippery as a trout.
I drive to work outside my body;
you slice tomatoes full of blood.
One evening, we share the only melon
ripe enough to harvest from the hail,
while our daughter, her red hair glistening,
dances to wind and light.

With Child

Mary Connor Ralph

I wait in an icy room for the doctor to come and take you, this bit of life, from my womb. He told me you are dead. I don't believe him. You have not moved or given me your heartbeat to hold, but I feel you there, a small beginning, reliant on me to become. Within minutes of your implanting, when you were cells splitting and regrouping, I felt you there. I would know if you died.

But there was the blood. So much blood, much too soon. I had to see the doctor, and he said you were dead.

I wait. Pregnancy is the waiting room. In this room, in six more months, you would be born. I would watch in the mirror as you slip from me into life. What will this be like, to watch them vacuum you out? I think I will go mad.

I am slipping away from this. Those pills, that nurse in the cheerful room, to prepare me she said. This nurse, another smiling one, unwraps a tray. Busy work until the doctor comes. Sterile tools. Are these what he will probe with when he hunts my womb to find where you lie hidden, my tiny aquatic gymnast? Tiny knife, large clamps, other shapes, other sizes. What are these things called? They must have names, recorded in a book, engraved in the doctor's memory. You have no name. You will be recorded as D & C.

I turn my head, close my eyes.

Someone else is here, whispering to the nurse. I fight my eyes open. He leans over me, "Curl into a tight ball."

The anesthetist.

I remember I did this when your sister was born, delivered to me by the same doctor who has pronounced you miscarried. I did not do this, miss carry you. I've cradled you in my body these months, curled tight around you, as I do now, to expose my back to the stab of needle.

The nurse rolls me over again. We wait. The anesthetist leaves. I want the spinal to take hold, want to feel my feet and legs go, to feel the unfeeling spread up to my barely rounded belly. Will you feel it? They tell me you are dead, you should feel nothing.

The numbness doesn't come all at once, only creeps up one side.

The anesthetist returns. Someone wheels in a machine, shiny and forbidding. I won't look at it. The doctor comes. I look at him. He is not the one who has pronounced you miscarried. He is another in the long list of names at the Ob-Gyn offices. We have not had time to meet them all. The anesthetist and nurse whisper with him.

I introduce us. "I'm not frozen. Please, not yet. I can still feel."

He pats my shoulder and turns to snap on plastic gloves. It echoes in the sterile room.

The anesthetist says, "You're fine."

No more drowsiness. I pump with terror. "No, I can feel."

"No," he says, "Wiggle your toes."

I wiggle my foot, shake my leg. "See? Look."

The doctors mumble unilateral something, something. "Roll over." Another injection.

We wait. They whisper, I cry. I hear my words in another voice, clogged with mucus. "Please don't do this. Don't take my baby."

I look up to the nurse. She is not smiling now. "Please," I whisper. She turns her back, back to the tray of tools.

I have run out of words, lie mute in sadness and fear, but I can't stop the tears. I sob and it echoes.

"I can knock her out," the anesthetist says. He fusses with a tube in my arm. I see it, but I don't feel it.

The doctor glances at his watch. "No. I think she'll be fine."

No, I want to tell him, I'll never be fine again. Never. The words become more tears. "Anyone examine her?" the doctor asks. The nurse turns to him. "Yes, not here. Your office."

He reads my chart as she tells him that his associate examined me, then sent me here for the D & C. He puts down my chart, checks his watch again.

"Almost ready," the anesthetist says.

The doctor decides to kill time by examining me again. I open my numbing legs and watch his gloved hand slip inside. I can't feel it. Can you?

He shakes his head at the anesthetist and the nurse. I look at the ceiling as he withdraws his hand.

"Cervix is tight, completely closed."

What?

"Who sent her? I'm not doing this."

What did he say? The snap of plastic gloves. As I start to float up to the ceiling, the doctor leans over me, pats my shoulder. "You haven't lost your baby."

I grip the sides of the metal table, blink, focus on his mouth. It says, "We'll keep you for a few days. Rest. You're threatening to miscarry. We have to wait and see."

Threatening. Wait. See.

The doctors leave. The nurse sits, monitors my blood pressure as it leaps and dives. I float and freeze, shake and cry, but you are alive. Wait. Hold on for the next six months. I promise you, when we enter this room again, you will have a birthday.

I wait in this darkened room for the sound of your key in the lock. There is the click of your heels on the stair. You cough, the door swings, the others, your friends and our family, spring from hiding. "Surprise," they shout.

I open my mouth, but no words, here come the tears. I stand in front of you with my offering, and stare mutely at your boy-becoming-man body. You tower over me, your shoulders broad enough to carry the weight of your growing. Your smile hugs me.

You might benefit from braces, but you've refused the orthodontists' dream. I like the way you've chosen to live out your life with this small imperfection, an oversight of Mother Nature. These crooked teeth were invisible buds in your gums when you were born. Wrapped in their womb of pink skin, these teeth waited patiently for their turn, waited through the birth of your baby teeth, pushed when their time came, crowded into the space they were offered. Now, I see how they shine as you suck in a deep breath to blow out your sixteen candles.

Lines For One As Yet Unnamed

Harry Brody

Birds argue over what water is,
and who can blame them as it has
been raining six days on and off.
So a second child wets my lover's womb.
Walking the beach at night with our
three-year-old son, we watch lightning
vein a storm still stalled at sea.
How fine our faces, floating
in the stale pools, feel, lit
first by those yellow forks, then cast
adrift in the darkness like embryos!
Mornings, you are not so certain.
The world lurches after sleeping late,
and birds learn to fly when they're thrown.
Today's week one. You sicken and say,
How I survive is last night's dream
of the child's face, then rise
and race in to release
that part of you the child's displaced.

Fist First

C. D. Runyon

The night before you were born, you kicked inside my enormous belly while I stabled the lambs. I tried bribing them into the barn with handfuls of grain, but they'd become suspicious in their last pasturing days. Finally I dragged them into the pen. That was the first night they didn't graze under the kitchen window while your father and I sipped our tea. All summer long, they'd interrupted our hushed evening conversations with their incessant bleating. The larger lamb broke into the grain shed and got a swollen belly in early autumn, nearly died, but he lived and fattened. The smaller lamb sensed danger in the frost tipped grass and the smell of wood smoke from the first fire of the season: wouldn't grain the last few days, refused to nuzzle my palm.

The slaughterer, keeping his strict schedule, pulled into the frost buckled driveway next morning. I told your sister and brother to stay inside. The slaughterer's hardy son jumped out of the cab and headed straight for the stalls, not breaking his stride as he loaded the pistol. The first lightning bolt shot through my womb, and I massaged my huge tummy. The slaughterer said, "We're only in the area for the day; next morning we'll be doing the Northeast Kingdom." He winked at me. "Tomorra you'll be doing diapers, I betcha," he said.

I was relieved; wanted them and their death tools as far away as possible when you came. We heard one shot, then the next and I felt sorry for the one that had to watch. The son dragged Wooly Bear (as your father named him) out of the barn by his hind legs, attached him to a meat hook and hung him. The blood steamed as it poured into the plank bucket. The slaughterer threw entrails to the chickens and your father dumped the rich, ruby blood on the slumbering garden. I called the midwife, and she raced over, thinking my third would come fast, parked her truck behind the slaughterer's. I morbidly imagined her truck battery dying, delaying the slaughterer's departure, your father scrambling for jumper cables, and offering them a cup of hot cider. I willed them far away. The midwife glanced at the bloody show in the barnyard and said, "You want to have this baby now?"

Now is never convenient although it is persistent. The present takes getting used to. I knew someday I'd laugh about all this, but I wasn't laughing then. Through the wall of my womb, I told you sternly that the lambs were being slaughtered and I had to get them to the butcher; so you should stay inside.

Your father didn't want to raise lambs. He was vegetarian until we married. He gave me a look that said: I won't have any hand in this. I told him you were coming, and I couldn't handle things alone. He softened and said, "The lambs are getting to be a pain in the ass anyway, breaking out of the pasture every other week."

Your father held the carcasses down while the slaughterer skinned them. Your father said, "She wants to make a baby bunting." The slaughterer grunted and tossed the bloody hides at my feet. I ran inside the house, trailing warm amniotic waters.

"Not long now," the midwife said.

"Feels like this baby is kicking my cervix," I said.

She had me lie down and palpated you. She found your round little behind pressed up near my ribs and said, "This baby is head down and ready to come."

I changed out of my wet clothes while your father loaded the meat into the back of the station wagon. The midwife pulled her truck out of the way, said she'd wait, and the slaughterer pulled his cap around his ears with his bloody paws. He advised us to get the pumpkins in. "It's getting cold in earnest," he said. He threw meat hooks, ropes and hanging tripod into the back of his truck. He said parsnips should winter in-ground to sweeten, warned us, "Take the skins to the tanner before they rot." His son patted his pistol holster as a goodbye gesture, and the slaughterer gunned the engine and sped away.

Your father drove, break neck, taking the curves like a pro. The thick smell of blood filled the car. He carried Lamb Chops (as I liked to call him), and I carried Wooly Bear into the butcher. "Want the organs?" the butcher asked. The contractions lessened. When we got home we sent the midwife away.

I took the pumpkins in that night and made a pie while your father fetched the lambs and installed them in the freezer. I asked him not to touch the pie until you were born, but later that night I saw that a slice was missing.

At dawn, I woke up. One shot. Then another. I told your father that they were killing again. He called the midwife and sent your brother and sister to the neighbor. Your father sat at the foot of the bed reading the sports page, and I asked him to help. He placed cool towels on my forehead and the midwife listened to your heart during a contraction. She frowned, but another contraction pushed me out of myself and I forgot to ask her about your heartbeat. When the pain subsided, I became aware of the midwife whispering to your father. I heard the word hospital like a curse.

"I feel like pushing," I said.

"Great," the midwife said. I thought I heard dread in her voice. She pulled latex gloves on and said, "This baby's in trouble, so you listen to me..."

I blanked out on what she was saying. I pushed. No feeling in this world compares with that urgency.

"It's a fist," your father said. I pushed again, but nothing happened.

"Again," the midwife said. She was clearly alarmed.

I pushed harder than I ever had with your brother and sister. Again, nothing.

I knew the danger signs; you were stuck. I said, "I didn't mean it. I was just too busy yesterday with blood, skins and meat. But the lambs are in the freezer now, and you should come."

"Listen to me," the midwife said. "We have to give this baby more room. On your hands and knees."

"I can't do it myself," I said.

It took all their strength, but your father pulled and the midwife pushed my bulky body into a hands and knees position while I contracted. She cut me open with a scalpel, reached inside me and pulled you out, squeezed blue as dawn, not breathing.

Naked and sweating, and still on my hands and knees, I prayed. I'd never prayed before, but I sensed for the first time in my life God's personal residence in me and you. God, if you breathe life into my baby I will remember for the rest of my life: thine will, not mine, be done.

Breathe! I said. Your father held his, and the midwife worked on you. Outside, it was snowing scattered flakes. Suddenly, I felt frightened, abandoned, cold and tired in that dreadful silence. Let me die, I said. I can't live if I lose this baby. When you finally cried, I cried and life flushed into us.

"She's crying," your father said joyfully. "She's crying."

We named you Rachel Fleeta, which means a swift ewe.

The midwife rubbed your skin until you turned pink, and I held you while the midwife stitched me up. Your eyes, calm, deep and searching locked with mine. We didn't take our eyes off each other, and I put my finger in your defiant little fist and I marveled at your grip on life.

I offered the midwife some pumpkin pie. She told me to rest, but I insisted. I wrapped you in a blanket and took you on your first visit to the kitchen. Your father put on his red plaid cap and said he'd be right back. He took the placenta and buried it deep where animals wouldn't find it. He dug up parsnips and gave them to the midwife in a paper sack along with her check. I nursed you while they had pie and tea together, the freezer humming its winter song.

The Bearing Woman

Judith A. Downey

With supple limbs and features fair
Goddess bless this babe I bear.

How many times had I sung the ancient birthing chant since the first contraction startled me out of sleep in the Hour Before Birdsong? Its rhythm had carried me through the morning and through the anxious moments when the fluid cradling my babe had gushed from between my legs.

The sunlight patterning the polished wood floor of my chamber told me it was not close to Even Hour, but it seemed this day had already lasted an eternity. I was as weary of the chant as of the grinding pain. My shift and the linen beneath me were sodden, as if I had lain too long in the midsummer grass and been drenched by the morning dew.

Eyes shut, I strove to gather my strength for the next contraction when the midwife's grating voice broke over me.

"I told you, dearie, you got to keep atop the pains. Don't let them bring you down! Breathe deep; then when one comes on, pant like a dog in the summer sun. And count—before you reach fifty, it'll be gone. I know you've had your schooling. You can count that high."

My eyes flew open as I readied a retort about trading places and letting her see how high she could count, but lost the opportunity to deliver it as she continued.

"You've hours yet to go and my man will be wanting his dinner. I'll leave you now, but I'll be back well before it's time. Davin can see to you for a while. He's handy enough with the mares, and it'll give him something to do for he's prowling around the door like a hungry cat. A lucky girl you are, Madrigal, to have a man like that."

I started to say I was no foaling mare and she was being paid to stay with me, but my words were lost in the bustle of her departure and her instructions to Davin.

"Just wipe her face with that cloth from time to time; let her wet her lips with the wine—but mind, no more than that. Yes, you can hold her hand, but it'll do more good for you than it does for her." Her grunting laugh followed her toward the door.

Experience she might have, but her fellowship was not to be cherished during the anxious hours at a bearing woman's side. What I wished most at that moment, more even than surcease of pain, was to rise from my bed and slap the laughter from her mouth. But if I tried, I'd most likely roll onto the chamber floor and burst open like an over-ripe melon.

"Keep your tongue behind your teeth, Sulfi, if you cannot speak gently," I heard my heart mate say.

Then another contraction swooped down, sharp-clawed as a hunting hawk, so that I panted like a bitch in heat, drumming my heels against the mattress straw, cursing aloud instead of counting. When it receded, I was alone with its memory and with my husband.

Before coming to my side, Davin washed his hands thoroughly, something the midwife had failed to do. He fumbled a cloth from a pottery bowl on the nightstand. Then, water still dripping to the floor, he turned to lay it on my forehead. His face was a mask, as if he were unsure if he should offer sympathy and unwilling to smile while I felt pain.

After placing the cloth across my brow, he took my hand as if I were a porcelain doll, the kind seen at the harvest fair, too dear to own and too fragile to be held. I knew he would not speak until I did.

"Thank you, love. It pleases me to have you near," I said and pressed his hand. It was then his smile came, unlooked for as a primrose on the path after a harsh winter, and more welcome.

"If I had known how it would be…I never thought it would be as bad as this…Madrigal, I love you so. If I could take the pain for my own, I would."

My heart mate, the father of my babe—how dear he was as he sought to comfort me, but no matter what he wished he would never know the pain of bearing. Nor would he feel the joy of carrying new life under his heart or the wonder of that first flutter of movement, like a tiny bird beneath his hand.

My Davin is a farmer. But how could even a farmer know such kinship with the fecund earth? Farmers spent hapless hours unconscious of the grain ripe fields, neglecting them for other joys or sorrows. But what bearing woman can forget the babe she carries when it makes its presence felt a hundred times a day?

I remembered watching our crops greening in the field, running my hands over my rounding belly and thinking, "My child grows strong and ripe as wheat. It will be born at harvest and will add to the wealth of the world just as the bearing earth does." Could any man feel or understand such joy?

And what man can share the fears a woman experiences as her time draws near—the threat of stumbling on the stairs and doing harm to the babe within; the dread that the child might be less than perfect; the senseless midnight terror that you carry a changeling child—and the dark desire to tear it from your womb.

So lost in musings was I that, for a time, the pain seemed a distant thing. I lay content—my heart mate near, my hand within his own; waiting—waiting for our child, my child to be born.

Then once again I writhed in torment—aware only of the strain of tortured muscles, as if my body must be split for the babe to come forth; the taste of blood upon my lips; and thoughts of dying close at hand.

There came the coolness of wine against my lips and Davin's voice sounding loudly in my ears, to distract me—or himself.

"If it's a boy, I'll see he learns to read and write. No mere farmer will he be, but a page to a great lord or apprenticed in the city, learning to work gold or be a scribe. And if the babe's a girl, I'll save my coin and dower her with gold enough to catch a prince. She'll never feed pigs or be a goose girl. She'll learn to be a lady."

"Let her be a woman first." My voice must have been a croak for Davin leaned toward me as if he had not heard. "She must be a woman, love, not a plaything for a man, however rich he is. A girl can shape her own life if she has the chance. My child will be a woman first."

His laughter followed the smile I treasured so. "Could she not be a little girl, for a short time at least? So I may buy her sky blue ribbons at the fair and dolls and other pretty things?"

I laughed too, and once again the pain moved back a pace. But in my most secret heart, I knew the things that I would teach if this babe were a girl.

"The cradle's here. All ready for the babe." Davin moved the newly made cradle toward the bed, lifting it so that I might see that it had been filled with well-washed lambs' wool covered by embroidered linen. At its foot was folded a snow white shawl. The burnished wood had been tenderly carved with leaping rabbits and gamboling lambs.

While I had sewn tiny gowns and pillow slips before the fire, Davin had labored nightly in its carving, rubbing the wood to a gleaming polish, handling the cradle as gently as he handled me.

The image of a child in that cradle, crying, drove me back inside the pain as if I sought escape from thought. For what did I know of babes?

I had been the youngest of my parents' brood. They farmed the plains with no Close Kin or neighbors within a two day ride so I had never minded younger children as most young women do. Oh, I had cared for lambs and brought home countless birds and such, tending them to health, cradling in my arms those that would allow, and crooning to them by the hour. I even had a piglet once—a tender little thing who let himself be loved until I dressed him in my shift and mother's best town bonnet.

But this would be my first child, my first babe. How would I know what to do?

Now that I lived near Peravay, there were mothers round me often. They told me tales and gave advice and even let me hold their babes. But, eventually, even the most cheerful child would cry and all my stroking and sweet words would not make it stop.

Then its mother would come and say, "Of course, he's wet and must be changed," or "She's a hungry little girl, that's all." But how was one to tell? What secret sense did they possess, the way each ewe can tell its lamb and every mare its foal? How could they know the babe wanted suck, or had wind, or needed to be changed? And yet they did, telling me that by its cry I'd know too, once my own was born.

I was afraid that I could give the child my breast but little else besides. And who would be there to assist me until I knew my babe and all its ways? My mother's spirit had long since been released from earthly cares, and Davin would be no help. He'd be back in the fields as soon as this was over, leaving me alone to cope. Swallowed up by fear were all the times he had done my chores as well as his own so that I might sit in the sun and dream, all the dinners he had cooked and all the evenings he'd spent at my side.

Spitefully, I dug my nails into his hand when the next contraction washed over me.

Then, like an unlooked for gift, a thought came to me. Of course! This child was mine alone to bear, mine to care for—if only I could offer up the comfort of my breast, then only I could cherish and could nurture. My heart mate would love the babe, playing with it in the evening before the warming hearth, but this child was mine—mine in a way no man could ever understand. Its flesh and bone were part of me—and carried beneath my heart for all this time, surely I knew it better than any could. When it cried, how could I fail to understand? I saw then that the other women spoke the truth.

And I felt such sadness that Davin would never know this joy that I took up the hand I had hurt and brought it to my lips to heal, filled with a tender compassion that I had not known before.

Time drew out. I wandered in a maze of pain out of which I struggled from time to time to sip from the cup Davin offered, to listen to his songs and praise his steadfast efforts at my side.

Gradually, the pain became a white hot fire and I grew so lost I knew not who I was or what I labored for. Then a contraction gripped me—fiercer than any that had come before, so that my body bent like a bow beneath the strain. And with it an urge to push so overwhelming I thought the babe must burst from between my thighs as a squeezed olive spits forth its pit.

Davin's exuberant cries echoed in my ears as if he were calling down a well. "That's right, push now. Push, Madrigal! I can see the head!"

Now, truly, I felt no more than a mare or ewe under his competent hands, doing what I could—pressing the babe out as if the entire world would burst from between my thighs. Crying—laughing—exulting in the strength with which my child sprang forth.

After an eternity, welcoming the sudden freedom from suffering's sharp claws, I must have drifted off. Davin's voice disturbed my hard won peace. Through barely open eyes, I saw him holding out the babe. Tears coursed down his cheeks and I must wake to hear his words.

"It's a girl, Madrigal, a daughter beautiful as you," he whispered, and laid her in my arms.

Exultation such as I had never felt swept over me as I gazed for the first time upon my daughter's face. This was the sum of anxious waiting and of agony—the ultimate expression of my female self. I thought senselessly of our half wolf bitch who howled her triumph at the moon each time she bore a litter. I knew I, too, could howl that way, ordering the world to rejoice in what it now possessed. And, with the same fierceness, I too would bare my teeth and growl at any who ventured too near or tried to take my daughter from my breast.

Without warning, I was engulfed with such longing for my mother that my cheeks grew wet with tears. Then, I seemed to hear female voices raised in jubilant song, as if every woman who had ever borne a child were gathered round the bed to bless my babe—and knew that she was near.

Kissing the wondrously tiny fingers curled about my own, I breathed a prayer of thanksgiving to the Lady, who herself had borne the world.

"My daughter needs a name. She needs a perfect name," I either thought or said. And clear I heard it, distinct as one can hear the chime of far-off bells in the silence before dawn.

"A name of power and of her womanhood to come. In-Whom-The-Goddess-Dwells...that is to be her name."

Infant Burial Room, Wupatki

Felicia Mitchell

Children were thus buried in their parents' home so their spirits would not wander too far. In Wupatki Ruin, seven burial pits have been found.

patience

The seventh child, still waiting to be born, hovered
for 800 years before it gave up and
followed a tourist from Arizona to Arkansas
and was delivered by Caesarian section.

ennui

The sixth child bore the spirit of the fifth,
so it rested heavy with two small mortal memories,
waiting, not sure it wanted to be born again
unless it could have its choice of lives.

inveteracy

The fifth, fragile, had little will to live,
was left to starve when it refused its mother's breast
and even ephedra didn't stimulate it to suck.
Craving a warrior's body, it spurned the next child
and waited its turn to be born again strong enough
to fight the Anasazi to the north.

sorrow

The fourth grew enough to crawl near the ball court
where its father's rituals were played out.
It died in its sleep so suddenly

its mother refused to relinquish the child at first,
to admit it wasn't sleeping and was dead.

felicity

The third was born to a girl who grew to a woman
who was known to start the chanting
when all the women would gather around
the courtyard to grind corn.
She remembered lying waiting,
and was never unhappy a day in her second life.

innocence

The second lived only a minute,
so it wasn't quite sure what life meant.
But when its mother made a new baby,
this one didn't hesitate even though
water was scarcer than usual this year.

joy

The first spirit was left alone in a cold place,
knowing its deformity had put it there.
When it was born again with a whole heart,
it paid homage to the sun.

Even after death, I will not forget how a newborn huffs and puffs when sitting slumped over

Hilda Downer

I am one with womankind
when loneliness names a hospital room
with its December filtered light
focused on my baby's breathing
and the mark he sleeps on
is the question of life or death.
Sometimes it has been a beauty recognized briefly,
but mostly, it is through suffering
that I have connected to all women,
all of us who have died countless times
anonymously in one individual skin.
Alone and woman,
I relate to pioneer women tearing out their babies
amid incompetence and antibiotics not yet discovered,
the memorization of cracks in log walls,
drafts clawing away frail blankets
to disclose a good look for death in awe of itself
as the babies eventually lay still in all their perfection.
I clasp spirits with these women for ancestral strength.
I think that as long as I can maintain eye contact with my baby,
even though he won't nurse,
I can keep him alive.
His stare like bullets,
he no longer cries when they draw blood,
but his eyes latch with mine as though asking for help.

Before he leaves me for sleep,
the stare becomes vague
as the meniscus striving for the edge of the glass.
Loneliness falls on me like an object from another dimension.
I do not know why I thought I could be a mother,
a lone warrior chosen to protect him
from a nurse who doesn't wash her hands
after changing him and before giving his injection,
the lab technicians who can't get blood the first time,
the doctor who can't get an IV started after three tries.

My baby was born healthy with his storkbites,
fat dimpled hands, and anger at being born so soon.
A week and a half later, he slept longer
than all the reassuring phone calls that day.
After six hours, I woke him and checked for a fever
that rolled his eyes back to sleep, unresponsive.
We were told he would not have awakened on his own.

Where do babies go?
Do they go back where they came from?
After majoring in Biology and nursing school,
I still do not understand where these babies come from.
They materialize out of air, a thing that can't even be seen.
They take up space where nothing was before.
Then, they look at you quizzically
as though you were not who they expected.
"Where is Raquel Welch?" they seem puzzled
as they take in your swollen and tear glazed face.
You study your babies but you cannot see what they look like
through the bright haze of love.

During the staggered days in the hospital,
I flip once through a National Geographic
where double pages open with penguins upon penguins
like standing babies in one-piece sleepers,
the sweet protuberance of bellies.
Penguins must love one another
to crowd so peacefully and well dressed
in their crystalline heaven,
perhaps with mint on their breath.
Maybe this is where babies go,

the arctic as a kind of purgatory,
disease resistant as snow.
Maybe this is where my baby would go
and I could go there and visit.

As my baby lies dying,
even the lifting of a water cup is prayer.
There is no governor to call who can grant my baby an extension.
I'm even more afraid when I recall kittens and robins,
their bodies rattling soft in shoe boxes for burial.
Even though I fed them with a dropper
and swaddled them warmly with fluffed socks and frayed towels,
baby opossums and rabbits caught by the cats
always laid stiff as papier-mâché in the morning.
My husband visits and friends call but I'm still alone.
My mother says it will be God's will if the baby dies
so this is between God and me.

There are certain feelings and memories that will carry
over death's threshold.
These are what I am and what will transcend—
the stamp of a Z-framed smokehouse door,
the lightning bugs that steer eyes everywhere at once,
and the quality of the voice in summer night air.
What is the solid part of me,
the granite molar root of the mountains,
is what I cling to now,
when I am truly alone.
Through the pain of all women
who could only turn to themselves to face God,
I have earned what I will take with me.
I will leave in return another strength
for those who will call out to the collective name of Mother.

Not a Trace

Jan Frazier

My six-year-old spent his allowance
on glasses with eyeballs on springs, bent
on making a teacher laugh. When the dog
ate one eye before the glasses even
made it to school, I scoured the house for something
small, round, and white, to draw pupil, iris,
and bloodshot lines on, and fit into
the gaping spring. A bob from his tackle box
was just the thing. I did it on the sly,
to surprise him. With a screwdriver I pried out
the metal loop. The magic marker pupil
smeared on the shiny plastic; crayon worked better.
The Sky Blue one made a perfect iris.
The bloodshot lines were passable.

He came in the kitchen just as I was
popping in the new falsy. I slid on
the glasses, noted the faint fishy smell,
said to my son, "What a mom!" He squinted
at the new eye, said, "Hey, what did you do
to my bob?" I made no effort to fight
the tears. "Throw the damn thing in the trash,"
I said, and then did it myself.
I checked his face for horror or remorse.
Not a trace. Later as I pulled
the glasses from the kitchen trash,
picking wilted spinach leaves from the springs,
I cursed the ingratitude of youth,
put on the glasses, and remembered

a doll's highchair, and how the tray wouldn't stay up
over the doll's head while she was sitting down,

but crashed like a guillotine. And how my father
said he'd fix it, it just needed a small block
of wood between the frame and the arm of the tray
to slow it down. And how he came out of
the garage smiling, good-as-new highchair
in his hand, and said all he'd done was cut
one of my wood blocks, just the right thickness it was.
He set down the highchair, showed me how the tray
would stay up now, said to get my doll, then
saw my face. "You cut my block?" I said,
like he'd cut out my heart and used that.
I checked his eyes for rebuke. Not a trace.

Cambodia

Alicia Ostriker

My son Gabriel was born on May 14, 1970, during the Vietnam War, a few days after the United States invaded Cambodia, and a few days after four students had been shot by National Guardsmen at Kent State University in Ohio during a protest demonstration.

On May 1, President Nixon announced Operation Total Victory, sending 5,000 American troops into Cambodia to destroy North Vietnamese military sanctuaries, in a test of "our will and character," so that America would not seem "a pitiful helpless giant" or "accept the first defeat in its proud 190-year history."

He wanted his own war.

The boy students stand in line
at Ohio State
each faces a Guardsman in gasmask
each a bayonet point at his throat.

U.S. air cavalry thrusts into Kompong Cham province, seeking bunkers. Helicopters descent on "The Parrot's Beak." B-52's heavily bomb Red sanctuaries. Body count! Body count high! in the hundreds. The President has explained, and explains again, that this is not an invasion.

Monday, May 4, at Kent State, laughing demonstrators and rock-throwers on a lawn spotted with dandelions. It was after a weekend of beer-drinking. Outnumbered Guardsmen, partially encircled and out of tear gas, began to retreat uphill, turn, kneel, in unison aim their guns. Four students lie dead, seventeen wounded. Four hundred forty-one colleges and universities strike, many shut down.

The President says: "When dissent turns to violence, it invites tragedy."

A veteran of the Khe Sanh says: "I saw enough violence, blood and death and I vowed never again, never again. . . . Now I must protest. I'm not a leftist but I can't go any further. I'll do damn near anything to stop the war now."

A man in workclothes tries to seize an American flag from a student. "That's my flag! I fought for it! You have no right to it! . . . To hell with your movement. We're fed up with your movement. You're forcing us into it. We'll have to kill you." An ad salesman in Chicago: "I'm getting to feel like I'd actually enjoy going out and shooting some of these people. I'm just so goddamned mad."

One, two, three, four, we don't want your fucking war!

They gathered around the monument, on the wet grass, Dionysiac, beaded, flinging their clothes away, New England, Midwest, Southwest, cupfuls of innocents leave the city and buy farmland. At the end of the frontier, their backs to the briny Pacific, buses of tourists gape at the acid-dropping children in the San Francisco streets. A firebomb flares. An electric guitar bleeds.

Camus: "I would like to be able to love my country and still love justice."

Some years earlier, my two daughters were born, one in Wisconsin at a progressive university hospital where doctors and staff behaved affectionately, one in England where the midwife was a practical woman who held onto my feet and when she became impatient with me said: PUSH, Mother. Therefore I thought I knew what childbirth was supposed to be: a woman *gives birth to a child,* and the medical folk assist her.

But in the winter of 1970 I had arrived five months pregnant in Southern California, had difficulty finding an obstetrician who would take me, and so was now tasting normal American medical care. It tasted like money. During my initial visit to his ranch-style offices on a street where the palm trees lifted their heads into the smog like a row of fine mulatto ladies, Dr. Keensmile called me "Alicia" repeatedly, brightly, benignly, as if I were a child or a servant. I hated him right away. I hated his suntan. I knew he was untrue to his wife. I was sure he played golf. The routine delivery anesthetic for him and his group was a spinal block, he said. I explained that I would not need a spinal since I had got by before on a couple of cervical shots, assumed that deliveries were progressively easier, and wanted to decide about drugs myself when the time came. He smiled tolerantly at the ceiling. I remarked that I liked childbirth. I remarked that childbirth gave a woman an opportunity for supreme pleasure and heroism. He smiled again. They teach them, in medical school, that pregnancy and birth are diseases. He twinkled. Besides, it was evident that he hated women. Perhaps that was why he became an obstetrician. Just be sure and watch your weight, Alicia. Smile.

I toyed, as I swelled and bulged like a watermelon, with the thought of driving out into the Mojave to have the baby. I continued my visits to Dr. Keensmile. I did not talk to Dr. Keensmile about Cambodia. I did not talk to him about Kent State. *Sauve qui peut.* You want a child of life, stay away from psychic poison. In the waiting room I found pamphlets which said that a newborn baby must be fed on a strict schedule, as it needed the discipline, and that one must not be moved by the face that it would cry at first, as this was good for it, to start it out on the right foot. And my daughters were laughing at me for my difficulty in buckling their sandals.

In labor, I discovered that I could have an enjoyable time if I squatted on the bed, rocked a little while doing my breathing exercises, and sang songs in my head. The bed had muslin curtains drawn around it; nobody would be embarrassed by me. So I had settled into a melody and had been traveling downstream with it for some long duration, when a nurse came through the curtains, stork white, to ask if I was ready for my shot. Since the pains were becoming strong and I felt unsure about keeping control through the transitional stage of labor, which is the hardest, I said fine, expecting a local. This would temporarily alleviate the pain of the fast-stretching cervix, leaving other muscles free.

Of course, it was a sedative. I grew furry. They lay me down. I was eight fingers dilated, only five or seven minutes away from the final stage of labor, where a woman needs no drugs because she becomes a goddess. Then Dr. Keensmile appeared to ask if I was ready for my spinal. A faint flare of "no" passed, like a moonbeam. Because of the Demerol, if they had asked me whether I was ready to have my head severed, I probably would have said yes. Drool ran from my mouth. Yes, I said.

When they wheeled me to the delivery room, I fought to maintain wakeful consciousness despite the Demerol, and fought to push, with my own body, to give birth to my child myself, despite the fact that I could feel nothing—nothing at all—below the waist, as if I did not exist there, as if I had been cut in half and bandaged.

A stainless place. I am conscious, only my joy is cut off. I feel the stainless will of everyone. Nothing red in the room. I am sweating. Death.

The black-hair head, followed by the supple limbs, emerges in the mirror. The doctor says it is a boy. Three thoughts fall, like file cards. One: Hooray! We made it! Finito! Two: YOU SONOFABITCHING BASTARD, NEXT TIME I'M GOING TO DO THIS RIGHT. Three: What next time?

Our bodies and our minds shoot into joy, like trees into leaves. Playfulness as children, sex, work with muscles, work with brains. Some bits survive, where we are lucky, or clever, or we fight. The world will amputate what it can, wanting us cripples. Cut off from joy, how many women conceive? Cut off, how many bear? And cut off, how many give birth to their children? Now I am one of them. I did not fight. Beginning a day after my son's birth, and continuing for a week, I have swordlike headaches, which I attribute to the spinal. I am thirty-three. In the fall I will be back at work, back East. My husband and I have two daughters, both all right so far, and now the son for whom we were hoping. There will never be a next time.

What does this have to do with Cambodia?

Morning Song

Sylvia Plath

Love set you going like a fat gold watch.
The midwife slapped your footsoles, and your bald cry
Took its place among the elements.

Our voices echo, magnifying your arrival. New statue.
In a drafty museum, your nakedness
Shadows our safety. We stand round blankly as walls.

I'm no more your mother
Than the cloud that distils a mirror to reflect its own slow
Effacement at the wind's hand.

All night your moth-breath
Flickers among the flat pink roses. I wake to listen:
A far sea moves in my ear.

One cry, and I stumble from bed, cow-heavy and floral
In my Victorian nightgown.
Your mouth opens clean as a cat's. The window square

Whitens and swallows its dull stars. And now you try
Your handful of notes;
The clear vowels rise like balloons.

Stumbling into Motherhood: A Few Words About Bonding & Mother-Women

T. J. Banks

When I came to, she was lying in my husband's arms. "We have a very pretty daughter," Tim said, "and she has your dark eyes." He offered her to me; but my arms were all trembly from the anesthesia, and I knew I couldn't hold on to her. There was a vague gladness in me, but there was also a sense of being disconnected from this tiny big-eyed girl-child I'd wanted so much.

The feeling lasted for a long time after Marissa's birth. A couple of months later, I was comparing notes with a woman from my childbirth class who'd had her baby naturally. "Don't you feel *cheated*?" she demanded. Her daughter had been whisked away immediately to have the meconium suctioned out, and she was still gnawing over the thought that they'd missed the chance to bond at birth.

"No," I said, and meant it. Still, I did ask myself sometimes if I would've had that strange feeling of disconnectedness had Marissa not been born Cesarean. During my short labor, I'd experienced enough of natural childbirth to decide it was highly overrated (when my daughter's pediatrician said he was sorry that I'd had to have a Cesarean, I shot back, "I'm not."), but I couldn't help wondering what I would have felt had we done the whole thing according to the pro-natural-childbirth books. Other than sore and exhausted, I mean. Prior to Marissa's birth, I'd read one of those take-back-the-birthing-process treatises and been very much swayed by it and by conversations with the friend who'd lent it to me. Yes, I will do this without medication! Yes, I will reach down and help pull my baby's head out during the crowning! Yes, Tim will cut the cord himself! Yes, I will go and plow the field afterwards!

Well, reality—in this case, Marissa managing to get the cord snaked around her head—cut in on those imaginings. Marissa is six months old and a happy, cuddly, opinionated baby despite the fact that we didn't do it by that particular book or even meet till almost an hour after she was born. And, as I've been getting to know her, I've had time to re-think this bonding business. Truth be told, I don't buy it. Loving your child, I learned, like any other kind of loving, comes with time. You love your child at first because she *is* your child. But it's all in the abstract. Only later, as her personality begins to emerge, do you begin to love her for *who* she is.

The bonding philosophy is tied up with the patriarchal notion that women must give all of themselves over to mothering the instant they conceive a child—that they must become, as Kate Chopin puts it in *The Awakening,* "mother-women." It's an insidious notion, and the people who espouse it often are the same ones who criticize working mothers and who believe that women should be denied the legal right to abortion. They are the folks who try to impress upon you the idea that raising your child is more important than anything else you can ever possibly hope to do.

My response? Yes, I believe that raising a child to be a loving, well-adjusted human being is a terribly important task; and I also believe, as Marge Piercy says in one of her poems, that every child born unloved is a bill that will come due twenty years down the line. But I do not believe that it can or should be the entire focus of a woman's life. Making it so isn't fair either to yourself or to the child. I know women—women in their early thirties like myself—who buy into this mother-woman doctrine. They channel so much of themselves into baby-making and -rearing, they're scary. I remember being with one such woman while I was diapering Marissa. Marissa was wriggling around and kvetching on general principle. My friend darted over *from across the room* and exclaimed, "Aha, just what I thought!" One of the fasteners on the baby's diapers had slipped from my fingers and stuck to the baby's hip. My friend could tell, she said, what had happened by Marissa's cry. And I could tell that I'd just failed the mothering litmus test as far as she was concerned.

Since then, I have given up attempting to be the all-knowing, all-giving Earth Mother. That, like the bonding doctrine, doesn't work for me. Like Chopin's heroine, Edna, I would give up everything for my child except myself. So I ad-lib as I go along, trying to tailor the day to meet both my needs as a person and Marissa's. It's a continual balancing act, of course. I'm learning to distinguish her lonely or "I-really-need-you-now" cry from her cranky one and to go to her when I hear it, even though I'm longing to be at my desk, working on an article or story. Sometimes she just wants to be near me, so I take her upstairs with me and put her in the cradle alongside my desk. I've done the same during phone interviews. On the other hand, I'm also learning that when I feel really overwhelmed, the best thing for me to do is to pack Marissa in her crib for a nap and get back to my writing. (Sometimes, I confess, I run the vacuum first to put her to sleep.) If I can't get even a few paragraphs in, I feel fragmented. Lost. And I'm no good to her then. As Brenda Ueland observes in her book *If You Want to Write*—in a wonderful chapter entitled "Why women who do too much housework should neglect it for their writing," to be exact—you cannot "teach, encourage, cheer up, console, amuse, stimulate or advise a husband or children or friends . . . [without] be[ing] something yourself. And how to be something yourself? Only by working hard and with gumption at something you love and care for and think is important." Ueland takes the idea a leap further. "If you would shut your door against the children for an hour a day," she exhorts the "worn and hectored" mothers in her writing class, "and say: 'Mother is working on her five-act tragedy in blank verse!' you would be surprised how they would respect you. They would probably all become playwrights."

Now Marissa is, naturally, a long ways from understanding the concept of being a playwright, let alone become one (although judging from the long cooing conversations she carries on with her favorite stuffed animal, Gray Bunny, I think she'll be acting out her share of stories with him and the other toys in a few years). And I cannot shut the door against her in quite the same manner that I would be able to with an older child. But I do think that Ueland's argument holds true. I want Marissa to be her own person, well at ease, and not an extension of me.

We have weathered the first six months—and each other—reasonably well. We may not have done things according to the childcare books or popular folklore, but we've discovered that we enjoy being together. That we can laugh together over her bath. I'm beginning to be able to read her moods, and I know that she likes music, bright colors, and cuddling with Gray Bunny & Co. in her crib. I read to her before her naps and bedtime; she doesn't understand the words, of course, but she likes the pictures and she follows the inflections in my voice till she tires. Our best time is in the golden glow of the late summer afternoon, the last burst of sunshine stippling the old scuffed-up maple bureau, the two large gray-striped toy cats in the child-sized twig chair, and the neatly turned posts of Marissa's crib as we relax in the large comfy gooseneck rocker with a book. Sometimes, though, I put the book aside and just hold her. She looks at me out of those large dark blue-gray eyes that seem to change their color constantly, then turns her head to the open window, listening to the birdsong. We sit there, outside of time, as close as it is humanly possible for two individuals to be.

Ironing

Judith Minty

Leaves and flowers blend, a river spinning over the cotton. It is my daughter's blouse. Green ripples under my fingers. Pink and blue blossom under the iron's steam. Tiny buds. The cement floor presses its back against the soles of my feet. The pipes gather pearls of moisture. I am a tree. I rise from the earth. I shade the ironing board. My hand passes back and forth, a branch in the wind. One sleeve, then the other.

Summer, but this basement remembers winter and holds loam to its heart. The water in these pipes wants to go underground, back to the dark. It is June, and my daughter sleeps in the heat of her dream. She is far from my belly now, on her white bed, still as a breath in the hospital wing. I have washed the blood from her blouse. Now this iron passes over a sleeve, it curls around a button. Colors intertwine, tangle. The petals blur. They bleed into leaves on the vines.

The car was thick with glass, little beads of glass, blue and yellow in the sun. The lace of slivers of glass, glistening on her skirt, under her bare feet. Glass clinging to her blouse, her skin. Glass in the upholstery, on the carpet, the dashboard. Prisms in the sun. A clink and tinkle like wind chimes when she stirred. Her hands gliding to her face. Glass glinting in her hair. Blood shining on the glass. Glass flowing, separating, as she stirred on the seat of the car.

I pass this iron over her blouse. Steam hisses. I hear her voice as she is lifted from the car. Steam rises from the flowers, the petals. The leaves. I am a tree. Her long hair matted with blood, the cut open on her scalp. My feet curl like roots on the floor. Sweat gathers on the pipes. I rustle over her blouse. Her hair unfurls on the pillow. The flowers blend, the leaves blur. My hand glides over the pattern, a river spinning. Her dream flows without sound. Steam hisses from the iron. Petals and leaves minglepink and blue. Green. I am ironing her blouse. Only this motion is left.

On the Inside

Eliza Monroe

Mandisa is Swahili for peace. Born in 1968, she was just the right age for pre-school when Sesame Street came out and filled up the Headstart programs. Sesame Street was the answer. So was television in general.

Mandisa's daddy had told me that the McAllisters were one of the first families in Kansas City to own a TV, which they replaced with five more when they migrated to California. For over three decades and two generations, television had saved them. Television and cards. Black jack, poker, crazy eights, gin rummy. If they could have built a bowling alley in their basement, they surely would have. The bowling alley and public school were the only two places the McAllister children ventured outside the home, and then never alone.

My orbit of Mandisa's world began when she was thirteen. She could read, but didn't like to. She preferred watching MTV. I was her stepmother for two years. It was easier to leave her father, Papa Hawk McAllister, than it was for him to be left. What made it worse for him, I'm sure, was that I was never able to let go of Mandisa, despite the advice of my counselor. "Face it," she'd told me. "Mandisa will never love to read." Still, I looked forward to her calls, her occasional long distance updates, as I patiently listened for some indication that I, the lover of books, had made a minute impression.

When I first met Mandisa, she said she wanted to be a singer and an actress and a dancer and a costume designer. I couldn't tell her that she'd picked four of the most competitive, insecure, low paying, shot-in-the-dark professions she could possibly pick. She hadn't had a lesson in her life. Both her parents worked and didn't let her take the bus alone, and I didn't have the heart to tell her that, at thirteen, it may be too late. It had been too late for me. I wasn't without talent and I'd started at age nine.

Still, I wanted Mandisa to know what I knew, not that it was too late, but the feeling of stepping out across the floor, kinetically, untelevisionlike. And I wanted to support the McAllister tradition of staying off drugs and out of gangs, which I considered a major accomplishment in this day and age for blacks in Oakland. That she was too old for the Olympics didn't matter to me. What mattered was that she was busy. I only wish that I'd met her sooner, that she were my own, that the McAllisters weren't such do or die Democrats, so adamant about sending their young to public school.

So I drove Mandisa and her cousin, Rochelle, to the studio with me.

"But I like modern jazz," she said as we entered Dancer Synectics, a studio converted from a marina style house that was embedded into a hill in San Francisco. The dressing room was in the garage, with curtained cubicles for changing, vintage posters of old musicals on the walls, and a green striped indoor-outdoor carpet on the slanted floor.

The inside of the studio itself teemed with long limbed, Lycra'd Narcissists not much older than Mandisa, each trying to intimidate the other by showing off a greater stretch, a more concave abdomen, a quick mark through of the current combination. They pushed in front of one another toward the mirrors. When the teacher appeared and the music began, I worked out somewhere in the center, Mandisa and Rochelle in the back, mostly watching the sweeps, punches and turns of the choreography.

When we went across the floor in lines of three, a woman who taught low impact aerobics at the Bay Club turned the wrong way and broke the arm of another woman who'd driven all the way from Walnut Creek, and never even said she was sorry.

"Is this modern enough for you?" I said to Mandisa after the class was over, and she nodded her enthusiasm. On the way home, I took the girls to the library and checked them out dance history books and biographies of famous dancers. I bought Mandisa a subscription to *Dance Magazine,* but she only looked at the pictures.

To understand Mandisa's aversion to the written word, I needed to understand Hawk's history. He'd been married four times. First to Bethany, who'd died. Second to Mandisa's mother, third to Camille, and last to me. Hawk is the kind of person who needs a woman in his life—someone besides his mother and his daughter to live for, to work for. His heart must have soared when he was with Mandisa's mother. They split up when Mandisa was five, but I've seen pictures and I can tell by the lift in his cheekbones how he felt inside: back on track.

On the rebound, as if to prove a point, he married Camille under a rented flower archway in Grammy and Grampy's backyard. Camille and Mandisa's mother were both tall and yellow and proud. I can see that he was trying to replace one with the other. I still don't know what his first wife looked like, nor what he saw in me.

Hawk never spoke of the one who'd died, only of those who'd survived him. Regarding Camille, he'd said that in seven short years she'd driven herself crazy trying to make Mandisa a baby sister or brother. She'd charged up all of Hawk's accounts—clothes mostly—then had declared personal bankruptcy and left him with the bills, clothes still in the closets with the price tags on. I know for a fact that Camille is still friends with some of the McAllisters. Some of the McAllister women sneak out and go shopping with her, but I was never included.

Mandisa was old enough to remember Hawk's slump after Camille. Lost his job, stayed at Grammy and Grampy's, smoked his pipe, moped. Then he got a job in marketing at Hewlett Packard. When I met him, the maitre d' at the Maya called him Senior Paquard. I was just about finished at Cal Berkeley, and was sneaking my literature homework in the salad station between waiting tables at the Maya. Hawk hung out there after work, drinking Glen Fiddich, sitting alone in the same red upholstered booth in the corner. He always left a twenty.

Some said I was too young for Hawk, too small. I doubt he warned his family that I was white. He just brought me to a McAllister holiday at his parents' home, a yellow stucco that needed painting on a quiet knoll between East 14th and Foothill. I could tell by the way his father unlocked three bolts on the front door for each group entering that the screen door was probably never used, not on the hottest Indian Summer day, though it had a lock of its own.

Mandisa ran past me to congregate with the other children her size. Hawk gravitated toward a poker game. I sat rigidly on a twenty-year-old overstuffed couch and stroked a doily that Grammy McAllister had carefully pinned to its arm. The colors spoke of the Seventies—olive green, gold and brown. Candy dishes and brandy decanters were full. The shelf above the fireplace sagged with the weight of bowling trophies. Card tables were set up in the living room. Every brand of cigarette was represented, second hand smoke blending permanently into the unlit air. ESPN played on the big TV.

I waited for a reaction to my presence, but heads turned only in forced delayed response. I didn't know these people and they didn't know me. Words flowed from each mouth, stating opinions regarding current events— no original opinions, just repetitions of one TV news broadcast or other or the commentary thereof. I felt invisible, as if I were some sort of anthropologist—an observer. I got the sense that they were trying very hard to give me a genuine view of what their holiday would have been like without me there.

Of course, things may have been different if I'd pulled up a chair and played cards. But games didn't interest me. Neither did television sports, soap operas or the new black music. Only good books interested me, and the good looks of my husband, Papa Hawk McAllister. I was disappointed that the rest of the McAllisters didn't favor him. Hawk was the oldest and the darkest and by far the most handsome.

I stood up and studied portraits of black faces on every wall representing the deepest gene pool I'd seen in any one family. Grammy and Grampy McAllister had twelve children, each a different shade of brown and bearing almost no family resemblance whatsoever. Except for the image of Hawk's double, which hung in an eight-by-ten frame in the dining room, they could have all been adopted.

Grammy McAllister shook my hand casually as if I were Hawk's hundredth wife, not merely his fourth. Then she tottered, slightly bow legged, a permanent half-smile set on her open face, and stooped to pick up empty soda cans from the mismatched end tables. Without a doubt, she had given birth to all the McAllisters personally.

"Would you like a soda?" she asked.

"Do you have any diet drinks?"

"Nutrasweet worse for them than sugar. We just give them regular sodas."

By "them" I figured she meant her grandchildren. She handed me a Coke. I thanked her, smiled and bowed slightly, like I'd seen Hawk do, then stared back at Hawk's double on the wall. Grammy stood next to me and I got the feeling she was accessing my soul.

She didn't have to say that somewhere there'd been white blood in the McAllister family. Hawk had a white man's nose. They'd made fun of him, he'd said, in the all-black schools he'd attended in Kansas City. The photograph of Hawk's ancestor revealed the same nose—long and bony and straight—a characteristic that seemed to skip generations in the McAllister family with more assuredness than any other feature.

"That's Hawk's grandfather, Lionell McAllister," Grammy said proudly. "He was a Buffalo Soldier, his daddy before him a breeder." Then she went about her business. Lionell McAllister, I noticed, held his head high in the portrait, as if he were black all over and through and through despite the nose. I could barely wait to drag Hawk home and set him up against a quiet, stark background, the only relative obvious in him his grandfather, Buffalo Soldier, offspring of breeders.

Mandisa practiced break dancing to a ghetto blaster with her cousins in the dining room. Hawk continued to play poker. I found a comfortable chair in the corner and buried my head in a murder mystery I'd brought. There was no dining room table, just a bar and one green card table, without which, I mentioned to no one in particular, a pool table would have fit nicely. But pool, Grammy told me as she passed holding a bowl of dip, was where the McAllisters drew the line. Lionell McAllister had come home from the war only to be shot in an alley outside a Kansas City pool hall.

"I decided," Grammy said, "that the way to keep my kids out of alleys was to keep them home with each other." They hadn't gone to the carnival when it had come to Kansas City, which was just as well. Black children were allowed in only the day before the carnival officially opened to test out the rides—as if the death of black children wouldn't be such a tragedy—and Grammy McAllister'd said, "I would rather my children not go at all than be guinea pigs for the white man."

After that, it was clear that Grammy McAllister's children, all twelve of them, and their children, and their children, would be protected from the outside world, would stay in behind locked doors, entertain themselves.

After meeting Grammy herself, I was beginning to understand. It was for their protection, their survival. It didn't matter that they grew up to be quite ordinary, not prone to do anything special to make the world outside a better place. What mattered was that the McAllister family, Grammy McAllister's flesh and blood—her babies—survived.

"Get yourself something to eat," Grammy McAllister said.

I followed her out of the dining room. *Days of Our Lives* played in the kitchen, which was also in greens and golds, the carpeted floor uneven. Coffee brewed perpetually. Grampy sat in the midst of a solitaire game, smoking and eating Grammy's deviled eggs in Tupperware at the kitchen table, a plastic lace tablecloth covering green Formica.

Every holiday was alike. The same people in the same positions, the same hands at cards, the same opinions, the same smoke, Grammy McAllister picking up the same empty soda cans. At Christmas, an artificial tree stood lit at the front window, a mound of wrapped presents underneath. At Thanksgiving there was turkey. In summer there were do-it-yourself hamburgers. Always, there were links, hot and mild, macaroni and cheese, deviled eggs and sweet potato pie.

I miss the McAllisters. Their predictability. Their noise. The sheer numbers of them. I would have expected to find more time to read without them, but I haven't.

I was pleased to find that Mandisa continued her dance lessons after I left Hawk. She got her own car at age sixteen and we met at the studio twice a week. By then, she'd changed her mind about wanting to be a dancer and a singer and an actress and a costume designer. "I want to be an astronaut," she said. "Why?"

"Because then I could fly in a rocket straight up in the air, away from Oakland."

"Mandisa," I said, "there are other ways to leave besides in a rocket ship. Have you considered moving?"

By that time I had moved south of the City and invited her to stay with me. It seemed the McAllisters were driving her crazy. She said she'd expected her father to go into a slump after I'd left him. That was the pattern. But this slump was noticeably longer and deeper, as if a compliment to the degree to which he'd been smitten. He walked off his job at Hewlett Packard, gave his handgun to his brother for safekeeping, and crawled back into the womb. That's what kind of mother Grammy McAllister is: always taking back her children, no matter how old they are. The McAllister twins, for instance, Joseph and Josephine—in their thirties—have also come back home, Josephine with a newborn daughter and Joseph with AIDS.

I wasn't surprised that Mandisa chose to stay in Oakland. After high school, she quit going to dance classes. I think she discovered men. I didn't hear from her for a long time, and then only to let me know she was six months pregnant. She was living with her cousin, Rochelle. She'd enrolled in a dentist assistant program, and would barely finish her internship before the baby was due. I wasn't invited to the baby shower, not with all those McAllisters there, so the day before the party, I picked her up at her mother's house—where she'd spent the night in her childhood bed—and I took her to Toys R Us. The baby had dropped and was kicking as we walked up and down the aisles, catching up, comparing strollers, exploring her options.

Mandisa stopped at the book section of the store and rested her hand over her abdomen. She picked out simple, first books and set them in our cart. "I already read to the baby," she said.

"What?"

"I read to her inside me. She can hear my voice. I read her stories now. Alexis is going to love to read."

After Reading Mickey in the Night Kitchen *for the Third Time Before Bed*

Rita Dove

I'm in the milk and the milk's in me!...I'm Mickey!

My daughter spreads her legs
to find her vagina:
hairless, this mistaken
bit of nomenclature
is what a stranger cannot touch
without her yelling. She demands
to see mine and momentarily
we're a lopsided star
among the spilled toys,
my prodigious scallops
exposed to her neat cameo.

And yet the same glazed
tunnel, layered sequences.
She is three; that makes this
innocent. We're pink!
she shrieks, and bounds off.

Every month she wants
to know where it hurts
and what the wrinkled string means
between my legs. This is good blood
I say, but that's wrong, too.
How to tell her that it's what makes us—
black mother, cream child.
That we're in the pink
and the pink's in us.

Crack in the World

Anne Waldman

I see the crack in the world

My body thinks it, sees the gaping crack in the world

My body does it for me to see

Blood flowing through the body crack

Body, send your rivers to the moon

Body twists me to the source of the moon

It turns me under a wave

It sets up the structure to make a baby, then tears
    it down again

Architecture of womb-body haunting me

Someone is always watching the ancient flow

It doubles up my mind

Ovum not fertilized

I see the crack in the world

Thoughts intersect in the body

He must not keep me down

Let me go my way alone tonight

No man to touch me

A slash in me, I see the slash in the world tonight

It keeps me whole, but divides me now

Out on land, to bleed

Out on street, to bleed

In the snow, blood

This is a South American song

Scent of oleander

Or this is a cactus song

Sing of blood flower a rose in the crotch
    O collapsible legs!

My body enchanted me to this

My body demented to this

It is endometrium shedding

I am compressed in the pressure of my heart

It is life pursuing the crack in the world

Between worlds

Between thoughts

A vacant breath

Words won't do it

Ovum not fertilized

The man hasn't done it

I cover every contingency
    the catty one
    or puritan walking in a fecund world

Words sing to me of endometrium collapse

Words go down to my belly

Back swelling, to put my body next to the earth

This is periodic

It comes at the full moon

Let me go howling in the night

No man to touch me

Don't fathom my heart tonight, man

No one wants to be around this factory,
*   this beautiful machine*
*   but I shun your company anyway*

My flexible body imagines the crack

Body with winds

See the crack in the universe

The curse, glorious curse is upon me

Don't come to my house

Don't expect me at your door

I'm in my celibacy rags

My anthropocentric heart says there's
*   a crack in the world tonight*

It's a long woman's body

It's a break in the cycle of birth & death

It's the rapid proliferation of cells
*   building up to die*

I make up the world & kill it again & again

I offer my entrails to the moon

Ovum not fertilized

Architecture haunting me

Collapsible legs you must carry the world

You get away from me

You keep your distance

I will overpower you with my scent
          of life & death

You who came through the crack in my world

You men who came out of me, back off

Words come out of the belly

Groaning as the world is pulled apart

Body enchanted to this

Body elaborated on this

Body took the measure of the woman
          to explain the fierceness of this time
          walking on the periphery of the world

What to Tell the Kids

Linda Vernon

If there is one thing that drives a mother crazy with a capital CRAZE, it is that kids expect an answer to everything. Even comments as simple as "the sun is shining" seem to require some sort of response. To prove my point, I wrote down an actual one-sided conversation my three-year-old had with me the other day which I believe illustrates perfectly just how far out of hand things can get when a mother does not respond as expected. I have recorded this soliloquy—if for no other reason than to use as exhibit A in my competency hearing.

"Mommy I want to play with those blocks up there. Can you get them down? I want to play with those blocks in the living room. Can you get them in the living room? Mommy can you? Mommy can you? Mommy can you? One for Mommy, one for Jackie, one for me, one for Daddy, one for me. Mommy how come all these blocks are here? Can you count them? One two three four five six. Mommy why are all these blocks here? Mommy can you take them in the living room? [Repeat ten times.] Can you? Can you? Can you?"

Right about now a mother is either (1) wondering how to tap into the geothermal energy coming out of her ears or (2) has become two personalities richer than she was this morning. It is for this reason that I have developed a list of answers guaranteed to make Mom look like the World's Greatest Mother to her children while simultaneously allowing herself a mental life of her own.

Instructions: Memorize the following phrases and use individually or combine as needed to satisfy your children's questions or comments.

"That's impossible! They've all gone to Mexico for the winter."

This phrase is perfect for children who can't sleep because they're afraid there is a *(pick one)* fly, bee, spider, wild animal, monster or grandparent in the closet.

"Well it's OK with me but just remember what happened to Uncle Fred."

This phrase works well in any type of hygiene situation, for example, when kids won't take a bath, brush their teeth or change their underwear.

"Do you want to be as flat as this?"

(Hold up something flat in conjunction with this, I find a tortilla works well.) This is an excellent pat answer when children ask if they can *(pick one)* cross the street, play in the street, ride their bikes in the street or run along beside the steamroller.

"Because of Supercalafragilisticexpialidocious!"

Use this explanation any time children ask about science, math or where babies come from.

"On August 1, 1986 at precisely 3:40 p.m."

Use this whenever children use sentences containing the word "when."

"I didn't become a parent to win a popularity contest."

An excellent comeback when children say *(pick one)* "you're mean" or "you make me sick" or the ever popular "I hate you."

"Because if God wanted you to have that you would have been born with a gold card in your mouth."

Repeat this every 15 minutes whether you need to or not.

But how?

Karen J. Donnelly

for Colleen and Cathy

At your birth
I became less
necessary, the shell,
stiff with age,
that you have blown.

The spotlight that was mine
now follows you.
I wait in the wings,
choreographing your dance,
amazed as the steps we
practiced together are left
behind, reborn in your burst
of spiraling joy.

I stumble along, unable
to match my clumsy gait to your
sway. Sometimes, you remember
and reach for my hand.

I know you sprang from me,
but how?

Yes, It is Possible to Love a Child Who Doesn't Have Your Eyes

Esther Cohen

We adopted Noah in the midst of two large-looming myths: that technology can solve infertility problems, and that biological children are somehow better. (Even the news media refer to biological children as "natural," implying that others are not.)

Both myths have deeply affected a large segment of society—people who want to be parents and who want the perfect child. Several hundred thousand people participate in fertility processes, a number that astounds even RESOLVE, the national organization dedicated to helping people cope with infertility in the same way that AA members, for instance, cope with alcohol.

But if you are able to love a child who might not have your eyes, there are many possibilities for adoption. And while the experience of adoption is strange, it is no stranger, maybe, than birth.

We became parents by telephone. I wrote down what a stranger told me about Noah on the back of an old envelope. She called us on the day he was born in Chile and said we had twelve hours to decide. We said yes knowing about him only as much as you can know about a baby: that he was a healthy boy. In the photograph they sent a few weeks later, we saw an out-of-focus baby in light blue pajamas. Imagining him was hard so we didn't talk about him much. We weren't sure what to say. I prepared for Noah by staring at people with children, trying to see how they did what they were doing. I felt odd, a little like someone who discovers the color green at thirty-five, and then notices, all at once, how much green there is.

Finally, my husband and I left New York in a heat wave, flew into a blizzard in Peru, and landed in Chile in the middle of a stormy night. During the layover in Lima, we wandered through the airport drinking coffee and selecting lucky charms, silver talismans and small painted mirrors.

Although we never said the words, we both felt we were somehow in labor. Dazed, tired and disconcerted, we seemed to walk in circles until we boarded another plane to land again in Chile, and to taxi through a dense, humid fog to the large, sanitized international hotel where a strange, kind, middle-aged woman named Dorys handed Noah to us.

Some moments in life should be full of music—Pachelbel's "Canon" or a Beethoven concerto. That was one of those moments. The anonymous room and incidental details, a green bedspread, a painting of flowers, are fixed in memory.

Becoming Noah's mother was instant. But, six years later, I am still a little dazed and often perplexed. It is the reaction to adoption that perplexes me. People say, "Maybe someday you'll have a real child," or, "I've heard of couples who adopted, and then they had one of their own." It is hard to imagine how one child could be less real than another, particularly to a parent.

People talk about families as though families are all harmony, station wagons and apple pies. In fact, we live in a time when families are changing dramatically, no longer limited by old definitions, by genes or sex preference, race or religion. Today everyone can have a child, be part of a family. In my kindergarten class in a small Connecticut town, family, more or less, meant only one thing. In Noah's kindergarten class in a New York public grammar school, there are nearly as many kinds of families as there are children.

We three are a family. We are connected through love, through choice and dailiness, through all those mysterious forces that brought us together. Not by blood or similar eyes.

Motherless

Carol Corda

"Winter will be," Kate always
said whispering, "all snow-bright."
Will winter be? I wondered
and watched the sun
pale under finger-thin clouds
that stretched toward me
in my hospital blue.
I struggled to see the child
of my center
laugh.

Margaret Kane children have her eyes:
dark-bright bowls, sun-tea clear.
Kate, tawny from summer's kiss
dances free, careless
that no mother sees. Motherless child
running swiftly among acorns strewn
like flowers across the wintry cave
as if thrown by mourners, grieves
not.

Brothers and Sons

Gus Pelletier

Adam The Brother, Adam The Son

Antiseptic, tense, the team stood by
while beams of surgical light landed
on your mother's lump of a shiny belly.
Soon enough a confident hand slid slowly
into the generous gash to fish you out,
wriggling and pink, your lungs impatient
with intrusive air, your brand new voice
impeccable proof of that sound delivery.

You thrilled your nearby father who saw
for the first time, flesh of his flesh,
his first-born son, future star of court,
diamond, classroom, track, a glistening
four-pound scrawn who soon enough would
sit, crawl, stand, walk and run, but who,
for the moment, felt his lifeline slit,
clipped at the navel, then and forever.

Your face was pure grimace, your cherub's
mouth puckering, as if on sour milk, salt.
"Where am I?" you seemed to ask. Someone
tallied toes, fingers, stethoscoped your
lub-dubbing heart. You kept angling back
for your other half, that long-time womb-
buddy who calmly slept in your common sac
while you butt out, delighting everyone.

You came off all spunk and holler, that
WHAA a primal squeal of cosmic proportion.

There seemed little wrong that incubation
wouldn't solve. Soon, one masked nurse
passed you on to another for yardstick,
scale: that ritual of vital statistics.
They sponged, aspirated you everywhere,
embraced you as if you were their own.

David The Brother, David The Son

On cue, an army of eyes rushed to your
mom's semi-pregnant paunch, the incision
savaged open by clamps of sparkling steel.
Again scrubbed fingers slid into wrinkles
of flesh, anxious for the prize that sat
in the gut-slime. Finding it, gentling
it forth into sterile air, they held it up.
This time it was you, you the kid brother.

Your dad's look telescoped your arrival.
Like some tracking camera, he followed
you everywhere as you emerged, scrunched,
squash-shaped, dripping of amniotic broth,
blood, what looked like mucous. A mess,
they cleaned you, wrapped you up in a kind
of cellophane. You kept to your fetal self
till medics unraveled your arms and legs.

In her sleep your mom looked like a ceramic
doll, her face pale and immobile. She slept
light years beyond the table where you lay,
cadaver-gray, half-alive, ready neither for
Kingship nor for Goliath. The earthly crew
hurried to finish the work begun by the gods:
huddling, hovering, calling on savvy, skill,
the patron saints of obstetrics, prime care.

"He's not in grave danger," they all chimed,
but you were not wriggling, nor in the pink.
Some distressing syndrome kept you in limbo,
your father ashen with funereal consternation.
In time, however, breathing freely, a scalp-
vein found for needled feeding, now bathed,

now bunked, you bloomed at last, so who would
not sing, not shout: PRAISE BE! PRAISE BE!

Loving Across State Lines

Meg Mott

On a hot day in the middle of July, Jacob's father came and filled up his shiny new Honda with boxes of Legos, bags of dusty animals, chess sets and train sets and remote control vehicles. All the amenities of a young boy's existence were packed in the trunk, squeezed in the back seat, their owner sitting independently up front.

I didn't want to, but I couldn't stop myself. The tears leaked out through the steel wall of my determination to be strong. Ducking into the bathroom as the third duffel bag went by, I silently heaved next to the bathtub, desperately reading a bottle of shampoo, willing the waves of sadness to stop so that I could go outside and say good-bye to my child.

A child psychologist had said to me, "It's time to think about his needs. You have to put your own needs aside. That's what parenting is all about." I put down the shampoo and willed myself through the door. I was determined to be a good mother.

I am a mother who loves across state lines. Because I respect Jacob, a thin, smart boy with spiked hair, one pierced ear, and a passion for winning at chess; because I see that he lives beyond the definition of "my son," I decided to let him go. I gave up custody of Jacob because I saw it would make him happy and because I believed he wouldn't talk about killing himself anymore.

I am a mother who does best by her son by not living by his side, by letting him go, by visiting him every other weekend and after school, once a week for 90 precious minutes.

There are some things a person cannot bear alone.

I live with monsters that rise out of the lonely hours of sleep and question my very existence. They send off a lethal lists of Interrogatories that call for a permanent darkness. "Why doesn't your child live with you? Why couldn't you make him happy? What sort of mother are you anyway?" These censures want to sentence my soul to life, life without parole. Somewhere inside of me I realized I needed a jury of peers.

Every Monday night, seven women get together in our barn. We light candles and sage, and call in the four directions to empower our space. We form a circle around the candlelight. In a process committed to care, we find our group spirit by nourishing the spaces between us. The group began because I asked a group of women I knew if they wanted to form a feminist spirituality group. Of the women who said yes, all but one are mothers.

They all know that Jacob moved away. I was cheerful in my presentation of the facts. He missed his father. They were very close. He can go to his old school where his artistry is encouraged. The women listened and nodded. The voices of mid-night descended upon me. Their unquestioning acceptance of my presentation became evidence of their judgment against me. If they thought I was philosophical about my son's departure then they must have seen me as an aberration of motherhood. If they thought I was capable of functioning without my son they must not see me as a real mother.

One of the women once said, "I could never do that," and the others quietly hummed in accordance. I wanted to say, "I can't do it either" but there I was, "doing it."

The other night, when the group was sitting around the candles and crystals and smoking sage, I used my time during check-in to describe how a friend had recently thrown a handful of tranquilizers into her mouth, a minute after I walked through her door. One of the women in the group, the eldest mother, turned to me and asked, "And how does this relate to Jacob?"

I stopped my narration. I looked around at a tribunal of mothers. "Jacob is happier now. I miss him but he's less at risk with his father." I looked around me. The women were holding me safe with their gazes. I continued, "Sometimes the best thing you can do for a child is to see their needs and recognize they can't be met by you alone." I took a deep breath and waited.

"You don't have to convince us, Meg, we know that you are a good mom."

A good mom. Those were the words I needed to hear to open a floodgate of tears. Those were the words that sent me swimming through deep waters. Jacob was thriving and content in his old neighborhood, in his old school with his old dad and his new step mom, and I was still a good mom. The jury had come back in my favor.

When I saw Jacob last week, I asked him about his suicidal feelings. My friend's drastic call for help had stimulated my concern for his well being.

"I don't feel that way anymore," he told me. "You know, mom, even though I talked about killing myself it was never my intent." Nine years old and he knows how to use the word "intent." "I just felt really bad and I didn't want to be sad anymore."

"Do you ever feel that way now?" I asked.

"No. I like it here in Keene. I mean, I miss you but it's better for me over here."

"I miss you too, Jacob," I said and gave him a squeeze, "but I'm glad to know that you are happy."

I meant it. That's how I know I am a good mom. My son can tell me what is best for him even if it isn't necessarily what's best for me. I think of the circle of candlelit faces, the respect and caring I saw in those mostly mother's eyes. They were watching me during that interchange with Jacob. They were humming quietly back to me the strong reflection of who I am. The kind of mother a person like Jacob needs.

The Glass Half Empty

Anna Quindlen

My daughter is two years old today. She is something like me, only better. Or at least that is what I like to think. If personalities had colors, hers would be red.

Little by little, in the twenty years between my eighteenth birthday and her second one, I had learned how to live in the world. The fact that women were now making sixty-seven cents for every dollar a man makes—well, it was better than 1970, wasn't it, when we making only fifty-nine cents? The constant stories about the underrepresentation of women, on the tenure track, in the film industry, in government, everywhere, had become commonplace. The rape cases. The sexual harassment stories. The demeaning comments. Life goes on. Where's your sense of humor?

Learning to live in the world meant seeing the glass half full. Ann Richards was elected Governor of Texas instead of a good ol' boy who said that if rape was inevitable, you should relax and enjoy it. The police chief of Houston is a pregnant woman who has a level this-is-my-job look and a maternity uniform with stars on the shoulder. There are so many opportunities unheard of when I was growing up.

And then I had a daughter and suddenly I saw the glass half empty. And all the rage I thought had cooled, all those how-dare-you-treat-us-like-that days, all of it comes back when I look at her, and especially when I hear her say to her brothers, "Me too."

When I look at my sons, it is within reason to imagine all the world's doors open to them. Little by little some will close, as their individual capabilities and limitations emerge. But no one is likely to look at them and mutter: "I'm not sure a man is right for a job at this level. Doesn't he have a lot of family responsibilities?"

Every time a woman looks at her daughter and thinks "she can be anything," she knows in her heart, from experience, that it's a lie. Looking at this little girl, I see it all, the old familiar ways of a world that still loves Barbie. Girls aren't good at math, dear. He needs the money more than you, sweetheart; he's got a family to support. Honey—this diaper's dirty.

It is like looking through a telescope. Over the years I learned to look through the end that showed things small and manageable. This is called a sense of proportion. And then I turned the telescope around, and all the little tableaus rushed at me, vivid as ever.

That's called reality.

We soothe ourselves with the gains that have been made. There are many role models. Role models are women who exist—and are photographed often—to make other women feel better about the fact that there aren't really enough of us anywhere, except in the lowest-paying jobs. A newspaper editor said to me not long ago, with no hint of self-consciousness, "I'd love to run your column, but we already run Ellen Goodman." Not only was there a quota; there was a quota of one.

My daughter is ready to leap into the world, as though life were chicken soup and she a delighted noodle. The work of Prof. Carol Gilligan of Harvard suggests that some time after the age of eleven this will change, that even this lively little girl will pull back, shrink back, that her constant refrain will become "I don't know." Professor Gilligan says the culture sends a message: "Keep quiet and notice the absence of women and say nothing." A smart thirteen-year-old said to me last week, "Boys don't like it if you answer too much in class."

Maybe someday, years from now, my daughter will come home and say, "Mother, at college my professor acted as if my studies were an amusing hobby and at work the man who runs my department puts his hand on my leg and to compete with the man who's in the running for my promotion who makes more than I do I can't take time to have a relationship but he has a wife and two children and I'm smarter and it doesn't make any difference and some guy tried to jump me after our date last night." And what am I supposed to say to her?

I know?

You'll get used to it?

No. Today is her second birthday and she has made me see fresh this two-tiered world, a world that, despite all our nonsense about post-feminism, continues to offer less respect and less opportunity for women than it does for men. My friends and I have learned to live with it, but my little girl deserves better. She has given me my anger back, and I intend to use it well.

That is her gift to me today. Some birthday I will return it to her, because she is going to need it.

Awaiting the Arrival of the Witch

Deborah Shouse

"I want to ask you a favor," my daughter Jessica says, when she calls me collect from college.

"Sure," I say. Hearing her voice makes me want to see her. "You may get upset," she says.

I clench the receiver and take a breath. "I'll try not to," I say.

"I'm coming home next week-end. I want you to come with me to get my nose pierced," she says.

I look at my coffee pot, my stove, the trail of milk left from this morning's hurried meal. I think of all the parenting and self-help books I read while raising Jessica. None of them has prepared me for this. I feel like Alice, falling slow motion down the dark rabbit hole.

"Sure, I'll come with you," I say.

All week, my daughter's request teases me. I sit in a marketing meeting and wonder if I should try to talk her out of this. I imagine her sitting across from me, a gold ring dangling from her nose. What happens when she gets a cold, I wonder?

I have been the first among my friends for a series of transitional events: the first to get divorced, to date as a mid-life woman, the first to deal with the intricacies of teenage sexuality. I am probably the first to be in a piercing parlor.

I park on the street and Jessica takes my hand as we stand outside.

"I'm scared," she says. The parlor is a small storefront, wedged between the adult theater boasting LIVE WOMEN NOON TO MIDNIGHT and an adult bookstore, featuring, ADULT PLAY THINGS MUST BE OVER 18. I want to whisk Jessica back into the car, lock the doors and race home.

But she tugs me inside. We stand in the middle of the shop, like Hansel and Gretel awaiting the arrival of the witch. I cannot quite look at the walls, which feature an amazing assortment of pierced parts. When I was growing up, men didn't even pierce their ears. Girls had just one dainty pierce, often filled with a simple pearl or rhinestone.

"May I help you?" a tall man emerges. He blends into the walls, with his white t-shirt and white slacks. I notice the three pierces in his ear and the delicate silver ring in his nose. As he talks, I am mesmerized by the soothing glint of the blue beaded ring that pierces his mouth and the silver ring in his tongue. I wonder where else holes have been bored into his body.

He and Jessica discuss the kind of jewelry she will need. He motions her to a small room and I follow.

"Don't look," the man cautions me as he lays Jessica down on a table and prepares his instruments.

"This will just hurt for a second," he says. I hold her hand and turn my head. The thought of something piercing my daughter's body hurts me. Perhaps that is the point—Jessica is separating herself from me with a ritual that marks her body as her own flesh, a flesh sacred and new.

As I stare at the wall, I think of the other small rooms I've been in with Jessica: pediatrician's, dermatologist's, dentist's offices. We have faced men with needles before, but this time seems different. This time, I am not a caretaker, but a witness.

"You're very brave," I tell her.

"Nothing's happened yet," she says, laughing.

I think of all the rituals that society validates with greeting cards, holidays and special products. My daughter's ritual is a personal one. I am the greeting card: I am to usher her from her old body to her new.

She squeezes my hand and I squeeze back.

"It's done," the man announces.

A stainless steel ring now quivers in my daughter's right nostril. I stare, wondering if it will become as familiar and normal as her freckles.

"It may be sore for a couple days," the man advises.

My daughter opens her purse and writes a check. Just last year, she would have asked me for the money.

I feel hollow as we get into the car. My daughter is grown, separate from me, totally in charge of her own money and her own body.

"Thanks for coming with me," she says. She smiles and the nose ring looks like a nice surprise on her face. It adds something mysterious, something dark and not easily understood, an unopened map to my daughter.

"What did you do this week-end?" my friend Judy asks me, Monday at work.

"I went with my daughter to get her nose pierced," I answer. I want to see how the words taste.

"Wow. What was it like?"

I describe each step carefully, as though I am a gourmet chef sharing a special recipe.

As a child, I had many rules about my body. I was cautioned not to be too sexy, too flamboyant, too brash, too carefree. My body grew up stiff and unpracticed, unaware of its graceful potential.

Perhaps I too tried to guard my daughter's body, to fill her with rules and keep her safe. But Jessica has created her own personal reclamation project. She has pierced my fences and said to her body, "I love you and you are mine." And she has said to me, her mother, teacher, nemesis, friend, her witness, "I love you and I am my own."

Ghost Child

Joanne Lewis Sears

To Steve, lost to schizophrenia

At half a year
Your cheeks were brown and round as the wheels
You turned interminably
On the upturned trike,
Too young to give your driving fancy
Words, or more than a round sound
Of power in the hum and roar
Where you played, safe at my front door.

By seventeen
The round had chiseled back to bone:
A length of cheek and leg and hand.
The hum of power now
Spilled from the foreign car
You slaved to drive;
A length of fingers
On the wheel of car
And on the strings
Of your guitar.

Lent me for nineteen years,
Your teasing fingers touched
My shoulder from the blind side,
Forever fooled, your catch could catch me
Every time off guard.
Which is, I reckon, why, when
Your mind sickened,
I balked at recognition.

Your long-boned body now
Still lopes and shuffles,
Picks at a guitar,
The round brown eyes have sunk,
The words come jumbled to your tongue,
Your chin, scarred from shaving,
Shaking, with cheap blades,
Diminishes.

I grow old, ghost,
Waiting for my son
Of the round cheeks,
Of the long bones,
To redirect the wheel
Now spun careening courseless
Through dark worlds.
Make the wheel turn, ghost child.
Return.

Learning the Firebird Suite

Nancy B. Miller

The curtain opens.
Darkness of poltergeist 'cellos
Punctuated by basses tiptoeing
               in descending tri-tones.
Ivan thinks he must catch the Firebird,
A talisman for his journey
               through the dark woods of monsters.
He swirls in an infernal dance
               with the subjects of Katchei, the magician.
He lulls the monster to sleep with a sweet
Berceuse.
Softly, safely,
He sneaks past with the princesses.
Everything important will happen on F sharp.
The Firebird promises,
               You will only need my one feather.

Program in hand,
I lean to touch my son's hand;
It rests on the wooden arm
Between our red velvet seats
that barely stay down with his weight.

My small, brave Ivan.

I cannot trust one feather.

That's My Girl

Marael Johnson

Men usually aspire
for sons who are
chips off their
old blocks, especially
when it comes to
sports or business.
Not so women—
particularly me.
My daughter is married
to a good guy,
pulls superb grades
at a prestigious university.
Eh, big deal.
Then one day
she says, Mom,
first thing I'm gonna do
when I graduate
and get a good job,
is to hire
a toy boy maid—
all for myself—
who walks around
in a pair of tight shorts
and speaks no English
except "yes, mistress."
My eyeballs
flash and explode,
all my pulses
pop and spark,
and my heart dances
an evil-woman jig—
I'm all awash
with motherly pride.

The Blessing

Carolyn Kizer

for Ashley

I.
Daughter-my-mother
you have observed my worst.
Holding me together at your expense
has made you burn cool.

So did I in childhood:
nursed her old hurts and doubts
myself made cool to shallowness.
She grew out as I grew in.
At mid-point, our furies met.

My mother's dust has rested
for fifteen years
in the front hall closet
because we couldn't bear to bury it.
Her dust-lined, dust-coated urn
squats among the size-eleven overshoes.
My father, who never forgets
his overshoes,
has forgotten that.

Hysterical-tongued daughter
of a dead marriage
you shed hot tears in the bed
of that benign old woman
whose fierce joy you were:
tantrums in the closet
taking upon yourself the guilt
the split parents never felt.

Child and old woman
soothing each other
sharing the same face
in a span of seventy years
the same mother wit.

I must go home, *says my father,*
his mind straying;
this is a hard time
for your mother. *But she's been dead*
these fifteen years.
Daughter and daughter, we sit
on either side.
Whose? Which? He's not sure.
After long silence
don't press me, *he says.*

II.
Mother, hysterical-tongued,
age and grace burned away
your excesses, left
that lavender-sweet child
who turned up the thermostat
on her electric blanket, folded
her hands on her breast:
you had dreamed death
as a sweet prince:
like marrying Nehru, *you said.*

Dearest, does your dust hum
in the front hall closet
this is a hard time for me
among the umbrella points
the canes and overshoes
of that cold climate?

Each week she denies it
my blithe mother
in that green, cloud-free landscape
where we whisper our dream-secrets
to each other.

III.
Daughter, you lived through
my difficult affairs
as I tried to console
your burnt-out childhood.
We coped with our fathers
compared notes
on the old one and the cold one,
learned to moderate our hates.
Risible in suffering
we grew up together.

Mother-my-daughter
I have been blessed
on both sides of my life.
Forgive me if sometimes
like my fading father
I see you as one.

Not that I confuse
your two identities
as he does, taking off
or putting on his overshoes,
but my own role:

I lean on the bosom
of that double mother
the ghost by night, the girl by day,
I between my
two old furies
alone but comforted.

And I will whisper blithely
in your dreams
when you are as old as I
my hard time over.
Meanwhile, keep warm
your love, your bed
and your wise heart and head
my good daughter.

Cornucopia

Frank Miller, Photographer

Frank Miller's interest in photography began when he was thirteen: "One Christmas morning, I received a 'Kodak Duraflex' from Mom. It was not only something I wanted but something I didn't expect to get. I photographed everything: the fellas playing stick ball, and hanging out in a Bronx park, along with cats, dogs and pigeons. Some pictures were too dark, blurred and others had heads decapitated. I was the block photographer, the cat you had to watch out for, always lurking about trying to capture an unguarded moment." He instinctively knows that catching his subjects when they are the least self-conscious is tantamount to perfection. In 1961, Mr. Miller attended the New York Institute of Photography. In 1966, his career was launched when he was hired as Photography Assistant at the Len Siegler Studios and in 1968, Studio Manager at the Roy Coggins Studio. He received a B.A. degree from Goddard College in Vermont in 1975. Since 1988, Mr. Miller has been employed as a Dropout Prevention Teacher, creating programs to guide students back into the mainstream. His art reflects himself; it is diverse in subject matter and unique in representation. Some of his photographs look like abstract art; others are so real they jump out of the frames. For *Our Mothers Our Selves,* Mr. Miller traversed different areas of Florida and came up with a collage of mothers and children "doing their thing." In October 1994, he had a successful exhibition of his work in West Palm Beach.

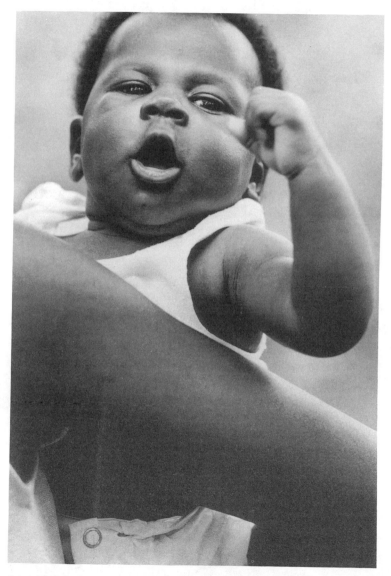

I Am Somebody

Cornucopia

We Are Family

Visions

Field of Dreams

Hula Hooping

We Wait, We Hope...

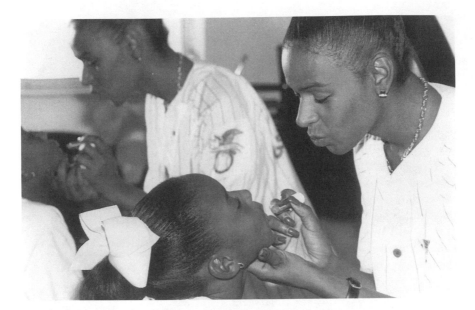

Pucker

Regina and James

Our Future Is in the Soil

Three Smiles

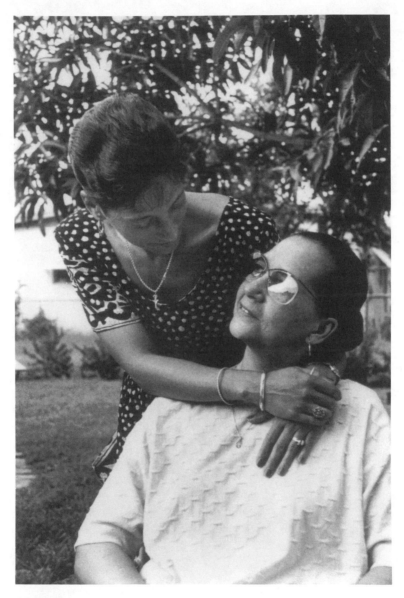

Admiration

II – Beyond Reflection

If knowledge is lacking you,
Seek inwardly
Your simplicity;
There you will find
Your mirror,
Always ready for you.

—Hadewijch of Antwerp

I Know Why the Caged Bird Sings (excerpt)

Maya Angelou

People walked along the streets as if the pavements hadn't all crumbled beneath their feet. They pretended to breathe in and out while all the time I knew the air had been sucked away in a monstrous inhalation from God Himself. I alone was suffocating in the nightmare.

The little pleasure I was able to take from the fact that if I could have a baby I obviously wasn't a lesbian was crowded into my mind's tiniest corner by the massive pushing in of fear, guilt and self revulsion.

For eons, it seemed, I had accepted my plight as the hapless, put-upon victim of fate and the Furies, but this time I had to face the fact that I had brought my new catastrophe upon myself. How was I to blame the innocent man whom I had lured into making love to me? In order to be profoundly dishonest, a person must have one of two qualities: either he is unscrupulously ambitious, or he is unswervingly egocentric. He must believe that for his ends to be served all things and people can justifiably be shifted about, or that he is the center not only of his own world but of the worlds which others inhabit. I had neither element in my personality, so I hefted the burden of pregnancy at sixteen onto my own shoulders where it belonged. Admittedly, I staggered under the weight.

I finally sent a letter to Bailey, who was at sea with the merchant marine. He wrote back, and he cautioned me against telling Mother of my condition. We both knew her to be violently opposed to abortions, and she would very likely order me to quit school. Bailey suggested that if I quit school before getting my high school diploma I'd find it nearly impossible to return.

The first three months, while I was adapting myself to the fact of pregnancy (I didn't really link pregnancy to the possibility of my having a baby until weeks before my confinement), were a hazy period in which days seemed to lie just below the water level, never emerging fully.

Fortunately, Mother was tied up tighter than Dick's hatband in the weave of her own life. She noticed me as usual out of the corner of her existence. As long as I was healthy, clothed and smiling she felt no need to focus her attention on me. As always, her major concern was to live the life given to her, and her children were expected to do the same. And to do it without too much brouhaha.

Under her loose scrutiny I grew more buxom, and my brown skin smoothed and tight-pored, like pan cakes fried on an unoiled skillet. And still she didn't suspect. Some years before, I had established a code which never varied. I didn't lie. It was understood that I didn't lie because I was too proud to be caught and forced to admit that I was capable of less than Olympian action. Mother must have concluded that since I was above out-and-out lying I was also beyond deceit. She was deceived.

All my motions focalized on pretending to be that guileless school-girl who had nothing more wearying to think about than mid-term exams. Strangely enough, I very nearly caught the essence of teenage capricious-ness as I played the role. Except that there were times when physically I couldn't deny to myself that something very important was taking place in my body.

Mornings, I never knew if I would have to jump off the streetcar one step ahead of the warm sea of nausea that threatened to sweep me away. On solid ground, away from the ship-motioned vehicle and the smell of hands coated with recent breakfasts, I regained my balance and waited for the next trolley.

School recovered its lost magic. For the first time since Stamps, in-formation was exciting for itself alone. I burrowed myself into caves of facts, and found delight in the logical resolutions of mathematics.

I credit my new reactions (although I didn't know at the time that I had learned anything from them) to the fact that during what surely must have been a critical period I was not dragged down by hopelessness. Life had a conveyor-belt quality. It went on unpursued and unpursuing, and my only thought was to remain erect, and keep my secret along with my bal-ance.

Midway along to delivery, Bailey came home and brought me a spun-silver bracelet from South America, Thomas Wolfe's *Look Homeward, Angel,* and a slew of new dirty jokes.

As my sixth month approached, Mother left San Francisco for Alas-ka. She was to open a night club and planned to stay three or four months until it got on its feet. Daddy Clidell was to look after me but I was more or less left on my own recognizance and under the unsteady gaze of our lady roomers.

Mother left the city amid a happy and cheerful send-off party (after all how many Negroes were in Alaska?), and I felt treacherous allowing her to go without informing her that she was soon to be a grandmother.

Two days after V-Day, I stood with the San Francisco Summer School class at Mission High School and received my diploma. That evening, in the bosom of the now-dear family home I uncoiled my fearful secret and in a brave gesture left a note on Daddy Clidell's bed. It read: *Dear Parents, I am sorry to bring this disgrace on the family, but I am pregnant. Marguerite.*

The confusion that ensued when I explained to my stepfather that I expected to deliver the baby in three weeks, more or less, was reminiscent of a Molière comedy. Except that it was funny only years later. Daddy Clidell told Mother that I was "three weeks gone." Mother, regarding me as a woman for the first time, said indignantly, "She's more than any three weeks." They both accepted the fact that I was further along than they had first been told but found it nearly impossible to believe that I had carried a baby, eight months and one week, without their being any the wiser.

Mother asked, "Who is the boy?" I told her. She recalled him, faintly.
"Do you want to marry him?"
"No."
"Does he want to marry you?" The father had stopped speaking to me during my fourth month.
"No."
"Well, that's that. No use ruining three lives." There was no overt or subtle condemnation. She was Vivian Baxter Jackson. Hoping for the best, prepared for the worse and unsurprised by anything in between.

Daddy Clidell assured me that I had nothing to worry about. That "women been gittin' pregnant ever since Eve ate that apple." He sent one of his waitresses to I. Magnin's to buy maternity dresses for me. For the next two weeks I whirled around the city going to doctors, taking vitamin shots and pills, buying clothes for the baby, and except for the rare moments alone, enjoying the imminent blessed event.

After a short labor, and without too much pain (I decided that the pain of delivery was overrated), my son was born. Just as gratefulness was confused in my mind with love, so possession became mixed up with motherhood. I had a baby. He was beautiful and mine. Totally mine. No one had bought him for me. No one had helped me endure the sickly gray months. I had had help in the child's conception, but no one could deny that I had had an immaculate pregnancy.

Totally my possession, and I was afraid to touch him. Home from the hospital. I sat for hours by his bassinet and absorbed his mysterious perfection. His extremities were so dainty they appeared unfinished. Mother handled him easily with the casual confidence of a baby nurse, but I dreaded being forced to change his diapers. Wasn't I famous for awkwardness? Suppose I let him slip, or put my fingers on that throbbing pulse on the top of his head?

Mother came to my bed one night bringing my three-week-old baby. She pulled the cover back and told me to get up and hold him while she put rubber sheets on my bed. She explained that he was going to sleep with me.

I begged in vain. I was sure to roll over and crush out his life or break those fragile bones. She wouldn't hear of it, and within minutes the pretty golden baby was lying on his back in the center of my bed, laughing at me.

I lay on the edge of the bed, stiff with fear, and vowed not to sleep all night long. But the eat-sleep routine I had begun in the hospital, and kept up under Mother's dictatorial command, got the better of me. I dropped off.

My shoulder was shaken gently. Mother whispered, "Maya, wake up. But don't move."

I knew immediately that the awakening had to do with the baby. I tensed. "I'm awake."

She turned the light on and said, "Look at the baby." My fears were so powerful I couldn't move to look at the center of the bed. She said again, "Look at the baby." I didn't hear sadness in her voice, and that helped me to break the bonds of terror. The baby was no longer in the center of the bed. At first I thought he had moved. But after closer investigation I found that I was lying on my stomach with my arm bent at a right angle. Under the tent of blanket, which was poled by my elbow and forearm, the baby slept touching my side.

Mother whispered, "See, you don't have to think about doing the right thing. If you're for the right thing, then you do it without thinking."

She turned out the light and I patted my son's body lightly and went back to sleep.

Reasons...

Sue Walker

Reasons to find my mother
I may need a transplant—
a kidney, bone marrow;
she could provide.
I could answer questions
on medical forms. Yes,
my mother had diabetes,
high blood pressure, T.B.
I would know why
I was near-sighted,
why my blood type was O.
I would recognize my crooked
fingers, understand my tendency
to over-eat. I could claim her
before it was too late, ask
her to my home. I could swear
forgiveness, if I could not give her
love.
Reasons not to find my mother
Past forty, I am too old for hunting eggs.
She has alzheimer, wouldn't remember.
Her children would hate me, say:
"That woman is no relation of ours!"
Perhaps she needs money; I could provide,
but I have my own family.
I don't want to share Christmas with her,
Easter, Thanksgiving, or the Fourth of July.
Or buy her a blanket for Mother's day.
No Mother gives her child away;
I don't want to know
the woman who birthed me—
not now.

The Woman Warrior

Maxine Hong Kingston

"You must not tell anyone," my mother said, "what I am about to tell you. In China your father had a sister who killed herself. She jumped into the family well. We say that your father has all brothers because it is as if she had never been born.

"In 1924 just a few days after our village celebrated seventeen hurry-up weddings—to make sure that every young man who went 'out on the road' would responsibly come home—your father and his brothers and your grandfather and his brothers and your aunt's new husband sailed for America, the Gold Mountain. It was your grandfather's last trip. Those lucky enough to get contracts waved goodbye from the decks. They fed and guarded the stowaways and helped them off in Cuba, New York, Bali, Hawaii. 'We'll meet in California next year,' they said. All of them sent money home.

"I remember looking at your aunt one day when she and I were dressing; I had not noticed before that she had such a protruding melon of a stomach. But I did not think, 'She's pregnant,' until she began to look like other pregnant women, her shirt pulling and the white tops of her black pants showing. She could not have been pregnant, you see, because her husband had been gone for years. No one said anything. We did not discuss it. In early summer she was ready to have the child, long after the time when it could have been possible.

"The village had also been counting. On the night the baby was to be born the villagers raided our house. Some were crying. Like a great saw, teeth strung with lights, files of people walked zigzag across our land, tearing the rice. Their lanterns doubled in the disturbed black water, which drained away through the broken bunds. As the villagers closed in, we could see that some of them, probably men and women we knew well, wore white masks. The people with long hair hung it over their faces. Women with short hair made it stand up on end. Some had tied white bands around their foreheads, arms, and legs.

"At first they threw mud and rocks at the house. Then they threw eggs and began slaughtering our stock. We could hear the animals scream their deaths—the roosters, the pigs, a last great roar from the ox. Familiar wild heads flared in our night windows; the villagers encircled us. Some of the faces stopped to peer at us, their eyes rushing like searchlights. The heads flattened against the panes, framed heads, and left red prints.

"The villagers broke in the front and the back doors at the same time, even though we had not locked the doors against them. Their knives dripped with the blood of our animals. They smeared blood on the doors and walls. One woman swung a chicken, whose throat she had split, splattering blood in red arcs about her. We stood together in the middle of our house, in the family hall with the pictures and tables of the ancestors around us, and looked straight ahead.

"At that time the house had only two wings. When the men came back, we would build two more to enclose our courtyard and a third one to begin a second courtyard. The villagers pushed through both wings, even your grandparents' rooms, to find your aunt's, which was also mine until the men returned. From this room a new wing for one of the younger families would grow. They ripped up her clothes and shoes and broke her combs, grinding them underfoot. They tore her work from the loom. They scattered the cooking fire and rolled the new weaving in it. We could hear them in the kitchen breaking our bowls and banging the pots. They overturned the great waist-high earthenware jugs; duck eggs, pickled fruits, vegetables burst out and mixed in acrid torrents. The old woman from the next field swept a broom through the air and loosed the spirits-of-the-broom over our heads. 'Pig.' 'Ghost.' 'Pig,' they sobbed and scolded while they ruined our house.

"When they left, they took sugar and oranges to bless themselves. They cut pieces from the dead animals. Some of them took bowls that were not broken and clothes that were not torn. Afterward we swept up the rice and sewed it back up into sacks. But the smells from the spilled preserves lasted. Your aunt gave birth in the pigsty that night. The next morning when I went for the water, I found her and the baby plugging up the family well.

"Don't let your father know that I told you. He denies her. Now that you have started to menstruate, what happened to her could happen to you. Don't humiliate us. You wouldn't like to be forgotten as if you had never been born. The villagers are watchful."

If my aunt had betrayed the family at a time of large grain yields and peace, when many boys were born, and wings were being built on many houses, perhaps she might have escaped such severe punishment. But the men—hungry, greedy, tired of planting in dry soil, cuckolded—had had to leave the village in order to send food-money home. There were ghost plagues, bandit plagues, wars with the Japanese, floods. My Chinese brother and sister had died of an unknown sickness. Adultery, perhaps only a mistake during good times, became a crime when the village needed food.

The round moon cakes and round doorways, the round tables of graduated size that fit one roundness inside another, round windows and rice bowls—these talismen had lost their power to warn this family of the law: a family must be whole, faithfully keep the descent line by having sons to feed the old and the dead, who in turn look after the family. The villagers came to show my aunt and her lover-in-hiding a broken house. The villagers were speeding up the circling of events because she was too shortsighted to see that her infidelity had already harmed the village, that waves of consequences would return unpredictably, sometimes in disguise, as now, to hurt her. This roundness had to be made coin-sized so that she would see its circumference: punish her at the birth of her baby. Awaken her to the inexorable. People who refused fatalism because they could invent small resources insisted on culpability. Deny accidents and wrest fault from the stars.

After the villagers left, their lanterns now scattering in various directions toward home, the family broke their silence and cursed her. "Aiaa, we're going to die. Death is coming. Death is coming. Look what you've done. You've killed us. Ghost! Dead ghost! Ghost! You've never been born." She ran out into the fields, far enough from the house so that she could no longer hear their voices, and pressed herself against the earth, her own land no more. When she felt the birth coming, she thought that she had been hurt. Her body seized together. "They've hurt me too much," she thought. "This is gall, and it will kill me." Her forehead and knees against the earth, her body convulsed and then released her onto her back. The black well of sky and stars went out and out and out forever; her body and her complexity seemed to disappear. She was one of the stars, a bright dot in blackness, without home, without a companion, in eternal cold and silence. An agoraphobia rose in her, speeding higher and higher, bigger and bigger; she would not be able to contain it; there would be no end to fear.

Flayed, unprotected against space, she felt pain return, focusing her body. This pain chilled her—a cold, steady kind of surface pain. Inside, spasmodically, the other pain, the pain of the child, heated her. For hours she lay on the ground, alternately body and space. Sometimes a vision of normal comfort obliterated reality: she saw the family in the evening gambling at the dining table, the young people massaging their elders' backs. She saw them congratulating one another, high joy on the mornings the rice shoots came up. When these pictures burst, the stars drew yet further apart. Black space opened.

She got to her feet to fight better and remembered that old-fashioned women gave birth in their pigsties to fool the jealous, pain-dealing gods, who do not snatch piglets. Before the next spasms could stop her, she ran to the pigsty, each step a rushing out into the emptiness. She climbed over the fence and knelt in the dirt. It was good to have a fence enclosing her, a tribal person alone.

Laboring, this woman who had carried her child as a foreign growth that sickened her every day, expelled it at last. She reached down to touch the hot, wet, moving mass, surely smaller than anything human, and could feel that it was human after all—fingers, toes, nails, nose. She pulled it up on her belly, and it lay curled there, butt in the air, feet precisely tucked one under the other. She opened her loose shirt and buttoned the child inside. After resting, it squirmed and thrashed and she pushed it up to her breast. It turned its head this way and that until it found her nipple. There, it made little snuffling noises. She clenched her teeth at its preciousness, lovely as a young calf, a piglet, a little dog.

She may have gone to the pigsty as a last act of responsibility: she would protect this child as she had protected its father. It would look after her soul, leaving supplies on her grave. But how would this tiny child without family find her grave when there would be no marker for her anywhere, neither in the earth nor the family hall? No one would give her a family hall name. She had taken the child with her into the wastes. At its birth the two of them had felt the same raw pain of separation, a wound that only the family pressing tight could close. A child with no descent line would not soften her life but only trail after her, ghost-like, begging her to give it purpose. At dawn the villagers on their way to the fields would stand around the fence and look.

Full of milk, the little ghost slept. When it awoke, she hardened her breasts against the milk that crying loosens. Toward morning she picked up the baby and walked to the well.

Carrying the baby to the well shows loving. Otherwise abandon it. Turn its face into the mud. Mothers who love their children take them along. It was probably a girl; there is some hope of forgiveness for boys.

Nursing the Adopted Child: A Different Pace of Bonding

Lisa Gayle

My mother has spoken about the magic that occurred the moment I was placed in her arms. For her, that instant was filled with inspiration and wonder. The culmination of nine months of pregnancy and a long difficult birth, it marked her passage into motherhood. She regards that time with awe and expected me to feel the same.

The night I first met Jacob, he was in a little ball, huddled in the corner of a crib in Guatemala City. He was eight weeks old and not yet my son. The room was dark, the surroundings strange. Although I had waited for this moment for years, the transition to parenthood happened in an instant. I was still wondering what it was like to be a parent while the child who was to be my son was cradled in my arms.

I made the decision to be a mom over and over again, after every period and throughout the adoption process, about two hundred times. I was absolutely committed to being a mom. But I didn't know Jacob, and he did not know me. I stroked his tiny fingers as I tried to shake the feeling that I was holding this baby in a dream.

In the foster home, Jacob had been physically provided for; emotionally he had been alone. His bottle was routinely propped. He spent his days lying in his crib, often crying. At eight weeks, he had difficulty cuddling and making eye contact. Infant massage, designed to relax, made him cry. The continuum, from safe womb to loving arms, from continuous placental nutrition to frequent suckling at mother's breast, was not his experience.

I also carried pain. I was not present at his birth, not able to help him through the separation from his birth mother, could not provide human warmth for those long eight weeks. I had missed an important time in my child's life and in my life as a mother. I felt a sore need to make our bonding as physical as possible. I wanted to nurse.

Lactation without pregnancy is a demand, demand, demand and supply process. Sucking alone can produce the hormones that change the structure of the breasts and create a milk supply, but it's a slow process and milk is usually less abundant.

When my husband and I received our referral from Guatemala, I rented a high-quality breast pump. Pump and think of your baby, La Leche League's literature proclaimed. I looked at the out-of-focus Polaroid snapshot and longed to be with him. I cried for the mother who had to relinquish her child and for the child who was in between mothers.

Many adopting parents find it too painful to prepare for bringing the baby home before they are certain there will be a baby to bring home. Painting a nursery, buying diapers or bottles are reminders of how much a child is missed. Pumping rendered me far more vulnerable than any other preparation. I stopped within a week.

When I arrived in Guatemala, warnings of nipple confusion and my lack of success pumping added to the nervousness of a first time mom. I didn't want to push nursing on Jacob. I wanted to respect his pace and how he had coped with being alone.

We walked the halls of his foster home, him crying in my arms at yet another change. After two days he began to nuzzle into my body. After several more days, he rooted at my breast. It was time.

Nursing is a learned experience passed from generation to generation. In our society where many mothers are reclaiming this ability, knowledgeable support is often an essential part of successful nursing. Studies show that adoptive nursing is overwhelmingly successful with the help of supportive professionals and when started within the first week after birth.

Adoptive nursing is also successful in societies where nursing is the way of life. A worker at the nursing home told me about a woman who nursed her sister's child. She lactated with the help of a Guatemalan drink and using hot compresses on her upper back.

On the other hand, the American mothers I know who have tried to nurse older infants report their babies protested and had difficulties latching on. These moms stopped trying when they felt the attempts to nurse were interfering with bonding rather than enhancing it. That was my initial experience.

I had purchased a Supplemental Nursing System consisting of a bottle that hung from my neck and thin, soft tubing leading from the bottle and taped to my nipple. I held Jacob in my arms and gently rubbed his cheek; his mouth opened. I tried to insert my aureola and the tubing; he screamed. I calmed both of us down and tried again. This time he fought me.

Nursing made Jacob angry. His mouth opened for a Gerber nipple, not wide enough to produce adequate suction to start formula flowing from the supplementer. He would suck and get no results. On top of that, each time we tried I was more nervous. If only I could keep the bottle from tangling in the tubing and "do it right." After a few more sessions, I put nursing on hold.

From time to time, Jacob would root at my breast. Eventually he did latch on, but without the supplementer, not at feeding times and with little body contact. Only when he was lying by himself, in a position imitating the one he was in when his bottle had been propped, could he accept the breast.

Back in the States we tried again with no success. I tried to remember my perspective: do what increases the bond. Jacob's wailing and my anxiety wasn't helping us. Our doctor, who had relactated to nurse her second child, discouraged me. "He's doing so well now," she said, "don't do anything to disturb that." With sadness, I put the supplementer away.

A month later I still felt something was missing. Amazingly, Jacob would still occasionally root. To hell with recommended positions and doctor's advice, it was time to use my head. Hoping to widen his sucking, I used a Playtex nurser for three days. Then I lay Jacob down and tried to duplicate the old bottle-prop position. I dangled my breast and the tubing by his mouth, tucked the supplementer bottle under my chin. He opened wide enough to securely latch on.

Jacob squealed with excitement; his bright eyes danced up at me, but when his mouth broke into a wide smile, he fell off the breast. Immediately, he lunged at the breast, latched on for three more sucks and dropped off to show his delight. Back and forth he went, sucking, smiling, dropping off, and sucking again. Within a few days, he was nursing in my arms.

For me, the skin-to-skin contact was compelling; no way could my mind wander to shopping lists and household chores. His sucking stimulated my production of prolactin with its soothing effects and increase in nurturant feelings. I was an intimate part of his nourishment and I felt it intensely.

At six months, nursing relaxed him enough to help him sleep. At eight months, he finished nursing and, still in my arms, rolled onto his back and looked directly into my eyes. His face had the bliss of contentment; love was in his eyes.

At twelve months, as other breast-fed children do, he would grab for my breasts when distressed. He also indicated his desire to nurse by bringing me the supplementer. At fifteen months, to distinguish nursing from the bottles he called "ba-ba," he named the supplementer "ma-ba." At seventeen months and ready to nurse, he curled into my lap and pronounced himself a ba-bee. Far from being an unwanted regression, this was a redoing of the painful time when he was alone, an act of healing.

When Jacob was a toddler, our nursing became the most direct way for us to reestablish closeness. Before naptime and bedtime, the skin-to-skin touch and full body contact eased him through his separation anxiety that would surface as he fell asleep.

Jacob is now three and one-half. We are no longer nursing, but the closeness that developed through that process has continued. I remember how our pain was transformed, through skin-to-skin contact, nurturance and love. My awe comes from our healing, my inspiration and wonder from our making a family when there was none before.

Sitting With My Mother and Father

Robert Bly

My father's hard breathing
We all three
Notice. To continue
To live here,
He must take air.
But taking air
Commits him
To sharing it
With the puma
And the eagle.
When breathing stops,
He will be free
Of that company.
He came reluctantly
From the water world,
And does not
Want to change
Again.
My mother is not sure
Where she wants to be,
But this air world
Is all she can
Remember, and nieces
Are here,
Friends, a son.
She sits with puzzled eyes,
As if to say,
"Where is
That reckless man
For whom I left

My father?
Is it this man
With gaunt cheeks
On the bed?
All those times
I drove into town,
Carefully, over packed
Snow, is this
What it comes to?" Yes,
It is, my dear
Mother.
The tablecloths
You saved
Are all gone;
The baked corn dish
You made for your boys,
The Christmas Eves,
Opening perfume—
Evening in Paris—
From your husband,
The hope that a man
Would alter his habits
For you—
They are all gone.
The nurse takes my father
For his bath.
"What sort
Of flowers are those?"
"Daisies," I say.
A few minutes
Later you ask
Again.
You and I
Wait here
For Jacob to come
Back from his bath.
What can I
Do but feel
Time
Go through me,
And sit here
With you?

Bending Over Roses at Twilight

Franz Douskey

my mother holds out her worn gloves.
her rusted trowel, that has fathomed
immeasurable underground arteries,
is motionless in the gauzy twilight.

the roses stretch toward an unknown
magnetic pole, as a blue vein
of cigarette smoke rises into
refractories of borrowed light.

an evening breeze arrives.
the hens, unusually quiet, lean forward,
the hammock billows like a green sail.

my mother bends over the ground she
has worked so many years,
soothsaying beneath the eastern moon
some great secret truth. and the roses,
suddenly flexible, nod agreement.

Mercy Killing

Margaret Fulton

I see the folds of my young flesh
open hungrily.

"My darling..."
Your vicious deceit
strokes my soul.

"Render me deaf, Mommy,"
I cried in anguished silence.
I tried to shut you out,
exile you,
assassinate your soul
at the very moment
my bludgeoned tears
screamed, and shucked
your innards clean.

Your raspy voice echoed back
in languid coos of drunkenness,
"My darling," you said softly,
"come closely now, come,
be Mommy's little whore."

Women and Other Mothers

Sarah Morgan

I have not always known that my mother is beautiful. It is something I think she has never known. Women see themselves in the past tense, gazing at photographs and thinking, God, I was beautiful at twenty, at thirty, at forty. See how my skin skims brownly over my ribs in the beach picture, see how my neck arches and my eyes glisten as I smile without a wrinkle in my bridal picture. At a bright mirror the woman sees the crepe that slacks from her neck and a tangle of lines that siphons the glisten from her eyes. In ten years' time she will look back at today's picture and say, God, but I was lovely then, why did I not know it? All her selves and images reflect like a mirror angled in back to one at front, and she is so busy comparing yesterday with tomorrow that she does not know today.

When I was a child I thought that other women were beautiful. The neighbor woman was my mother's age and red haired, legions of freckles splattering her face and shoulders. She sat me on the counter to chat while she swept and cleaned. When I paused for a breath she murmured, "Is that right? Is that right?" and kept on sweeping, her hair frizzed wires and her fingers wide. I stayed in her kitchen as long as she would have me. At times she let me play with her jewelry box, an ornate white one. A plastic ballerina in pink turned slowly on the top of it, its skirt tattered but stiff, while tinny music creaked.

My mother's skin was olive and clear; her things were not so beautiful to my child-eyes. Her jewelry box had been her grandmother's in Germany, heavy and wooden. It had no ballerina, no music. My mother wore an old sweater from high school and sloppy socks and pants. She wore dresses only on Sunday and did not permanent wave her heavy hair.

My aunt was quite beautiful, I thought. Her dark hair waved tightly against her skull and her lips always were red. Her mark of singular beauty was a blue vein that crossed her cheek, bold and pulsing. She was the only one in our family with skin so thin; the vein gave her a startled fragility, I thought, and I told my mother that drawing such a vein across her face would make her pretty. What my mother replied I do not know, but she gave me a permanent wave and tied my curls in a red ribbon.

Now, in this hospital, I am the most beautiful. My son tells me I am lovely; on my face he sees his brows and chin but his blue and pale eyes come from the past of his grandfathers. When he was in kindergarten he told me his teacher was beautiful because she had fat thighs. I had spent a lifetime avoiding such a description. I had wanted not fat or round thighs but sleek and smooth ones, the thighs of a young boy whose muscles are just finding shape.

My father's friend Shari had such thighs, thighs of enough substance only to skim her bone and muscle. Her body had that sense to it, a sparse and lean beauty. Her face was sharp but smooth; had it been crossed with a vein she would have realized my childish ideal of perfection. I came to admire Shari most; she surpassed my freckled neighbor and my aunt. I often liked Shari more than I liked my own mother; Shari's hair came to a neat end at her shoulders; it did not jumble and fall the way my mother's did. Shari wore broad black hats and gloves, red suits, glistening pearls.

I told my mother that when I grew up I would buy her a string of pearls like those that Shari wore. My mother asked me not to. The only pieces of jewelry she ever wore were her wedding ring and a pair of silver starfish earrings. Other pieces lay in the wooden box she had gotten from her grandmother, but my mother never wore them. When I had grown she gave the box of jewelry to me; I wore none of it. For many years I preferred the string of pearls Shari gave me for my eighteenth birthday.

I have the wooden box here at the hospital. It is filled with the dime store jewelry my son gave me over the years of his childhood. He saved allowances and raked leaves, spending his quarters and dimes at counters of cheap beads and hammered tin. I wore each gift happily and often, no matter how gaudy. I wear them now sometimes. It is painful to see the blue and gold beads around this neck when I can feel them around a neck so many years younger.

The way my father looked at Shari seemed to me to be the way the handsome men in movies looked at the women they loved. I saw Shari through my father's eyes and thought her perfect; through these same eyes I saw that my mother was lacking. My mother lacked pride in her appearance: she grocery shopped in hair curlers. My mother lacked a sense of propriety: she would not wear high heels. My mother lacked the model's figure:

she was short and curving. My mother lacked an easy social grace: she could not converse with strangers. She was not the woman I longed to be. My father was devoted to my mother, I believe, but he loved Shari.

The year I became den mother is the year I discovered how beautiful my mother was. An instant's remembrance of my mother in a blue uniform, the skirt straight and tight across her narrow hips, the jacket close at the waist and straining across her chest. Her hair was thick and auburn, a nest upon which her cap rested. In one instant I saw myself and raised my hand to volunteer, for, once having realized my mother's beauty, I wanted it for myself.

To become her I had to become different, to leave Shari behind me. In such moments are lives changed. Or, perhaps, only diverted.

My first roommate here was a girl of twenty who would not eat; she drank diet cola all day. For two full weeks she did not eat; she hid empty drink cans all over the room, in my closet and my dresser and the pockets of my jacket. Each day she spent hours dressing and making up her face. She looked young and lean and healthy, thinner than Shari ever could have hoped to be. Finally they moved her from my room to shadow her: every minute an attendant stays by her side. They confiscated the plastic bottle that she kept filled with diet drink in order not to go mad. Still she hoarded cans of soda and would not eat. Only when they threatened to send her to the state hospital would she take some soup.

The boy in the Daffy Duck slippers is being sent away. He tries to kill himself. He threw a wooden chair through the back fire exit and sliced his wrist with the glass. He tried to hang himself with the drapes but he was too tall and the rod crashed down. Every night I lend him my credit card so he can call his mother. She knows where he is but will not call him because she is disappointed.

I was disappointed but never in my son.

I hope my son is never hard on himself. The boy in Daffy Duck slippers and the girl who will not eat, they are hard on themselves. Were they older they would realize that cruelty is not something they need to practice against themselves, that cruelty is the function of others. That is why we have these others, why we love them and take them into ourselves, because they need to be cruel against us.

I would like to say it is another's cruelty that brought me here but it was not. Perhaps like the boy in the Daffy Duck slippers and the girl who will not eat, I turned my cruelty inward.

We had a daughter, my husband and I, when our son was eight. Her beauty enthralled me. Her eyes were grey and her hair light and straight;

she moved with a fragile and strong grace and spoke in a voice deep and rich. In school Ariane charmed, her mind and heart filled with words and warmth. She was to have become a dancer; two summers she had spent in New York studying. The autumn of her death was to have been the beginning of her career.

Ariane knew me only after I had become my mother, only after I had abandoned the sleekness of my father's friend Shari to practice my mother's peculiar beauty. The peculiarity suited Ariane; she never compared me to the other women and measured what I lacked. Unlike my son, she did not criticize my thighs. Instead, she molded herself in my image, as I had become my mother's. I was pleased and thought my love for Ariane unbound.

"Look at this!" she would croon, rising sharply on the toes of short brown boots in a shoe store downtown.

"You like ugly clothes?" I would laugh, happy in her differences.

"I do like ugly, my Mother, I do, I do!" she would reply, sweeping her arms in an arc.

"You want to wear Army boots with a skirt of lace?" I would ask.

"I do!" And so we would buy the boots or the lace or the joker's pants.

Ariane was nothing like Shari or the me that had been Shari. Ariane did not work at beauty. She seemed herself, always, a perfection I reached much later in life. When Ariane looked at photographs of me taken before she was born she crumpled in delight: "This is not you! This cannot be my funny, sweet Mother!"

I thought that I had given her a self of value, a self to make and own that no part of this world or life could steal or force into disguise.

I became disappointed because of Ariane, not with her.

She died after several weeks of injury, her face slashed and twisted, her body snapped bones—a car's quick rush of metal and speed. My husband and son and I went to New York. Both my husband and my son hoped for her life, hoped once more that her eyes would see and her voice would sound.

My eyes saw her deep blue gashes and gnarled red seams. I tried to sort her fairness and her life from the mangled net her body had become. Somewhere within the bandages were bones that would perhaps meet and move again but never again with nature's grace. From her had gone all that she was. Ariane lay crushed into ugliness, and I prayed to God for her death.

I became more disappointed in God with each of her breaths. At night I prayed, laying awake next to my husband. I waited for the doctor's call, waited to know that God still listens and could still act. For six weeks I prayed in silent diligence, watching Ariane. Each day I expected my answer. Each day I waited. I had no sleep.

Then Ariane died. Still I did not sleep.

At night I walked for hours, from our neighborhood to the next and the one after that. I liked walking the quiet darkness of the night and the far feeling of sky. On wet nights I kept my head down and watched as the gathered rain separated and closed around my feet.

I could not sleep with the knowledge that God listens.

The last night I walked, the sky's full moon gave me a shadow, a straight and slender night shadow that resembled Shari, the friend of my father that I thought I had abandoned before Ariane's birth. I moved my arms and the arms of the shadow moved; I shook my head and her head shook, no hair displacing. I ran home, my hair wild and my heart large in fear, resting only when I came to my own front lawn.

Shari followed me.

I tried to make her go but she would not. Her feet stepped into mine; she stretched upward to my face and to my thoughts. I kicked at her and I pushed, trying to send her back into the night. She would not leave me. I fell to the ground and curled around myself, thinking to make her small and easily to strangle her. She only sank closer and whispered in my ear. Her shadow wrapped more tightly around me and I feared she had strangled my mother and not me.

All night I did not move upon the lawn. I called once to my husband who slept inside the house but he could not hear. In the morning he found me still there, awake in silent horror. He spoke and I heard his words. I wanted to warn him that it was Shari, but she tightened around my mouth and I could not speak.

My husband tried to move me but could not, for the heavy lead of her weight was within me. He called for an ambulance and they lifted me, still curled, and drove in speed to a hospital. After that hospital, another one. Now this one. I have been here a short while and do not care how time lengthens.

Nurses give me medicine and doctors talk to me. The boy in the Daffy Duck slippers wanders the halls to create his death and cries into the phone for his mother in the evenings. I am happy to lend him my credit card. I call no one.

The girl who will not eat may finally grow so small that she is able to fit into the space she searches for.

My son visits, and my husband. I can look at them and smile, but I pity their love of me.

Once each week my mother visits. She is old and wears the same beauty. Her hair is grey and long; she uses no rouge for brightness. When I feel her standing in the doorway I turn away in my bed, curling inward. She walks to my bed and sits, stroking my hair. I cannot look into her face. I cannot speak to her.

But when she lies next to me I let her hold me. I think I should have stayed always in her arms and should never have let Ariane away from mine. I know I will talk no more to God, and I dare not speak within His hearing.

Spring of '42

Peter Desy

It could be 1942, as a man
drives his truck down the street
crying Fresh strawberries, asparagus,
flowers. The housewives come out
in their summer dresses and
pinch the strawberries and dip
two fingers into their black changepurses
for quarters, like a priest for the round
host into his chalice.
And the ice man and his truck,
a square of black leather over his
shoulder, tongs gripping a wet block
and beads of water splash in the dust.
I am eight years old. I take a sliver
of ice from the truck and suck on it,
loving its clarity and its slipperiness
in my mouth. My mother picks me up,
tells me in child talk that I will never
die, for I am her child, her baby.
The men gather under the giant elm
telling of rumors of kamikazes revving up
on the decks of aircraft carriers heading
for San Francisco and the Golden Gate.

Then a hum from the sky. It is the sun
announcing its benediction.
The houses, white cubes of wood glowing,
fall against each other as if
leaning to embrace. We look up
and surrender ourselves to the light.

The Body Market

Elizabeth Cohen

1.
I learned how to wear my body
in my mother's closet,
an amphitheater of shoes and hat boxes
where shiny purses were wrapped in clear plastic,
sacred as embryos.

In air tricky with static
and the strange, dry sweat
of moth-balls and cleaning chemicals,
each hem and fold
had memorized her.

In the full length mirror
on the closet door,
I pushed my toes and skull
inside her shape,
stretched my whole self out in her.

Swooning, serenading,
I practiced Woman, and Beautiful Woman,
drunk on the way
the mirror could still see me
when my head was turned away.

2.
The next year magazines went crazy
with hairstyles and warnings about thighs.
A body was a job, each part had duties,
creams, little businesses
involving soap and spray.

Real Beauty had arrived with its own government
tribunals and bureaucracies
and I was dissected
into a list of things to take
to its marketplace:
Breasts. Shins. Teeth.

Ankles. Neck. Fingernails.
I learned each one
could make serious mistakes.

Holding onto my face
of eyelashes and bones,
I was just a spirit
carrying a bag of human parts,
waiting for the world to decide.

Foreword from The Measure of Our Success

Jonah Martin Edelman

The 8 × 10 photograph of my parents' wedding occupies a prominent place in both the living room of my house and the recesses of my mind. A record of the pivotal event in the lives of my father and mother, it also signifies my strikingly diverse heritage. In the middle of the nuptial scene stand my parents, with my uncles and aunts, now long since gray, and grandparents, some since gone, at their side. To my father's right, the group are Minneapolis Conservative Jews, three generations removed from Russia, one generation removed from poverty. My grandfather, stern as always, beckons me to persevere as he did. Grandpa supported his entire family from age twelve, when he peddled papers on the freezing corners of St. Paul for nickels and dimes. He exudes the satisfaction of having raised both himself and others up, but grimaces as if to tell me that the fight is far from over. To the left of my mother, the wedding participants are Black Baptists from Bennettsville, South Carolina. They stare fiercely into my eyes, urging me to carry on a tradition forged with sweat, toil, and pride in the cotton field and the pulpit.

My mother, Marian Wright Edelman, has carried on the values of her father and mother, dedicating her life to helping others as a child advocate. Probably one of the most honest people in the world, she is tirelessly devoted to both her children and her cause.

The legacy of our parents and ancestors influences each of us in different ways. Unlike many people my age, I am acutely aware of my family's past. It has for me proven both overwhelming and motivating, burdening and uplifting. I wonder how I would have reacted if I had come up against the obstacles that so many of my relatives struggled to overcome. And I am aware that my mother's is an especially difficult and challenging example to follow, especially in a time in which causes are easy to find but hard to champion effectively, and in which children are earlier and earlier conceived but more and more difficult to nurture.

Our eras as well as our legacies shape us, and in this certainly I am no exception. Born in 1970, I am indebted more than most to the civil rights movement and the struggles of many, like my mother, who exposed and fought racism despite inordinate risks. In fact, I think, had there been no civil rights movement, I would not be the person I am today. My parents might still have met in Mississippi in 1967, gotten married in 1968, and had three children. Josh first, Jonah (me) in the middle, and Ezra last. In the absence of the civil rights period, though, the person that I have become—the cultural mulatto, the well-to-do Black liberal wary of the political process, the sheltered Bar-Mitzvah boy who has struggled with his blackness—never could have existed. Society, I do not believe, would have allowed someone of such a diverse heritage to develop.

My parents raised me as an individual, letting me make my own mistakes and supporting me when I did. When I spelled m-e-n wrong in the first grade spelling bee (with a capital M as on public bathrooms), they immediately informed me that they were proud of me anyway. Similarly, when I committed three errors in one inning during the biggest varsity baseball game of my young career, they consoled me gently. I did not realize it then, but the phrase, "We are *very* proud of you," always with the emphasis on *very*, boosted me immeasurably through the years. It still does.

Just as I have gained an appreciation for the praise heaped upon me, I also now value the mix of discipline and understanding exhibited by my parents. For instance, my stuffing peas, beans, and other greens in various pockets so as to avoid having to eat them was a minor offense and was dealt with as such by my parents. To them, though, my stealing a candy bar from a store was not a trivial matter. My giving my dad "the finger" from my shortstop position in Little League for bench-coaching me—in front of every parent in the neighborhood—met with surprising reserve and humor. My coming home in high school at 4:00 a.m. and trying to convince my mother, after frantically stripping off all of my clothes when I heard her calling me, that I had been sleepwalking did not meet with a similar reaction. Though comical, it was blatantly dishonest and resulted in one of the only two groundings I ever received. Through such punishments and my parents' lectures, I was made to learn the importance of honesty and forthrightness. Just as my parents' praise transformed itself into self-confidence, so their lectures became part of me as well.

The publication of my mother's book is a project I have both feared and welcomed—feared because everyone will realize the legacy to which I am tied and the standards I feel responsible to uphold; standards by which few except my mother could live. But I welcome it for the same reason, as it will spur me on. My mother's book is a written testament to her beliefs, from which everyone, including myself, can benefit. Many of her lessons for life strike a chord in me, but three in particular represent what I have come to see as the legacy of my ancestors:

1. Don't feel entitled to anything you don't sweat and struggle for.
2. Never give up. You can make it no matter what comes. Nothing worth having is ever achieved without a struggle.
3. Always remember that you are never alone. You are loved unconditionally. There is nothing you can ever say or do that can take away my or God's love.

When I am feeling paralyzed by a task that seems too difficult, I remember the love that lies at the core of my family and their legacy to me. The love gives strength, and I can move again.

Mother's Voice

Robert Creeley

In these few years
since her death I hear
mother's voice say
under my own, I won't

want any more of that.
My cheekbones resonate
with her emphasis. Nothing
of not wanting only

but the distance there from
common fact of others
frightens me. I look out
at all this demanding world

and try to put it quietly back,
from me, say, thank you,
I've already had some
though I haven't

and would like to
but I've said no, she has,
it's not my own voice anymore.
It's higher as hers was

and accommodates too simply
its frustrations when
I at least think I want more
and must have it.

Autumn Roses

Elizabeth Engstrom

Winter approaches. I lie in bed, taste the tang in the air from the open window and recognize the urge to breed—like the coyotes and the bears, the foxes and the deer, rutting before the winter sleep. Resting before spring birth.

I arise, stretch, and look out the window. My rose garden, too, is ablaze with the plants' procreational hopes.

This frosty morning, I rummage in the winter clothes box for the first time and emerge with a thick, soft, stained and torn fleece shirt, my winter gardening favorite.

With basket, clippers and leather gloves, I step out the door, see my breath and blink away frosty tears.

The first rosebush is new this year, its tiny salmon colored buds appeared sporadically this past season as the rose concentrated on its roots instead. All summer I gently pinched off the tiny buds, helping it grow to maturity instead of misspending its youth on unwanted seed. The bush is now vibrant and green, its glossy foliage plentiful, its barbed canes thick and purposeful.

I slip off a glove and squish a few hearty aphids on fragile newly emerging red leaves. I don't poison the aphids—that's too impersonal. Growing roses is a commitment, like raising children. One must pick the aphids off by hand.

The next rose has three spent pale pink blooms which have perfumed the air for over a week, and two rich, newly opening buds. I snip the old blossoms with a sharp angled cut, but soft whitish petals cascade to the compost below, leaving me holding prickly green stems with brown curled sepals around hard green hips. The essence of autumn in my hand.

My mother sent pink roses to me when my daughter was born.

I crush two fat aphids on a stem.

The next rose is blue—its petals thick and leathery, barely like a rose at all. The blossoms last an impossibly long time, and this is the rich, spicy fragrance I first smell on lazy summer mornings. I tend the bush, one of my favorites, and in this morning's chill, I remember a late-season outing at the lake many years ago. I heard, "Mommy, I'm cold," and turn to see my tall, thin five-year-old, all elbows and stringy hair, goosebumps and lips the blue of these blossoms. I wrapped her in a dry towel and hugged her, rubbing her icy form and holding her close.

The next rose is prom-yellow, slightly fragrant and only when the buds are freshly open. Not my favorite, and its brittle, spotted leaves reflect my opinion. I tend it just the same, but it reminds me of the tiny bud my daughter's prom date started in her and the yellow roses my mother sent when I arranged to have it nipped.

White roses next, a deep, heady fragrance that filled the church and competed with the organ music for attention. Their degrees packed along with their dreams, I envied their youth and cried when white roses slipped into white limo and they moved to Texas to begin their own.

But roses don't grow in Texas, at least they didn't. Three tries—three deep red roses in a row in my garden, planted with first blush of hope. It's a wonder I didn't rip them out by the roots when hope died on monthly tide. They overbloom every year, these three roses, blaming me for prom night damage. I hurry past them. They are too healthy and need no tending.

At last. The Double Delight. A full, double-petaled white rose, delicately tinged with red, the fragrance dark and domineering. One blossom scents the whole house.

My mother sent this rose on the birth of my granddaughter. She sent one to my daughter as well. A double delight, she said, is a daughter with a daughter.

I tend this bush carefully. It is fragile and prone to aphids carelessly sucking its juices and deforming its brilliant fruit. It has given us a common ground—if nothing else, one can say, "So how's the rose bush?" and we both know it is a growing salve.

The sun has come over the neighbor's garage and my fleece shirt is too hot. I clip a couple of opening buds for kitchen vases. I pick up the shears and the basket of waste and as I walk past the new little bush again, I look at its fresh healthy green. Vigor literally vibrates its canes. I wish it a calm winter sleep, knowing with a parent's mysterious wisdom, that next spring it will awaken fresh, forgiving, and fruitful.

Passing Away

Dusty Sklar

I think that my mother is trying to get ready to die. She is trying so hard that it appears as if she is trying to live.

I am trying to get ready to live without her. She has very little heart muscle left, her doctor told me. Very little. Not even enough to take a shower without a pill or two under the tongue.

Each time I go to see my mother, I memorize the visit, thinking it may be the last.

This time, I ask if she wants me to bring any food, knowing that she can barely cook any more.

"I will make us a little something," she offers.

I remind her that if she cooks, she will be too weak for our visit.

"A little something," she pleads.

My mother is leaning back in her reclining chair, gasping for breath, like a beached fish, when I arrive, but the smells in her kitchen are divine.

"This is crazy," I admonish. "It costs you too much to cook."

"It will be the last time," she promises. "The last time, I swear it. Next time I let you feed me. Is this a life? I can't even wash my hair."

I insist on washing her hair after lunch. She says no, says that our time together is all too precious for that.

After lunch, I do not wash my mother's hair. She totters into her living room, and I notice how much greyer and smaller she is than last time. She stretches out in her reclining chair, her ankles thin enough to break. She was always a small woman, but there was a roundness to her, a fullness that is all gone now. Now, my mother is the size of a small child. A slight child. She has on a flowered blue house dress which I bought for her months ago and which is already too large for her.

I pace around the room, noticing slight films of dust on her precious Italian Provincial furniture, which I always thought was too grand in this modest apartment, in this building where the elevators are always breaking down, on this street where broken glass lines the curbstones. It is the first time I have seen dust on anything belonging to my mother.

When she shuffles into the bathroom, I search in her linen closet for a dust cloth. In her linen closet, everything is still arranged neatly. I take the dust cloth and quickly glide it over the surfaces of tables. My mother slowly slips into the room and catches me at it.

"Oh my God," she cries out. "What are you doing?" She tries to take the dust cloth away from me, but I hang on tightly. Tears form in her eyes. I drop the dust cloth. "Mama, please," I say. "Is it so terrible if I help you?"

"Just talk to me," she says. "Just be a guest."

She sits in her reclining chair in the Italian Provincial living room, and I sit opposite her on the plastic-covered sofa and try to think of something to say to lessen the pain of growing old and becoming a shut-in and having nothing to look forward to except death. The sun streams in through the windows and illuminates the motes of dust covering the table tops. All I can think of to say to my mother is that she still looks good, as good as when she had a lot of heart.

It seems to bother her to be told that she still looks good.

"Look at my hair," she says. I see her pulling at a wisp of short thin grey hair. "You think this looks good? Come on." Tears form in her eyes again. She blinks them away and looks at my hair. "Thank God you still look beautiful," she says. "Let me wash your hair, Mama," I say. "I will do it in the kitchen sink, the way you used to do mine when I was little." I get up from the sofa and go over to the reclining chair, tugging at her arm. "Come, let me wash your hair."

She pushes me away. "Leave me alone," she says. "I can't shop. I can't cook. I can't clean. I can't go out. I can't eat. I can't sleep. But so far, I can still manage to wash my hair."

I remind her that she said she could not. She had told me herself.

"I can. If I take a couple of pills, I can. And if I stay in bed two days after, I can."

I pace back and forth in front of the window, glancing down at the children skating in the playground below, and wondering how I will endure life when this frail old woman is gone. I turn and face her.

"Then I'm leaving," I say. "If you won't let me do this simple little thing for you so you don't have to take two pills and stay in bed two days, then I'm going right now, and frankly, I don't know when I'll come again. You see? You make things so much harder for yourself."

"You're not scaring me," she says. "If you want to go, go."

"Then I'm going," I say. I go to the clothes closet and open the door to remove my coat, and the smell of moth balls overpowers the room.

"Oh, I forgot," my mother says. "I wanted to give you some things to take home." She points to the Italian Provincial credenza which looms over the room. "There. I put them all in the bottom drawer, in a box."

I say that I will not take them unless she allows me to wash her hair.

"Will you stop being such a pest?" She gets up from the reclining chair and walks with halting steps to the Italian Provincial credenza. She is about to stoop down and tug at the drawer, but I reach it before her, yank it open, and remove the box.

My mother is divesting herself. I remove the contents of the box: a mink collar; a pearl necklace with a broken clasp; a black ribbon sweater; a tape recorder which I had given her, the use of which she had never mastered.

She orders me to take them home, says she will never have need of them again. But first, she wants to see how I look in the black ribbon sweater.

I put it on. It does not look well on me, makes me look too matronly, but I do not tell her that I do not fancy it.

"Beautiful," she sighs. "How beautiful. Now, let us have a cup of coffee." Clumsily, she struggles to lift herself from the reclining chair.

I kiss her on the cheek, which is paper-thin against my lips, and stroke her hair with my hand, feeling the scalp underneath.

"My hair is so dirty," she murmurs. "I need to wash it."

I sip her good strong coffee and marvel at how, even in trying to get ready to die, my mother is still in command.

Breast Fed

Larry Schug

I think of my mother,
Twelve year's dead,
understand how, as a woman
She was waitressed until weary
And finally, cashiered to death
By the mercilessness of a life
She embraced like the drunken husband
That she cured with love.
I feel a sadness today,
Deep as an oak tree's roots,
That the very breast
That fed my hungry stomach,
Was cut away from her.
Her womanhood, cancerous, was discarded,
Not even buried with her.
I feel a duty, born of milk,
To stand with all the world's women
Opposing brothers, sons and husbands,
Men who have ransacked their own nests
And forsaken the sacred breasts
Of women and Mother Earth that nursed them.

The Annuity

Marge Piercy

1.
When I was fifteen we moved
from a tight asbestos shoebox
to a loose drafty two-story house,
my own tiny room prized under the eaves.
My privacy formed like a bud from the wood.

In my pale green womb I scribbled
evolving from worm to feral cat,
gobbling books, secreting bones,
building a spine one segment
at a time out of Marx and Freud.

Across the hall the roomers lived,
the couple from Appalachia who cooked
bacon in their room. At a picnic
she miscarried. I held her
in foaming blood. Lost twins.

Salesmen, drab, dirty in the bathroom,
solitary, with girly magazines,
detective stories and pads of orders,
invoices, reports that I would inherit
to write my poems on;

overgrown boys dogging you
out to the backyard with the laundry
baskets; middle-aged losers with eyes
that crawled under my clothes
like fleas and made me itch;

those who paid on time and those
with excuses breaking out like pimples
at the end of the month.
I slammed my door and left them,
ants on the dusty plain.

For the next twenty years
you toted laundry down two flights,
cleaned their bathroom every morning,
scrubbed at the butt burns,
sponged up the acid of their complaints

read their palms and gave common
sense advice, fielded their girlfriends,
commiserated with their ex-wives,
lied to their creditors, brewed
tisanes and told them to eat fruit.

What did you do with their checks?
Buy yourself dresses, candy, leisure?
You saved, waiting for the next depression.
You salted it away and Father took control,
investing and then spending as he chose.

2.
Months before you died, you had us drive
south to Florida because you insisted
you wanted to give me things I must carry back.
What were they? Some photographs, china
animals my brother had brought home from
World War II, a set of silverplate.

Then the last evening while Father watched
a game show, you began pulling out dollar
bills, saying Shush, don't let him
see, don't let him know. *A five-dollar*
bill stuffed under the bobbypins,
ten dollars furled in an umbrella,

wads of singles in the bottom of closet
dividers full of clothes. You shoved
them in my hands, into my purse,

you thrust them at Woody and me.
Take, *you kept saying,* I want you to have
it, now while I can, take.

That night in the hotel room
we sat on the floor counting money
as if we had robbed a candy store:
eighteen hundred in nothing larger
than a twenty, squirreled away, saved
I can't stand to imagine how.

That was the gift you had that felt
so immense to you we would need a car
to haul it back, maybe a trailer too,
the labor of your small deceit
that you might give me an inheritance,
that limp wad salvaged from your sweat.

What She Left Me

Judy Doenges

A COMPLETE SET OF BARWARE. Including: twelve each of highball, old-fashioned, martini, and mint-julep glasses (for the Derby, brought out once a year); sixty champagne flutes bought for an anniversary party canceled because of divorce; fifty etched wine glasses, sets of cordial glasses, brandy snifters, aperitif glasses, mugs for toddies, sixteen cut-glass water tumblers (all chipped); swizzle sticks from (among other places) The Palmer House, the Pump Room, Cape Cod Room, and the Bali-Hai in Arlington Heights; and finally, the silver-plated cocktail shaker, well-used, well-loved (because martinis were her drink of choice, always), now so badly tarnished that the monogram of my mother's initials looked like a crooked scratch across the finish.

My mother housed all of this glass in The Bar, an iconographic, highly varnished walnut affair with thick, spotlit glass shelves along the wall and a black leather bolster across the front. When I was a child, The Bar was a rarely used area of the family room that looked out on the backyard. By the time I finished junior high, my parents had divorced, the pool had replaced most of the lawn, and my mother had put in French doors to open the family room out onto the patio. Mother was like a workhorse back then—her appetite for parties, though she had few friends, driving her like one of those faithful creatures that walk the same furrows every day because they love the work so much, or because there's little else to do.

The summer I turned thirteen she began inviting her poor relations over for "swimming parties." On one occasion, her sister Olga and her husband Oscar, a meat cutter, sat uncomfortably in the gingham-backed kitchen, smoking and drinking beer, while my mother sailed back and forth from the pool to the table, something iced and highly alcoholic in her tinkling glass, her gold sandals snapping against the bottoms of her narrow, brown feet to the rhythms of Sinatra on the record player. My cousin Jimmy slumped in my father's green leather armchair, his dirty jeans and motorcycle boots giving off a gritty smell of motor oil. "For God's sake," my mother said, stopping by his side. "Use a coaster, honey." And she handed him a pink Lucite circle to put under his beer.

I sat silently on the couch—wrapped in my faded Snoopy towel, wearing a damp polka-dot tank suit, hair plastered to the sides of my fat face—shivering and watching. Jimmy was my only cousin. He waited until my mother left the room, and then he pinched cigarettes from the lacquered box on the coffee table with the concentration of a surgeon picking shrapnel from a wound. It was that same singular precision that cost Jimmy his life in a South-side liquor-store robbery a year later. Once he saw the money, he was blind to caution: he got shot by the owner while artfully assembling each pile of bills at the bottom of a paper bag.

For Jimmy's funeral, my mother wore a black linen dress and silk pumps, carried a black straw bag. She stroked the upswept hair at the back of her neck so she wouldn't cry. "Does my slip show when I sit?" she asked herself, pulling at her dress. "Did you shine those shoes, Sandra?" she asked me without looking in my direction.

Olga and Oscar, in the front pew, tilted their doughty, pink faces to the minister. Behind them sat several of Jimmy's buddies, bulging and awkward in the polyester suits, hair curling over their collars, acned jaws working gum.

The minister went on about diminished lives, those cut down in their prime. But they didn't *have* to be diminished, I thought. Clearly my mother, who nearly glowed beside me, knew something that the rest of my relatives didn't, for, unlike them, she had a house and a great deal of possessions, and she knew how to care for them. Some piece of knowledge had fallen to her, and it was hers to nurture and cherish. I wanted this same power, so I vowed that day to watch carefully how my mother kept the world running, how she employed her possessions to achieve the grace of a smooth and even life. Jimmy didn't have this strength. Jimmy didn't have many things—that's why he had gone to such lengths to get them.

When my mother and I came back from the funeral, our house seemed bigger than the church: straining at the walls with heavy furniture and marble table lamps, laid over with thick carpeting, everything clean and operating, the whole downstairs full of the scent of my mother's lilac bushes outside the window. As we sat in the family room that afternoon, sniffling and talking idly about mundane subjects, I felt something in me reverse: the tiny craft that had been speeding through me for years—carrying me from dependence to independence and on to adulthood—had stopped and was now prepared to take me back. I would never leave this house, I told myself, because only here could I learn my mother's secrets, avoid the fate of Jimmy, embrace all the objects surrounding me that my mother presented.

Attentive, the tears resting in her eyes, my mother concocted her martini. Like a scientist she lifted, then examined, the bottles, the shaker, the glass. These things are yours, her movements said. All you need is in them.

A LARGE LEATHER ADDRESS BOOK. Tan calfskin, dictionary size, thick, the pages cream colored and trimmed in gold, the front bearing a monogram, also in gold: *DCM,* David Charles Millan.

When I was twelve my father left without a fight, without much noise or warning, in the middle of the night, carrying his extensive wardrobe to the car in leather suitcases and cardboard cartons. My mother helped him. I know because I watched them from my second-floor window. The crickets sawed away, a thumbnail moon sliced across the trees on the horizon—it was the perfect night for a backyard party. My mother and father laughed about something as they put the last of my father's things in the back seat of his Lincoln. Staggered piles of boxes crammed the car; in the dark they looked as if they were climbing out of the seats. My mother walked around patting the boxes, adjusting them, while my father watched. Then she kissed my father good-bye, waved, and he was off.

The next morning she sat with me at the breakfast table. Pink roses in a white vase, eggs and bacon and toast on bone china, white frilly place mats, and my mother in a white eyelet robe, her blond hair tied in a yellow ribbon. She looked as if she'd slept. "Don't eat so fast, Sweetie," she said, pointing at my plate with her cigarette. "We're going downtown later today. Chicago. To the bank."

I tapped my plate with my fork and stared at her.

"What?" she asked. Then brightening: "Oh, honey, a wonderful thing has happened to your father. You'll never guess."

"You're right," I said. "I'll never guess."

"Your father has fallen in love. Yes, really. Isn't that great! She's a wonderful woman—Janet. You might remember her: tall, black hair, a terrific figure. She was at our Christmas party last year."

"Do you think I'm dumb?" I asked, my mouth full of eggs. "I saw you last night. You're breaking up, and you might as well tell the truth about it."

"That's what I'm saying, yes. I mean, your father can hardly be in love with two women at the same time, can he? It wouldn't be fair, either to Janet or me. He had to make a choice, and considering your father's happiness, I think he made the best choice." She looked out the window to the backyard full of rose bushes and lawn and a perimeter of maple trees. Perhaps she was already planning the pool.

I hated my mother with a piercing righteousness at that moment. It was impossible to tell when she was real. Sometimes she just seemed to be another bright fixture in the house. Maybe my father just forgot about her one day, and there was this Janet instead. "What did you do?" I asked, narrowing my eyes.

To my mother's credit, she never cracked. "I didn't do a thing, darling. I think you know that. No one does or doesn't do things to make a relationship work. You feel things and your actions hopefully follow. So it was for your father. For Janet, that is."

"And look," she continued, opening her arms to the kitchen, to the buttery sunlight, the waxed linoleum, my garish finger paintings in frames on the wall. "He could have left us with nothing. Instead, he said he'd take care of us the rest of his life. So many men don't, you know. They just leave. But we have all this."

We did have everything: the house, the big Chrysler, all the furniture and heirlooms, and my father's family holdings—which were considerable since he was an only child like me. And frankly, I never missed him that much. I remembered him as clean-smelling, rather handsome, and so short that he always seemed dwarfed by our huge house. But he wasn't active like my mother, either in memory or in real life; I marked what he did for us by new chairs, rugs, a car. When my father left us, he also left his job with the Chicago firm. And eventually he left Janet to travel as a vocation—circling the country, dropping into work at various law offices along the way before he finally disappeared when I was safely in college. He called sometimes from LaGuardia or Logan, or even O'Hare, and he talked to me over the pay phone about school, boys, clothes—all the subjects he thought I wanted to discuss but about which I had little to say.

Around Thanksgiving the divorce papers came. They sat on my father's leather-topped desk near The Bar for almost a month. One week before Christmas my mother got out the address book, made herself a shaker of martinis, and wrote season's greetings to each person my father had known. She opened each card, flattened it with the side of her hand, sipped her drink, and wrote "Yours, Dave and Evelyn."

"Honey, pour me another drink, will you?" she asked after the fourth card.

"No," I said from the big leather chair, turning my eyes back to my book.

"Oh, you're at the age, aren't you?" my mother said, going to The Bar.

"What age?" I mumbled.

"Your father's age," she said. "Suspicious. Not caring. Ah." She settled back at the desk, but after a few more cards she said quietly, "That's when they cut you."

"What?"

"Read your book. I'm busy." She made another shaker of martinis.

"Don't you think you've had enough?" I asked, never looking up, only hearing more ice rattling, the gin pouring. Actually, I found these sounds reassuring; they meant that my life would hum on as it always had. I'd asked the question because people on TV always asked it at this point in the drama and because my mother's movements had a sharp, shaky edge that scared me. No matter what, she was never out of control.

"Who asked you?" my mother snapped at me. "Do you want to end up with nothing?" She sat down again, ignoring me as she signed more cards and sealed more envelopes. Then she got out the stamps. She licked each one, placed it on an envelope, then raised her right fist and brought it down with a bang.

"Mama?" I asked quietly. I was afraid to go near her.

Finally she stacked and straightened her pile of envelopes and slid them off the desk into the wastepaper basket. I watched as she lit a fresh cigarette, dropped her flaming match after the envelopes, and then picked up the papers from my father, and dropped them in, too.

"Mother!" I screamed, jumping up.

"Good night, Honey," she said, rising from her chair, the address book in her hands. By the time she was on the stairs, flames had appeared over the top of the basket.

"Mother!" I screamed again. "Crap," I said next, grabbing the can with one hand. I ran for the French doors, opened them, and rushed across the patio with the fire stinging my fingers. I flung the basket in the snow and held it upside down until it stopped spitting and smoking. I could hear my mother up in her bedroom, singing an old song.

DOGS: Two. Great Danes, male harlequins, now elderly and arthritic: Kramden and Norton.

We had a routine, that summer when my mother insisted I come home from Madison when I was a freshman in college, majoring in nothing. My roommate was getting married anyway, leaving school, as all my roommates in college seemed to do. A professor had offered me an easy research job, but my mother insisted that I not work and instead stay with her to "have fun." She was right, of course: we did have fun. My four college summers became the best parts of my life, hanging like ripe peaches in my memory: pastel perfect—pink, orange, and gold against a blue sky, never falling.

Every day we got up late, ate, put on makeup, took our time; there was none of that bitter rush that precedes a dreaded task. Then my mother and I slipped into the new Cadillac, blasting cold air, and floated to the bank where we withdrew crisp, fresh money.

At the mall, in Marshall Field's—our only stop—we didn't have to say a thing because we savored the same details: the hushed slide of the display-case doors, the sound of our heels on the tile, the shine of the lip gloss on the clerks. "Hello, Mrs. Milan," they said. "And Sandra." I got a nod, a puzzled expression: the thickset daughter following her elegant mother—trailing after an inheritance, they probably thought. What they didn't understand was the shared ritual of our days. My mother and I each bought something small that we wanted, paid for it with our stiff bills, walked out eating the tiniest Frango bars the store sold.

At home, we'd unwrap our purchases from lightly scented tissue paper, lay them on our beds or put them in place around the house to admire. All the while our dogs, yearlings barely out of puppyhood, jumped and woofed around our legs or drank out of the toilets with big, noisy laps. Kramden and Norton had their own room in my old nursery, now filled with enormous bags of dog chow, gaping food dishes that seemed cast from concrete, and two ratty Turkish prayer rugs with damp and shredded fringe. And now, in summer, the whole house smelled of wet dog: my mother left the French doors open, so Kramden and Norton were in and out of the pool constantly, cooling off their huge, solid bodies—like film stars on an estate, at home, in command.

My mother and I spent the rest of the afternoon in our lounge chairs, sunning, traveling between the pool and The Bar. Kramden and Norton leaped into the pool, heads up, paddling and blowing air, huge jaws biting water, until they were ready to dry. Then they clambered up the graduated cement steps in the shallow end, their great testicles swinging as they struggled like horses getting out of mud. They immediately ran for my mother and shook off the water, making her shriek.

"Good boys," she said as they settled down like sphinxes between us. Legs straight out in front of them, smacking their lips, they lowered their heads to their paws.

There was usually a sour moment late in the afternoon as the sun sunk behind the trees, but it was only a moment. Soon my mother went into the house and came out again with a tray bearing cheese and crackers, the martini shaker, and a cold beer in a frosted glass. The new alcohol pushed us over that invisible line again—the one that separated us from worry or loneliness. The house loomed silently over the patio.

We became sleepy. My mother usually dropped off at dusk, snoring quietly, the glass still in her hand, her long, brown legs drooping over the sides of the lounge chair. I rested but kept one eye on Mother. She seemed to have calmed the world, slowed it down, wrapped it around me, and I felt that if she were disturbed, the earth would shudder in sympathy.

Periodically, the dogs lifted their heads and looked towards my mother, then glanced nervously at me. They seemed to be waiting for her to give them a signal, though she had never had them trained. They couldn't even be walked, as I learned again every time they dragged me around the streets of our suburb. Unlike most other dogs, they were always anxious to get back home.

My mother adopted the dogs because I was gone. "I'm so lonely!" she had said into the phone each week for six months or so, until one time I heard yapping when I picked up the receiver. "You'll never guess," my mother said. After that, it was the dogs this and the dogs that. I didn't really mind—they were just dogs, after all—but every detail of my mother's anecdotes spoke of the dogs' devotion to her, their loyalty, their dependence. I was falling behind somehow. Madison began to feel too free and wild, one hundred and eighty miles too far away, until the rescuing summer came and I could join my mother again.

The dogs padded over to my lounge chair and whined quietly, finally sitting next to me. They gazed at my mother, brows wrinkled. Kramden sniffed the air, Norton stiffened his ears; they were on guard. We all were. I sipped my beer while we waited in the hot dark until my mother finally awoke.

"Your brothers," my mother said, her voice rough. She held out her bony hand for them to lick.

A BOX OF ASSORTED SWIMWEAR. Including: five bikinis with matching coverups, four tank suits, three newer swimsuits with attached skirts and built-in prostheses, three terry-cloth robes embroidered with the crests of various hotels, one pair of men's swimming trunks, and seven rubber bathing caps—one ringed with curls of real hair.

She wore the bikinis and coverups throughout my childhood when she was tiny, slim, even muscular from her long walks and the exercises she did along with the TV every morning. The swimming trunks were my father's: navy blue, with the words "Chicago Athletic Club" across one leg. He never swam in our pool. The modest tank suits were mine.

The skirted swimsuits, all three, and the curl-fringed bathing cap came from a store in Palm Beach near where my mother took me on a vacation about a year before she died. I was twenty-five, ready to be trained as my mother's caretaker. I spent the first day in Florida holding her elbow, guiding her out of the plane, into cabs and stores and lobbies, and finally into our hushed hotel room with the fan ticking overhead.

My mother dressed for the beach the next day as if for battle, slowly, with heavy sighs, her hands shaking. The suit went up over her skinny, brown legs, over her one breast; she positioned the prosthesis over her scar; then I helped her work the tight cap over what little hair she had left. Together, we lined up her pill bottles on the dresser. I whispered dosages as she took each medication from her bag. Then, after she applied her moisturizers, makeup, and sun cream, we were ready to descend to the beach.

We lay, slick and browning, near our rented cabana. Mother was wearing her new yellow one-piece suit with attached pleated skirt and her new cap with the curls that looked like eyelashes all around her face. She placed a seashell over each eye.

"You can smell the salt, Mama," I said, opening our tiny cooler to take out the martini Thermos and a beer.

Blindly, she lifted her head just a little to sip her drink. Her face was drawn and tense under her makeup, her mouth set in an irritated line. Glancing at her out of the corner of my eye was like watching a movie running on in front of me, a set of small scenes designed to make me remember her. Memories were like this: slips, faults, small gestures loaded with meaning. That was all I wanted—just the opportunity to guess in private about the meaning of my life with my mother. I already knew that as I got older, these poses, these memories, would become pieces of what I thought I'd known all along.

Coming to the bottom of her thermos, my mother began to cry. "Oh, damn," she said, tears squeezing out from the sides of the seashells. "Oh, shoot, now."

"Mother, what is it? Do you feel sick?"

She put both hands on the place where her breast had been and pressed down hard. The rings were loose on her wrinkled fingers, but her nails were still perfect, rounded, frosted pink. "It's coming, Sandra," she said. "I can feel it—right where it left off, too. You know, where it is, you'd think it was a heart, giving out blood, but it's just there to take me. It'll take me, honey! Oh!" And she pressed down harder, sobbing.

"Mom, jeez." I tucked a terry-cloth robe around her legs as if that would help. She was like liquid, running out of the shape that usually held her.

"Feel it, Sandra. Sweetie, put your hands here!" And she lifted her own hands off her chest and reached blindly for mine.

"Now, Mama," I said, "I . . .don't. . . ."

She grabbed my hands and flattened them on top of her yellow swimsuit. The prosthesis collapsed under my palms, and I closed my eyes in embarrassment. Under my eyelids I saw our dream of a hotel room—plush, scented, quiet, and dark against the sun's glare. Here, I had to watch her cry. It was as if the bareness of the sand, our lack of cover, had brought it out. I was paralyzed by my lack of any appropriate feeling.

"Can you feel the cancer coming out?" my mother asked. "Tell me you can. I'm not that strong. I can't fight this again, you know."

"Mother, shut up," I said, lifting off my hands, but she pulled them back again. "Shouldn't drink in this heat," I added quietly, more to myself.

"I know someone else has to be able to feel this sickness coming," my mother whispered, holding my hands down. "It's got to be you."

I tried but I couldn't feel anything, no death waiting, not the rumble of tumors forming, no blood spurting, not even her heartbeat. There in the coming shadow of the shiny buildings behind us, all I felt was the sun my mother had brought me to see.

A WANT. Not a thudding ache, wanting appeared rather as a jolt, followed by an inevitable change in my life that allowed me to escape from a place where I cared for nothing to a place where too much mattered.

Six months after my mother died, I found myself in the kitchen at work with a waitress, Jensine. Three other sullen waitresses in green smocks pushed through the door from the dining room, their angry faces framed in the porthole before they gave a kick and stormed in. Cookie's was the kind of restaurant that employed miserable people. They stayed on for years—sometimes, like Jensine, for a lifetime—just to gripe. It gave them energy. As assistant manager, I was responsible for all trouble, unprotected from all misplaced rage, and uncredited for any success. Jensine held a plate under my nose.

"Sandy, honey," she said. "The dick on twelve returned his dinner. He says there's a hair."

"So give him a new one. Why are you asking me?" I had a long shift that day, so I had filled six pill bottles with scotch instead of three. I fingered four full ones in the right pocket of my cardigan.

Jensine sighed. "Mr. Giaco said no returns without checking first. Remember?"

"No. I don't remember a thing from one day to the next, Jensine," I said, smiling. "That's my plan anyway." Giaco's bald bullet head appeared in the porthole and he pushed his way through.

"What's the holdup here?"

"Hair problem," I said. I couldn't seem to stop smiling. Jensine and Giaco just looked at me. This wasn't work, it was a long list of petty grievances.

Giaco folded his arms. "Jensine, go. A new dinner. Sandy, my office."

I followed him back behind the kitchen, past aluminum tables that held towers of plates and bowls; past the pantry stacked with cans of ketchup, sliced beets, green beans; past the freezers full of beef, chickens, veal steaks. Giaco was ostensibly the man in charge of all this, but he did little besides clap the shoulders and kiss the cheeks of various nameless associates as they made their way to meetings in the banquet rooms. One of them owned the restaurant, Jensine told me. A tax dodge, I told her, knowing money.

It was painful sitting under the lights in Giaco's office within earshot of the kitchen noises—painful to be so close to anything that kept me separate from my mother's house, even now that she was gone. She had tolerated my job during her final nine months of invalidism, tolerated it just barely, even though I gave her a visiting nurse. "I'm sick," my mother would say every morning as I went off to work, leaving her crying in her rented hospital bed, the gin and chemical treatments surging through her blood. Next to her, on the nightstand, was an eerie still life of her existence: rows of medication, martini makings, an ice bucket, a Styrofoam head wearing a gray wig set in an Ann Landers style. Some mornings, if my mother was too weak to sit up, I would turn from the doorway when she said goodbye and imagine that it was the fake head that had called to me.

"We've got a problem, Sandy," Giaco said, sitting down behind his desk.

At home, the walls creaked and sighed, the clocks chimed, the dogs panted. At home everything had a place and a meaning—as if before my mother died she had left on each of her possessions a card discussing the value of each item and how to weigh its significance. I got this job, and kept it, because that's what people did. They "stayed involved," "went on," no matter what—just as my mother had gone on with her house as long as she could. But all the time I was at work I felt as if I'd left my real life at home. Work was like a bad TV show, minus the laugh track. I was surprised, as usual, by how ghostly other people were, how difficult to place, and I was surprised at how uninterested I was in figuring them out. My boss's presence now was as light as breath, irrelevant, as if he were from a land I'd never even imagined.

"I'll get right to it," Giaco said. "I don't like to beat a dead horse."

"What?" I asked. Behind Giaco's desk hung a huge photograph of him kissing the Pope's hand.

"You're on the sauce," Giaco said, his eyes closed.

"Yes?" I asked, waiting for more. For a second I had a familiar feeling of fingers tugging at my clothes, of an insistent hand that could pull me in a direction, any direction the way my mother used to.

"Well?" Giaco waited. "I think this needs some explanation."

"Oh. Well, then, I guess I quit," I said, rising, disappointed. "Okay?" I asked, looking back from the doorway. He remained silent as I walked out and dropped my plastic name tag next to the bowl of moist, crumbling mints by the cash register.

Now I could organize things, I thought, as my key scratched at the lock of my mother's Fleetwood. Now I could sort and inventory what I had.

It's not as they say: it's not money that talks, it's the things that money can buy. These things talk loudly; sometimes they yell. I wandered about my mother's property with a clipboard and made lists of what was in the house, the garage, the yard. I even have the dogs marked down, though they're probably not long for this world. Norton and Kramden lie next to my chair as if they've never noticed that my mother is gone. It's the old leather smell, the scratched wooden legs, and the simple shape they cling to. I have accounted for most items on my list, but lately, at night, when the moon comes through the French doors and I pour another drink, I wonder whether I should start over and go through it all one more time, in case I missed something.

Rubberband Dances

Delisa Heiman

Sometimes I am grateful for the physical separation of California and Washington, D.C. It assumes a barrier which I don't control, yet constantly stretches the grasp of my mother's arms. I pull on those arms. Sometimes I stretch them to their limit, yanking the rubberband ligaments from their sockets. Other times I fall frozen into their warmth and comfort. This whole independence dance that I choreograph to my liking leaves my mother confused yet understanding. She stretches her nature to encompass my fluctuations. Sometimes it would be easier if we didn't see so much through the same telescope. So I create separation. I rebel, I fight, I purposely push her to her corner. Demanding that my edges be sharp and clean-cut from hers. And yet I love her.

Her hands have changed as they age. She's sixty-one, though she embraced her forties and never relaxed her grasp. Choosing instead to internalize a youth which seeps through her pores and keeps her young.

Her hands are old, though they seem to soften more each time I see her. The flesh loses its elasticity and liquid-filled pockets cushion themselves on her palms and knuckles. Brown kisses on satin freckle the overside of her hands. I want to tell her that I love her hands, but I hesitate.

I coolly build glass walls, panes which tease at closeness. Letting the viewer see, but which delineate separation. Then in moments of insecurity and doubt—I smash through the glass and splinter my self-imposed limits. And she is there. I'm trying now to find a nurturer within myself. My own internal parent.

Last January she remarried. I forgot her anniversary. She seemed to start life again. We would call each other up when she was courting and compare notes on our relationships. She, always understanding, ready with a way out of a crisis. For eight sinewy years she struggled to untangle herself from depression. I see those years in images of her standing by a window crying, migraine headaches pulling half her head into war and angry accusations at my detached father. She worked so hard to provide, worked harder at being my mother and father both. Putting herself aside and focusing on me, who ineffectually wavered in my father's shadow. We both were inadequate at being someone other than ourselves. We forgave each other for being human and moved on into the present.

I call her up sometimes and tell her I think of her dying. I wonder how I will fill the millions of crevices that would suddenly chip and crack open inside me. The places which have been bandaided closed. Then we cry and tell each other how strong and fortunate we are to have each other and pass back into tellings of unimportant goings on. She clutters me with coupons, articles and vitamins in her letters—all love.

Sometimes I feel her fingers making indentations on my arching neck. I circle round with my feelings, as she patiently waits.

Shooters

Leo Connellan

Hey Momma I'm going to know Brooklyn
just because we live here. Nothing's happening,
dying is living, so we drive by and shoot
because nothing is ours, you don't destroy yours.
Sometimes we hit and sometimes we get hit. A
bullet just rolled off my roof. You go to
Columbia University, I go to the undertaker.
I explain the bullet I keep on my dresser
to my momma, she worry more than she
already thinkabout . . . so don't tell her
I'll be here until I'm not . . . oh, momma
you birthed us abandoned by men, any man, a
couple of steady sleepovers who could buy
shoes, food, clothes to keep coming. You
did what you could for us and now all you
got for it is headstones.

Writing My Mother's Life

Elayne Clift

"I want you to have my typewriter," she said from her nursing home bed.

Not "Take my typewriter." As in "Take my pictures. I won't need them anymore. Take my jewelry. Take my good coat."

This time she said, "I want you to have my typewriter." I heard the difference and it was deafening and this time, I took the typewriter.

Soon after, she said, "I want you to write the story." By the time she told me this, "the story" in her mind was about nurses poisoning her and conspiracies of cruelty and eviction. I promised to tell the story. Not that one, of course, but her real story.

I have known for a long time that I needed to tell the story of my mother. I have needed it so that I could reconcile her life, and in so doing, could begin to put an end to fear and great sadness. At first I thought I should have to gather many more facts. I would go in search of a great oral history, I thought, and in her roots and her childhood, I would discover my mother and would come to make sense of her life.

But in my mind, it was still one life, one story to be told. Now I know that that is why I could not begin. Because the telling of my mother's life is two stories, and the cruelty of that reality is that they can never be reconciled.

The first story is a fiction, and it contains the facts. It begins with a female child being born to Russian Jews in the year 1904 somewhere in Eastern Europe, and close to, but preceding the High Holy Days of Rosh Hoshana, so that her birthday was celebrated on August 25th each year. Her Hebrew name was Brona, but she chose to be called Reba as she grew up in small town, anglicized New Jersey where she had emigrated at the age of two. Her father, a tailor, was distant in the years of her growing up, but her mother, for whom she felt an almost painful love, was devoted. They were friends, which for my mother, was a great tragedy in the end. There were also two brothers.

Reba, a good student, went from eighth grade straight to secretarial school, where she excelled. After graduation, she worked as legal secretary to "Pepper, Bodine, Stokes and Shock," until Mr. Bodine, old enough to be her father, chased her around the office with a strand of real Parisian pearls and a litany of promises.

One could understand his devotion: My mother was a real beauty. For all the years of my growing up, I cherished the photograph of her swathed in pastel blue and pink, her large dark pools of eyes peering mysteriously out from under the frame of rich black curls which she later had bobbed. (Her mother would not speak to her for three weeks. Then she had her hair bobbed as well.) She must have been about eighteen in that picture, but there were others, later, equally stunning. In one, wearing green satin and velvet lounging pajamas, she looked just like a young and glamorous Indira Gandhi; in another, at the Chicago World's Fair in 1936, she is the epitome of New York chic in a black suit and saucy hat dipped over one eye. My mother had true class.

She was also talented, energetic, full of humor and high hopes, everybody's dream girl. Which is why she began to contribute to her own fiction.

In her brilliant book, *Writing A Woman's Life,* Carolyn Heilbrun, to whom I am deeply indebted for helping me to understand (and tell) my mother's story, explains the fiction of women's lives and of their autobiographies. Gertrude Stein and Jane Austen and Eudora Welty wrote fiction as autobiography because they had not the language, nor the forum, nor even the perception of their own lives to write with truth for public consumption. The essence of their own experience, recorded if at all only in private letters and journals, had no place in traditional accounts of female lives. No language existed in the male experience or in the male paradigm of literature or life to allow for the diversity, the ambition, the passion of women's lives. Traditional accounts and conventional chronicles of women were built upon layers of concealment and closure. Women had therefore to find beauty in pain, and to make of their rage spiritual acceptance, becoming in the final analysis, female impersonators. My mother neither wrote, nor lived, her own life for the very same reason. Instead, she tried vigorously and with valor to be the best of impersonators.

She waited at first, continuing, I believe, to know somewhere in the recess of her heart and her intellect, that there was more. But with no language to express it, no literature to validate it, no friend with whom to explore it, she put away her dreams, her aspirations, her intellectual curiosity. Finally, at the age of 36, she gave up ideas of leaving her needy mother for a career in New York. She no longer believed in adult love as she had dared to imagine it. She began instead to embrace myth, which is why, as Carolyn Heilbrun knows, the telling of women's lives has always ended with marriage and children. And when, in her passivity, she married a man she should not have done, and began a life she did not really want, she did not even question the emptiness of having it all.

Although, of course, she did find great joy in her three children, to whom she was the greatest of mothers.

Until, no longer able to sustain what was forbidden to her—anger, and the desire for power and control over her own life—and unable to find a voice in which to publicly complain or privately comprehend, she began, like millions of other women who take themselves to be the only one, to take refuge in depression, which in the end, became lucid madness, inherent in which was a terrifying power, pervading her presence like bitter irony in a tasteless joke.

It didn't happen all at once. And in between the "bad spells" there were some good moments: the joy of working in my father's haberdashery at Christmastime, trips to Florida and Canada, the laughter of children and the ceremonies of life. She took joy in her grandchildren, with whom even a McDonald's hamburger was a cherished treat. And she loved writing great long letters full of humorous anecdote and colorful detail. "I'm going to start a book!" she would say, pulling out her Smith Corona portable. But those moments were not many in the whole fabric of her life. She deserved more, much, much more.

She did not deserve to be incarcerated in institutions designed and run by men who saw in women's depression only depravity and not longing and diversity and depth. She did not deserve to have electrodes put to her head so that in the end she could not remember the date of her children's birthday. She did not deserve meaningless labels like "involutional melancholia" and "manic depressive" and "bi-polar disorder." She did not deserve in her old years to become ugly, even grotesque, and crazy and difficult to be with because of the perversities of her life.

These are not easy things to say about your mother, or to remember, but they must be said and remembered, because they are true and the truth about women's lives must be told.

There is another truth about my mother's life, and that truth can only be told in another story, which we must come to recognize and cherish (for many women) as unrealized biography.

In that story, my mother has the same chance beginnings. But the childhood passion which is female, and Russian, and unique to her as well, is nurtured like a seedling from whose sprouting the whole world will be fed. She is encouraged, like her brothers, to study, to "make something" of herself. She is rewarded for independence, action, curiosity. Her budding world view is encouraged, even if it can only be in New York. Her desire to delay marriage for travel and career (to try being a writer?) is not frowned on or laughed at and her successes, small though they may be, are cause for excitement and celebration, which is not restricted to wedding receptions and a "bris" insofar as women are concerned. When she grapples with the essence of female experience, or the human dimensions of anger, grief, fear, uncertainty there is a feminist community to share it, to say "You are not alone," to serve as midwife to the birth of spirit. No surgeon tries instead to excise it, as if it were an aberrant growth because it only grows in women. Later, when she marries, it is with the joy and maturity of friendship and the sensuality of full being. She continues to work, not as handmaiden to her husband, but as fullbodied Self, in whatever realm she chooses. She is devoted to, but not defined, by her children. She takes pleasure in a McDonald's hamburger with her grandchildren, but she feels worthy of dinner at Maxim's. She grows old with intellectual and physical elegance (which does not mean she is still slender). Her mind is clear, she is still a woman of taste and vision, and when she lets go, it is not out of defeat, or defiance. It is the letting go of peaceful demise, knowing that life, in all its richness, has been hers, not by chance but by the design of a life self-determined and well lived.

This unrealized biography, and not the fiction of my mother's life, is the story I promised to tell and that those of us who love my mother, who is Everywoman, must celebrate. It is the one she always meant to write, on her typewriter and on her palette of possibility.

It is the life she deserved to live.

Feminism, Art, and My Mother Sylvia

Andrea Dworkin

I am very happy to be here today.* It is no small thing for me to be here. There are many other places I could be. This is not what my mother had planned for me.

I want to tell you something about my mother. Her name is Sylvia. Her father's name is Spiegel. Her husband's name is Dworkin. She is fifty-nine years old, my mother, and just a few months ago she had a serious heart attack. She is recovered now and back on her job. She is a secretary in a high school. She has been a heart patient most of her life, and all of mine. When she was a child she had rheumatic fever. She says that her real trouble began when she was pregnant with my brother Mark and got pneumonia. After that, her life was a misery of illness. After years of debilitating illness—heart failures, toxic reactions to the drugs that kept her alive—she underwent heart surgery, then she suffered a brain clot, a stroke, that robbed her of speech for a long time. She recovered from the heart surgery. She recovered from her stroke, although she still speaks more slowly than she thinks. Then, about eight years ago, she had a heart attack. Then, a few months ago she had a heart attack. She recovered.

My mother was born in Jersey City, New Jersey, the second oldest of seven children, two boys, five girls. Her parents, Sadie and Edward, who were cousins, came from someplace in Hungary. Her father died before I was born. Her mother is now eighty. There is no way of knowing of course if my mother's heart would have been injured so badly had she been born into a wealthy family. I suspect not, but I do not know. There is also of course no way of knowing if she would have received different medical treatment had she not been a girl. But regardless, it all happened the way it happened, and so she was very ill most of her life. Since she was a girl,

*Delivered at Smith College, Northampton, Massachusetts, April 16, 1994.

no one encouraged her to read books (though she tells me that she used to love to read and does not remember when or why she stopped reading); no one encouraged her to go to college or asked her to consider the problems of the world in which she lived. Because her family was poor, she had to work as soon as she finished high school. She worked as a secretary full-time, and on Saturdays and some evenings she did part-time work as a "salesgirl" in a department store. Then she married my father.

My father was a school teacher and he also worked nights in the post office because he had medical bills to pay. He had to keep my mother alive, and he had two children to support as well. I say along with Joseph Chaikin in *The Presence of the Actor:* "The medical-economic reality in this country is emblematic of the System which literally chooses who is to survive. I renounce my government for its inequitable economic system."[1] Others, I must point out to you, had and have less than we did. Others who were not my mother but who were in her situation did and do die. I too renounce this government because the poor die, and they are not only the victims of heart disease, or kidney disease, or cancer—they are the victims of a system which says a visit to the doctor is $25 and an operation is $5,000.

When I was twelve, my mother emerged from her heart surgery and the stroke that had robbed her of speech. There she was, a mother, standing up and giving orders. We had a very hard time with each other. I didn't know who she was, or what she wanted from me. She didn't know who I was, but she had definite ideas about who I should be. She had, I thought, a silly, almost stupid attitude toward the world. By the time I was twelve I knew that I wanted to be a writer or a lawyer. I had been raised really without a mother, and so certain ideas hadn't reached me. I didn't want to be a wife, and I didn't want to be a mother.

My father had really raised me although I didn't see a lot of him. My father valued books and intellectual dialogue. He was the son of Russian immigrants, and they had wanted him to be a doctor. That was their dream. He was a devoted son and so, even though he wanted to study history, he took a pre-medical course in college. He was too squeamish to go through with it all. Blood made him ill. So after pre-med, he found himself, for almost twenty years, teaching science, which he didn't like, instead of history, which he loved. During the years of doing work he disliked, he made a vow that his children would be educated as fully as possible and, no matter what it took from him, no matter what kind of commitment or work or money, his children would become whatever they wanted. My father made his children his art, and he devoted himself to nurturing those children so that they would become whatever they could become. I don't know why he didn't make a distinction between his girl child and his boy child, but he didn't. I don't know why, from the beginning, he gave me books to read, and talked about all of his ideas with me, and watered every ambition that I had so that those ambitions would live and be nourished and grow—but he did.*

So in our household, my mother was out of the running as an influence. My father, whose great love was history, whose commitment was to education and intellectual dialogue, set the tone and taught both my brother and me that our proper engagement was with the world. He had a whole set of ideas and principles that he taught us, in words, by example. He believed, for instance, in racial equality and integration when those beliefs were seen as absolutely aberrational by all of his neighbors, family, and peers. When I, at the age of fifteen, declared to a family gathering that if I wanted to marry I would marry whomever I wanted, regardless of color, my father's answer before that enraged assembly was that he expected no less. He was a civil libertarian. He believed in unions, and fought hard to unionize teachers—an unpopular notion in those days since teachers wanted to see themselves as professionals. He taught us those principles in the Bill of Rights which are now not thought of very highly by most Amerikans—an absolute commitment to free speech in all its forms, equality before just law, and racial equality.

I adored my father, but I had no sympathy for my mother. I knew that she was physically brave—my father told me so over and over—but I didn't see her as any Herculean hero. No woman ever had been, as far as I knew. Her mind was uninteresting. She seemed small and provincial. I remember that once, in the middle of a terrible argument, she said to me in a stony tone of voice: You think I'm stupid. I denied it then, but I know today that she was right. And indeed, what else could one think of a person whose only concern was that I clean up my room, or wear certain clothes, or comb my hair another way. I had, certainly, great reason to think that she was stupid, and horrible, and petty, and contemptible even: Edward Albee, Philip Wylie, and that great male artist Sigmund Freud told me so. Mothers, it seemed to me, were the most expendable of people—no one had a good opinion of them, certainly not the great writers of the past, certainly not the exciting writers of the present. And so, though this woman, my mother, whether present or absent, was the center of my life in so many inexplicable, powerful, unchartable ways, I experienced her only as an ignorant irritant, someone without grace or passion or wisdom. When I married in 1969 I felt free—free of my mother, her prejudices, her ignorant demands.

---

*My mother has reminded me that she introduced me to libraries and that she also always encouraged me to read. I had forgotten this early shared experience because, as I grew older, she and I had some conflicts over the particular books which I insisted on reading, though she never stopped me from reading them. Sometime during my adolescence, books came to connote for me, in part, my intellectual superiority over my mother, who did not read, and my peership with my father, who did read.

I tell you all of this because this story has, possibly for the first time in history, a rather happier resolution than one might expect.

Do you remember that in Hemingway's *For Whom the Bell Tolls* Maria is asked about her lovemaking with Robert, did the earth move? For me, too, in my life, the earth has sometimes moved. The first time it moved I was ten. I was going to Hebrew school, but it was closed, a day of mourning for the six million slaughtered by the Nazis. So I went to see my cousin who lived nearby. She was shaking, crying, screaming, vomiting. She told me that it was April, and in April her youngest sister had been killed in front of her, another sister's infant had died a terrible death, their heads had been shaved—let me just say that she told me what had happened to her in a Nazi concentration camp. She said that every April she remembered in nightmare and terror what had happened to her that month so many years before, and that every April she shook, cried, screamed, and vomited. The earth moved for me then.

The second time the earth moved for me was when I was eighteen and spent four days in the Women's House of Detention in New York City. I had been arrested in a demonstration against the Indochina genocide. I spent four days and four nights in the filth and terror of that jail. While there two doctors gave me a brutal internal examination. I hemorrhaged for fifteen days after that. The earth moved for me then.

The third time the earth moved for me was when I became a feminist. It wasn't on a particular day, or through one experience. It had to do with that afternoon when I was ten and my cousin put the grief of her life into my hands; it had to do with that women's jail, and three years of marriage that began in friendship and ended in despair. It happened sometime after I left my husband, when I was living in poverty and great emotional distress. It happened slowly, little by little. A week after I left my ex-husband I started my book, the book which is now called *Woman Hating*. I wanted to find out what had happened to me in my marriage and in the thousand and one instances of daily life where it seemed I was being treated like a subhuman. I felt that I was deeply masochistic, but that my masochism was not personal—each woman I knew lived out deep masochism. I wanted to find out why. I knew that I hadn't been taught that masochism by my father, and that my mother had not been my immediate teacher. So I began in what seemed the only apparent place—with *Story of O,* a book that had moved me profoundly. From that beginning I looked at other pornography, fairy tales, one thousand years of Chinese footbinding, and the slaughter of nine million witches. I learned something about the nature of the world which had been hidden from me before—I saw a systematic despisal of women that permeated every institution of society, every cultural organ, every expression of human being. And I saw that I was a woman, a person who met that systematic despisal on every street corner, in every living room, in every human interchange. Because I became a woman who knew that she was a woman, that is, because I became a feminist, I began to speak with women for the first time in my life, and one of the women I began to speak with was my mother. I came to her life through the long dark tunnel of my own. I began to see who she was as I began to see the world that had formed her. I came to her no longer pitying the poverty of her intellect, but astounded by the quality of her intelligence. I came to her no longer convinced of her stupidity and triviality, but astonished by the quality of her strength. I came to her, no longer self-righteous and superior, but as a sister, another woman whose life, but for the grace of a feminist father and the new common struggle of my feminist sisters, would have repeated hers—and when I say "repeated hers" I mean, been predetermined as hers was predetermined. I came to her, no longer ashamed of what she lacked, but deeply proud of what she had achieved—indeed, I came to recognize that my mother was proud, strong, and honest. By the time I was twenty-six I had seen enough of the world and its troubles to know that pride, strength, and integrity were virtues to honor. And because I addressed her in a new way she came to meet me, and now, whatever our difficulties, and they are not so many, she is my mother, and I am her daughter, and we are sisters.

You asked me to talk about feminism and art, is there a feminist art, and if so, what is it. For however long writers have written, until today, there has been masculinist art—art that serves men in a world made by men. That art has degraded women. It has, almost without exception, characterized us as maimed beings, impoverished sensibilities, trivial people with trivial concerns. It has, almost without exception, been saturated with a misogyny so profound, a misogyny that was in fact its world view, that almost all of us, until today, have thought, that is what the world is, that is how women are.

I ask myself, what did I learn from all those books I read as I was growing up? Did I learn anything real or true about women? Did I learn anything real or true about centuries of women and what they lived? Did those books illuminate my life, or life itself, in any useful, or profound, or generous, or rich, or textured, or real way? I do not think so. I think that that art, those books, would have robbed me of my life as the world they served robbed my mother of hers.

Theodore Roethke, a great poet we are told, a poet of the male condition I would insist, wrote:

Two of the charges most frequently levelled against poetry by women are lack of range—

in subject matter, in emotional tone—and lack of a sense of humor. And one could, in individual instances among writers of real talent, add other aesthetic and moral shortcomings: the spinning-out; the embroidering of trivial themes; a concern with the mere surfaces of life—that special province of the feminine talent in prose—hiding from the real agonies of the spirit; refusing to face up to what existence is; lyric or religious posturing; running between the boudoir and the altar, stamping a tiny foot against God; or lapsing into a sententiousness that implies the author has re-invented integrity; carrying on excessively about Fate, about time; lamenting the lot of woman...and so on.[2]

What characterizes masculinist art, and the men who make it, is misogyny—and in the face of that misogyny, someone had better reinvent integrity.

They, the masculinists, have told us that they write about the human condition, that their themes are the great themes—love, death, heroism, suffering, history itself. They have told us that our themes—love, death, heroism, suffering, history itself—are trivial because we are, by our very nature, trivial.

I renounce masculinist art. It is not art which illuminates the human condition—it illuminates only, and to men's final and everlasting shame, the masculinist world—and as we look around us, that world is not one to be proud of. Masculinist art, the art of centuries of men, is not universal, or the final explication of what being in the world is. It is, in the end, descriptive only of a world in which women are subjugated, submissive, enslaved, robbed of full becoming, distinguished only by carnality, demeaned. I say, my life is not trivial; my sensibility is not trivial; my struggle is not trivial. Nor was my mother's, or her mother's before her. I renounce those who hate women, who have contempt for women, who ridicule and demean women, and when I do, I renounce most of the art, masculinist art, ever made.

As feminists, we inhabit the world in a new way. We see the world in a new way. We threaten to turn it upside down and inside out. We intend to change it so totally that someday the texts of masculinist writers will be anthropological curiosities. What was that Mailer talking about, our descendants will ask, should they come upon his work in some obscure archive. And they will wonder—bewildered, sad—at the masculinist glorification of war; the masculinist mystifications around killing, maiming, violence, and pain; the tortured masks of phallic heroism; the vain arrogance of phallic supremacy, the impoverished renderings of mothers and daughters, and so of life itself. They will ask, did those people really believe in those gods?

Feminist art is not some tiny creek running off the great river of real art. It is not some crack in an otherwise flawless stone. It is, quite spectacularly I think, art which is not based on the subjugation of one half of the species. It is art which will take the great human themes—love, death, heroism, suffering, history itself—and render them fully human. It may also, though perhaps our imaginations are so mutilated now that we are incapable even of the ambition, introduce a new theme, one as great and as rich as those others—should we call it "joy"?

We cannot imagine a world in which women are not experienced as trivial and contemptible, in which women are not demeaned, abused, exploited, raped, diminished before we are even born—and so we cannot know what kind of art will be made in that new world. Our work, which does full honor to those centuries of sisters who went before us, is to midwife that new world into being. It will be left to our children and their children to live in it.

1. Joseph Chaikin, *The Presence of the Actor* (New York: Atheneum, 1972), p. 126.
2. Theodore Roethke, "The Poetry of Louise Bogan," *On the Poet and His Craft: Selected Prose of Theodore Roethke,* ed. Ralph J. Mills (Seattle: University of Washington Press, 1965), pp. 133–134.

Going Deeper into the Album

Larry Rubin

Your photos past my birth date I can frame
Within a memory that fuses film
With candles, every conscious moment its
Own flare. But your girlhood pictures,
Taken when my brain was still unformed,
Frighten me with flashes of the void,
A time that never was, returning you
To some black hole my mind cannot explore.
For you to be so young, and me so old,
Defies the logic of both clock and genes.
That danger in your eyes I don't recall—
And did you wear that pirate headband
Like some flapper modeled after Theda Bara?
Am I some Oedipus you taunt with sex
Just to warn me what can never be?
So out of reach in times I've never known—
I'll wrench the pillars of the universe
To fracture clocks, to pull your days into
The orbit of my own, to hold you hard
Within the zone that I command:
                                    come, child

On Learning of the Death of My Great-Grandmother in Childbirth at Age 18

Em Case (Droppo)

My bed is soft tonight, with down and scented lace,
And I am filled with life and love
Because long years ago—a century
And a half—they tell me now,
You came, all dewy-eyed in youth,
With dreams and hopes unspoken yet—
To that dear task, for which is woman made.
                A bride of just a year; your cup was full
                To be a mother—joy was running o'er.
Words found no utterance in those days long past,
There was no need. The eye was steady—
Even proudly so, as roughened hand touched yours,
Reaching in love to comfort and caress.

I do not think you cried aloud,
Such pain and fear can be too deep for tears;
As all your strength and all your will you gave
To him instead. Even to spare your own
Did not one pulse or breath withhold.
Dear mother-girl, I hope you were so blessed,
Awhile to hold your new born son within your arms;
And I would wish that you mistook the tide
That bore your life away, for love's fulfillment
Rich beyond the bounds of sight and sound.

Grandmother

Ruth Harriet Jacobs

My grandmother, Marmita
was given the name Minnie
at Ellis Island
and carefully traced it
on the report cards
of five children.
It was all the English
she could ever write.

When her oldest child
my mother, died at thirty
she took a ten year old
and a three year old
and traced Minnie
on our report cards
and on all those forms
to get legal guardianship
and state aid to feed us.

She crocheted doilies
for the social worker
begged clothes and camps
and within a slum
kept a shining house.

Half crazed
by her daughter's death
and endless poverty
she cried, screamed,
had no patience
with my brother

and even threatened me
good, too good, though I was.

But every spring
somewhere in that slum
she stole lilacs
to put upon my dresser
and trace her love
forever on me.

Making the Wine

Marisa Labozzetta

Angelo is in the bathroom now, shaving. I can hear him singing "Gli Stornelli," belting out the same stanza over and over again in his deep robust voice just the way he used to back in Italy. It is the only song he ever bothered to learn at all. Soon he will come into the kitchen for his orange and cup of black coffee. Peeling the rind in a circular fashion as though he were carving one of his fine pieces of wood, he'll say, "Caterina, take some; it's good for you," and hold out a slice with the same hand that is still gripping the sharp paring knife.

I try to steady my hand as I lift the cup of coffee to my lips. Steady. Steady. Ah! I have spilled some on the table and Sophie must help me put the cup down. She wipes the table—her clean table. Now, Tom, Sophie's husband, has that look on his face as he sits across from me. He always looks like that when I spill something, or eat with my hands, or—almost all the time. I want to say to him, wait, you have no idea what it's like. You can't walk, you can't work, you can hardly think. But all I can manage are the same words each time. "I'm sorry." He gets up and walks out of the room.

Angelo is putting on his lumber jacket and going out to the garden. I tell him that I would go with him but my legs are very swollen. I have not been to the garden in years. Angelo goes religiously every day. He plants and weeds and keeps the rows of tomatoes, beans, eggplant and squash neat like church pews. Then, at the end of the season, we can five hundred jars of tomatoes for Sunday gravy. Angelo has to have his pasta on Sunday. He loves to wake up to the aroma of his tomatoes seasoned with sweet *basilico* simmering for hours in the thick red sauce. When the children were young, they used to come home from church and dip chunks of thick-crusted bread in the bubbling hot gravy. "It's not done yet!" I warned them, but they loved it anyway. Then, it was the grandchildren. They would walk over on Sunday mornings after church and do the same.

I never went to church. I wish I had. I made sure the children went, though. Children need religion, I used to think; but now I see it is old people who need it. Sophie won't take me. She says the Mass is too long and

I will have to go to the bathroom. Once she brought the priest here to hear my confession. It was the third time I had gone to confession in my life. The first time was my First Holy Communion in Italy, all of us dressed like little brides. The second was fifty years later. I don't know what possessed me, but I wanted to go. Angelo laughed at me. He said I had nothing to confess. He said priests did not deserve to hear anyone's sins. When I came home, I told Angelo all about it, how I said it had been fifty years since my last confession. He called me a fool and, cursing, left the room.

Angelo taught me everything about life. I married him when I was almost sixteen; I didn't know anything. I didn't want to marry him but my parents made me. He was really very kind to me. With so much blond hair, blue eyes and a Roman nose, my sisters thought he was wonderful. I thought he was too short. I didn't like any men; all I wanted to do was sit in a corner of the kitchen and read books. When Angelo came calling, I would pretend I was tired and go to bed. But he was so gentle, he took me to America and taught me everything. He told me there were diseases that people could get from making love. He knew because one of his *paisanos* had gotten sick from a town whore. She had wanted Angelo to make love with her but he wouldn't. He is so smart, Angelo.

Angelo is always hugging me and every night he wants to have a love affair with me. I don't like it so much. I'm tired at night and the heaviness of his body on my chest is suffocating. Sometimes I think he will crush my lungs. And it is messy; he soils my clean sheets. Angelo is disappointed but I just don't like it. But there was one time. I don't like to think about it. Angelo was so angry. Father Cioffi had come to visit; Angelo was at the barber's. The baby was only six months old then, and Father Cioffi kept bouncing him onto our bed, then lifting him high into the air and down onto the bed again. When Angelo saw the rumpled bedspread and the priest's black shirt pulled partly out of his black pants, he was furious. He ordered him to leave without an explanation; then he called me *putana*, "whore," he said. I cried and explained that nothing had happened but he left the apartment cursing. I was already in bed when he came back. He undressed quickly and began stroking my hair. When he climbed on top of me and pulled up my nightgown, I didn't mind; I was thinking of Father Cioffi, what it would be like, his tall strong body, his curly black hair.

I think I will wash the dishes for Sophie. I want to but where is the soap? I know it's here on the sink. Is this it? No. That's Sophie's china ashtray. Now she's grabbing it out of my hands. "I only wanted to wash the dishes," I tell her. "Just sit down, Mamma, she says, "just sit down."

Angelo will be coming in for lunch soon. He will want a plate of escarole, a piece of fresh Italian bread and a large glass of red wine. I hope Sophie has remembered to fill the small bottle with wine from the basement.

"How is the garden?" I ask him, as he comes in the door. "It will be a good garden this year, Boss." Boss. He has called me Boss forever. I do tell him what to do often. Maybe sometimes too much. But he needs it; he is too easygoing. There are always things to be done. You must work. Angelo likes to drink wine and laugh with people. His laugh is high pitched, almost hysterical. He does everything totally. I don't laugh too much. I have to work. Work is important. You can't have anything without working. Do you think we would have this land if I had not saved all our money? Oh, Angelo worked too, six sometimes seven days a week in the lumber yard, but he never made much money. Every night, he came home with splinters and he and Sophie would sit by the coal stove under the kitchen light. Sophie would take a sewing needle she had sterilized with the flame of a match and poke at his callused hand while he screamed. He is very strong, Angelo; but if he is hurt, he cries out a lot just like a baby. Like when he has attacks of the gout and screams when I walk into the room because vibrations make the sheet touch his foot. I stay awake all those nights. I want to sleep on the couch, to get some rest; I have to work the next day. But Angelo will not let me. He says I have to sleep with him in his bed every night. I am his wife.

I think I will put some coffee on for Angelo. Just turn on the gas. There. It will be done soon.

"Mamma, what are you doing!"

"What are you doing?" Damn you, Sophie! You are always taking things away from me. Damn you! I'll slap you! Again! Again!

"This is an electric coffeepot, Mamma. You've ruined it!"

But I never use an electric coffeepot. Angelo likes me to use the drip maker for his espresso. I keep it warm over the flame just before I pour it into his favorite demitasse. Then, he puts in a few drops of *anisetta* and a twist of lemon rind. I never use an electric pot. And that man sitting across the kitchen table keeps staring at me with that look again.

"Sophie, who is that man?"

"It's Tom, Mamma."

"Why don't you let go of my hand? Sophie, you're hurting my hand!"

I must turn on the radio now. After lunch, Angelo likes to listen to the news and then the stock market report. We don't own many stocks, just a few of AT&T, but Angelo likes to know what's going on. I don't understand it very much. Still, if it weren't for me, Angelo would never have been able to buy those stocks. I work hard, day after day, in the machine shop sewing clothes. Even though Angelo is retired, I still work, and he drives me to the machine shop in town every morning and picks me up each evening. I look out of the fourth story window of the factory and see him sitting in the old black Dodge. He is always there twenty minutes before quitting time. He is never late.

But Angelo spends too much money. Like the time he bought a sixty dollar typewriter for Sophie during the Depression, and in cash! He could not turn away the young salesman standing in the doorway of our apartment. Or the time he bought me the diamond brooch for our fiftieth wedding anniversary. I was angry. He should not have ordered a custom-made brooch from Italy. I yelled at him for spending so much money. And I showed him, I never wore it until the day he died; since then, I have never taken it off.

Angelo is going outside now to work on the trellis he is building for my roses. He knows how much I love flowers. "Be careful," I tell him.

"Don't worry, Boss," he laughs.

"And the grape arbor, don't forget to fix the grape arbor!"

Every year Angelo and I make gallons and gallons of wine. The last time we made the wine it happened. I knew I shouldn't have made it; I felt the pressure mounting in my chest; it was getting hard to breathe. But we had to make the wine. If we didn't, the grapes would go bad. All that time and money would be wasted. We had to make the wine; and we did. And it happened. My heart. I remember the first time I opened my eyes after the attack. Angelo was standing over my hospital bed like a frightened schoolboy on his first day of class. Suddenly, he threw himself across my still body and wept even harder than when the baby died, harder than I had ever seen him before. I took his hand in mine and held it as tightly as I could. "Don't cry, Angelo," I said, "I made it. Didn't I?" He nodded. "I made the wine, Angelo. I made it."

Angelo loves living here in the country. It reminds him of our *paese* in the mountains of Rome. Thanks to me, we were able to save the money to buy it. I used to cook cheap meals and sew the children's clothes so we could save. And little by little, we saved enough to buy a few acres, then a few more. And we never owed anybody—nobody. Angelo is different here with the grandchildren. In the city he was mean and strict with our children. He was afraid for them—this new country with all of its freedom. There were so many things to get in trouble with—gangsters, cars, subways. If the children were not home on time, he would go out looking for them; and then, when he got them home, he would send them from one side of the kitchen to the other with a single slap. But here in the country he plays with the children, chasing them around the farm with his belt folded in half and snapping it, pretending he will catch their fingers in it if they dare to stick them in. But we are not in the country anymore, are we? And work? I can barely lift myself from this chair which has become a part of me, an extension of myself.

"I have to go to the bathroom again," I tell Sophie.

"It's too late, Mamma. Look what you've done!"

I don't remember doing it. One minute I had to go to the bathroom and the next minute I called Sophie. Maybe it wasn't the next minute. Maybe it was a long time after. Is that possible? I keep looking at Sophie, waiting for her to tell me if it was a long time after.

It is almost four o'clock. I have to turn on the television because Angelo will be in soon and he will want to watch our story. This and wrestling are the only programs he loves. When he watches wrestling, he screams and laughs as though he were right there in the audience. Oh, and "Gunsmoke," he loves to watch "Gunsmoke." But our story is his favorite. It's on every day and is about a nice girl named Nicole. Nicole has a lot of problems. Right now she is pregnant but can't find the father of the baby, who really loves her, but doesn't know she is pregnant. Every afternoon, we watch to see what Nicole will do. I hope Sophie is making stuffed peppers and sausage for dinner. Angelo likes to eat stuffed peppers and sausage on Monday nights. I think I smell sausage.

After dinner, Sophie gives me a bath. I wish I could bathe myself, but I can't seem to remember what to do. I get into the tub and I am fine. I go for the soap and I get confused. I get so confused. Then my head begins to hurt and I am dizzy. I'm afraid I will fall. But I'm sitting. My head hurts so much.

"Sophie, it hurts."

"What hurts, Mamma?"

"I don't know."

I always feel good after my bath, but I never want to take one. Sophie tells me it's good for me, but I'm afraid. Tom tells me I'm dirty and smell. I never know what will happen to me there in all that water. I don't care if I smell: I'm afraid.

Yesterday, or maybe it was last week, Sophie took me to a nursing home. It wasn't really a nursing home but something better. The floors were very shiny, and it smelled like a hospital. There were groups of people sitting in wheel chairs singing old songs. They looked so young; I like to sing.

We sat in an office and a man behind a desk asked me a lot of questions. I knew I had five children, but I couldn't remember any of their names, just Sophie's. I couldn't remember one other name.

"She knows the words to old songs," Sophie said right away.

"Fine, then, let's hear one," the man said.

So I started singing "Ramona," but when I looked at Sophie, she was crying, without a sound, just tears streaming down her face. Don't cry, Sophie, I can remember the words. Don't worry, I thought, I know the words.

Then, a funny thing happened. The man said "no" to Sophie; he said I didn't qualify. And Sophie helped me out, and she was smiling.

Tomorrow is the anniversary of Angelo's death, and I want Sophie to take me to church to the Mass they will say for him. Angelo never went to church after the time with Father Cioffi, but they will say a Mass for him anyway. I didn't tell the priest he never went to church. He should have gone; we both should have gone.

I sleep with Angelo tonight as I have for all these years. He snores loudly and rhythmically to the noisy ticking of the alarm clock on the night table. I have never known any other man in this way except him. I want to have a love affair with you tonight, Angelo. What? No, I cannot promise I will like it, but I won't complain. Please, can we have a love affair tonight?

Dead Baby Speaks

Toi Derricotte

Everybody knew what she was called, but nobody anywhere knew her name. Disremembered and unaccounted for, she cannot be lost because no one is looking for her, and, even if they were, how can they call her if they don't know her name.
　　　　　　　—Tony Morrison, *Beloved*

i am taking in   taking in
like a lump of a dead baby
on the floor   mama kicks me
i don't feel anything.

i am taking in   taking in
i am reading newspapers
i am seeing films
i am reading poetry
i am listening to psychiatrists, friends
someone knows the way
someone will be my mother
& tell me what to think

the dead baby wants to scream
the dead baby wants to drink warm milk
the dead baby wants to go to lunch with her mother, woman to woman,
*　　　say*
i can't always say the right thing
sometimes i've got to say what feels best
i'm not perfect
but i will not be a lump on the floor
the dead baby wants to kick her mother
the dead baby wants her mother to lie down & let herself be kicked
why not   she let father do it

how to separate
me from the dead baby
my mother from me
my mother from the dead baby

nothing is expected
nothing is expected
of you
you don't have to do this or say that
nothing is known
just be   be who you are
a little defiance   a little defense
say, if you want
i lifted up a little

there is that stunned moment when she shuts up & lets me speak
i have nothing to say

then i say
rotten mother who opened your legs
like iron gates & forced me into this prison
who lay among lilies & pressed me to your breasts, saying i will never be
*   alone again*
who wanted my soul for company, used my body in the place of your soul
who brought me up to the surface by straining off the rich dark broth
until what remained was as vaporous as the shadow of a shadow
whose breasts were bruised fruits
whose legs were swollen tree trunks, but when you were shaken, only one
*   red apple fell*
whose genitals hold me tethered, a string like a primate's tail, so that i
*   am your monkey in the red hat, you are my organ grinder*
cease your desperate paid music

if you say do not write about me
i will write more
there are many more mouths to feed
than yours
my life is juice pouring
out of me
let it find a channel

i could knuckle under & be good

i could pray for her & turn the other cheek
i could live in her house with her sickness like a stinking body in the
        stairwell
i could bake bread until my hands puff off
i could sweep the floor
i could suck misery out of my teeth like stringy meat
i could poison her with a plate of sorrow
i could leave the door open on her corpse so that no breath would warm
        her back to resurrection
i could throw myself at her feet
i could languish like a whore in colored rags
i could lie as still as a still life
i could be cut up & served on her table
i could go to my father & beg for her life
i could dance the seven veils while she escapes
i could give to the poor
i could close my legs like a hardened corpse
i could grow into a hag & compare myself to her pictures
i could eat her while she's sleeping
i could put her in the oven & burn her into a lace cookie
i could roar like a gored dragon
i could come crawling like a sexless husband
i could beg her to touch that scratch between my legs which should open
        in a flower

every time i question myself, i say
mother did not believe me
she thought i was making up my life to torture her
i take off the layers of pain for her to see the teeth marks in my soul
she thinks i can be born fresh once my rotten desires are removed

the desire to touch
the desire to speak

i could clean house until it is empty
i could put everything in the right place
but what about the one mistake i always make

i could love her
i could love her every time she is mistreated
i could love her every time someone forgets to pick up a plate from the
        table

i could love her weeping in church with a light on her face
i could love her stinking on the cot of ben gay waiting for my father to
> *come*
i could love her roaming from room to room in the dark with a blanket
> *on, trying to be quiet*
i could love her white breasts
i could love her belly of scars
i could love her insides which are half of a woman's
i could love her with the dead baby in her
i could love her even though the dead baby could be me
i could love her even if she wants some part of me dead
some part that invades her with sorrow she never understands

for the mystery of her childhood
for being too white & too black
for being robbed of a father
for wearing the cast-off clothes of the rich
for eating figs & cream on silver that wasn't hers
for putting the comb & brush neatly in place because they were the only
> *things she owned*
for learning to make up lies & make everything pretty
(she never believed her own body)
i could love her ocean black hair
i could love it in a braid like a long black chain
i could love her kneeling over the tub cleaning the scum out with a rag
i could love her standing in the doorway, thinking she's made the wrong
> *choice*
as frail as i
as strange to herself as i
as beautiful to herself as i
as ugly as i
i could love her as i love myself, imperfect mother

worse was done to me *she said* & i never told
i always told
in the body out the mouth
everything from insults to penises
needed words to make it real
be still   you make me suffer
i thought it was i who would die
i thought silence was a blessing
& i was its saint

i was prepared for
a higher calling

my mother is on my mouth
like a frog
be good be good
she points her finger, that old spinster teacher
she points her stick at my tongue
she knocks some sense into it across its red handle
half of my tongue hangs like a limp dick
a flag of my mother's country
half rises like a bridge
words might leap across that great divide, a daredevil driver
but i am the driver
& my mother is peeping out of the back like a baby
her eyes big & black with fear

my mother is on my mouth
like a gold frog
she is sparkling & quick as sin
with terrible humped breasts
that nothing can suck at
the black spots on her are universes you could walk on
if she were flat & sound as a board
i take her on my tongue like a lozenge
& roll her around
then i bite down.

50 Mothers of a Renowned Wolf

Evelyn Roehl

Most people think they have only one mother. I know the names of 50 of mine.

Oh yes, I have my birth mother. Bless her soul, she's still living on the family farm near Foreston, a fly speck on the map north of Minneapolis. I'm her youngest child, the eighth daughter of ten siblings, of German lineage (or so we'd been told). Of course we were Catholic, and God must have wanted my mom to pop babies on average every eighteen months, for fifteen years, so my pop could cuss at us to milk cows and drive tractors and get off our *hinders* to pull weeds in the garden ("Don't give me a lip of sass or I'll swat your mouth like a fly on the screen door"). Love was not a common term in the family vocabulary. Neither parent spoke Kraut, except when Dad called us *Dummkopf* or *Scheisse*-ass, although Mother and her sisters would gossip with guttural intonations at family reunions—to keep their kids' ears clean of muck about the cousins, I guess.

She too was the youngest of ten, raised on a family farm in a German-Catholic hamlet west of the Cities. My grandmother, or "Ma" as my mom called her, was the last of nine, widowed at Mother's age of three, and dead before my birth. Her mom, an immigrant from Germany, was *filia octava,* born of a mother who became a widow one and a half years later. So I'm the youngest child of the youngest child of the youngest child of the youngest child—all farmer's daughters, all "the Baby" of the family. Don't even think of asking me the psychological ramifications of those traits; I'm certainly not going to perpetuate them. I live in the city. I'm single and sterile by choice.

My great-great-grandmother's options were not so propitious. Of her eight children (who knows if they were "wanted"), only four survived after age three. Another great-great-grandmother (not an "only child" as the family legend contended) watched her mother deliver two sisters and a brother, all of whom died the same day they were born. In the 1800s, babies dropped like flies into little cemetery holes—or, if they were lucky, grew up and hopped on a boat across the Atlantic. Even then, they may have had to bury an infant at sea (as the "only child" did) or bear a child on the boat (as the mother of another relative did).

Thanks to the priests and civil servants who kept vital records, I know the names of five of my matrilineal mothers—Antoinette, Margaretha, Elisabeth, Bertha, and Carola—whose surnames disappeared when they joined in holy bonds. But resurrected, I become part Judge (Richter), part Rope Maker (Cordes), part Field Pea (Vetsch), part Keeper of the Treasure (Kasper). And thanks to my dad's father's papa, I am a Renowned Wolf (Rudolf>Rolf>Röhl>Roehl), hunting for documents about my great-grampa's original romping grounds in Prussia. (Oh Laurentius, dear Lorenz, from what den did you come? What was the bitch's name who raised you and your pup brother, before you came to the U.S. then lost track of each other after the Mexican War? What was his name? I'm trying to find him so you can rest in peace, so I can find more of our pack.)

I also know the names of my maternal grandmother's paternal grandmother, and her mother, and her mother, and her mother, and their mothers-in-law—all of whom were ultimately *my* mothers—back to Maria Anna Covigin's marriage to a farmer in Niederlauterbach, Austria, Alsace, a town about as far northeast as you can go in France before the Rhine River separates the wine sippers from the beer guzzlers. Then there's the lady from Ohio (!), mother of my mother's father, whose mama and grandmamas came from Schirrhoffen, a *dorf* upriver from Niederlauterbach. Farther north, some clan on my dad's grandmother's side (coincidentally named Roehl, reportedly not related to Lorenz) were farming in the Rhineland, raising babies, all going to Catholic churches in little villages throughout the hilly countryside. Just think of all those mothers' feet stomping on grapes or through the hop and barley fields, or on the cabin floors to get their kids to obey, or to Mass every Sunday to pray to the Blessed Virgin to stop the soldiers from stomping through the pastures with muskets and wagons and silly uniforms and killing their 19-year-old baby boys who should've been tending sheep in the *scheids,* not feeding their blood to the grass. (Damn Messieurs Bonaparte for their stupid *révolutions,* changing our borders and allegiances—and for what? And damn the men for their drunken foolhardiness in the *biergartens* and slapping us around when we were with child. God how could you subject us to such a life?! I ask your forgiveness, *in Nómine Patris, et Fílii, et spíritus sancti,* Amen.)

Fifty mothers. That's just the *known* names, only a tenth of what we all have in ten generations: 511 mothers—and fathers—1,022 parents of parents of parents. . . . With every past generation there's an exponential increase in the number of parents. It's a reverse population explosion—a genetic implosion. Their voices echo in passenger lists, church books, census rolls, and military records; from photos of stern pioneer women in black, high-collar dresses and somber men with beards; in our blood.

We are all hybrids. We carry physical traits of hundreds of beings who played in the sand, wandered in the woods, sang, dance, fought with their siblings, ate cabbage and sausage and strawberries, got married, made love, and had babies. We carry behaviors learned and repeated in our families for decades. And many of us now carry the babies that will carry on the human species.

Thank you, Mother, for suckling me, changing my dirty diapers, feeding me mushed up carrots, and training me to pee in the potty chair. Thank you for telling me the words in my Dick and Jane book and letting me visit Darla after school. Thank you for the Ginger doll from a cereal box offer and for not making me wear dresses in winter. Thank you for explaining what I pointed to on my body was called a vulva, and for throwing the *Growing Up and Liking It* booklet on my bed when I got my period. Thank you for forcing me to go to church until I was 18 so I could learn to hate it with a passion and open my mind to other beliefs and rituals. Thank you for all the homegrown potatoes and corn and apples you urged me to take to my apartment that I couldn't wait to get back to so I wouldn't have to listen to your disapproving remarks about the man I was living with whom you'd never met, whose son helped me realize that kids are okay—it's their parents who perpetuate unhealthy living patterns. Thank you for giving me reasons to change. Thanks for all the birthday and Christmas gifts; I'll spend the money digging up more bones of our ancestors.

But most of all, Mother—all 50 or 511 of you—thank you for my life. I love it. May you howl at the moon with me someday.

Beautiful Bellies

Daryn Stier, Photographer

Daryn Stier, a mother, photographer, and therapist, lives in Oakland, California. Her photographs are part of a larger series entitled *Our Beautiful Bellies: Portraits of Pregnant Women,* a project that reflects an affirming and powerful vision of pregnancy to replace the negative stereotypes and fears that are in place in society.

Honoring women's lives is one of Daryn's lifelong commitments. Through her gallery shows, cards, private photography sessions, and in her psychotherapy practice, she strives with women to reclaim their magic and strength.

Daryn is gathering short memoir and fiction pieces from women across the country to accompany her photographs. Her book, *Our Beautiful Bellies,* will document women's insights and wisdom as they travel through the pregnancy journey.

Stargazing

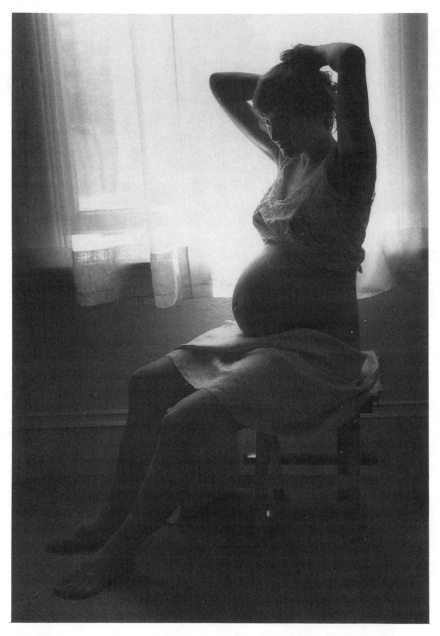

Unfolding

Centered

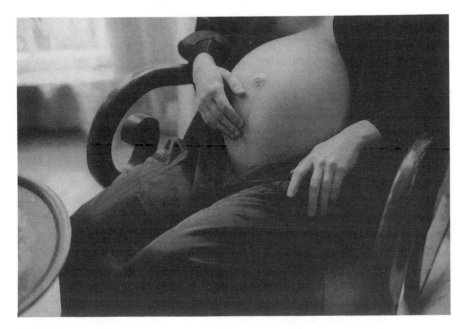

Listening

Beginning

Parallels

Silhouette

Babydreaming

Bellylaugh

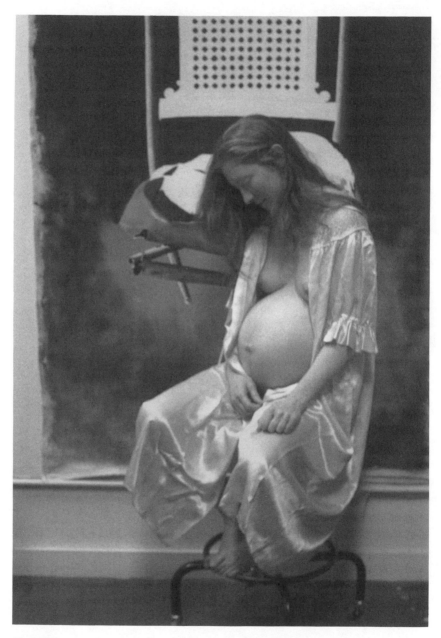

Heartful

III – Beyond the Whole

Her thought,
In its silent chase,
Which makes it boundless,
All in all,
Will find again
the uncircumscribed Whole.

—*Hadewijch of Antwerp*

Mother and Daughter, A Dynamic Duo Indeed

Jackie Fitzpatrick

When Rosa L. DeLauro was sifting through piles of family memorabilia—dog-eared photographs, scrapbooks and letters—as she prepared for her first Congressional campaign, she stumbled across a letter written by her mother, Luisa Canestri DeLauro, back in 1933.

Her mother was 19 at the time and secretary of the Tenth Ward Democratic Club in New Haven. She wrote to encourage the female members of the club to take a more active role. "We are not living in the Middle Ages when a woman's part in life was merely to serve her master in her home, but we have gradually taken our place in every phase of human endeavor and even in the heretofore stronghold of the male sex: politics."

Rosa DeLauro, elected to Congress in 1990, tucked the letter away and still keeps it for inspiration. Not that she needed a source. Some children are weaned on books or baseball, but it was politics that flowed like water at her house in Wooster Square. A pot of coffee was always on, the kitchen table was a makeshift social service agency, Italian immigrants unfamiliar with the language and life in the States would sit down with her parents, Luisa and Theodore DeLauro, and talk of their difficulties during those Depression years.

Ted, as the Representative's father was known, would leave the house and return with a basket of food. Luisa would ask around the neighborhood then jot down an address, a place for the person to live or find work. Ted became Alderman for a short time, then Luisa gave politics a try. She lost her first election, but the second time around, her husband gave her some campaigning tips.

"He gave me a stack of 5 by 10 cards and said, 'Go and see all these people. Look them square in the eye and that way you'll know if they're gonna vote for you,'" Mrs. DeLauro said.

"When I got back he'd ask me, 'So what did so-and-so say, what did the other one say,' and I said, 'I don't know.' He said 'Why didn't you write their comments down?' So that's what I started to do. Wooster Square was heavily populated then so I got to know what a lot of people thought. It was scary as all sin that first time running because in those days people figured most women stayed home and cooked."

Luisa DeLauro was elected in her second run for office in 1965 and has been on the Board of Aldermen ever since. New Haven Mayor John DeStefano said hers is the longest term ever in the city. "She's been a strong advocate for people all her life," he said. "And it's very natural she would have a daughter like Rosa who would go on to work for people. The genuine pride they have in each other's work is something to see."

At the age of 80, Luisa DeLauro still knows how to work a room. "Hey, how's that new baby of yours?" she asks a woman as she walks into a communion breakfast of the Santa Maria de la Virgine Society of New Haven with her daughter, Rosa. Luisa is a tiny burst of a woman in strawberry blond curls, glasses, a long strand of pearls and a smile that makes her whole face crinkle.

Rosa, meanwhile, is a United States Congresswoman, an F.O.B. (friend of Bill Clinton), a member of the House Appropriations Committee and every bit Luisa DeLauro's daughter.

Now people come to her asking for help, as one woman did at the breakfast. She said her grown son needed Prozac but he had no health insurance and couldn't afford it. "I just don't know what to do," the woman said. Representative DeLauro took both of the woman's hands in hers and said, "He must be eligible for something, ConnPace, something. We'll check into it and call you."

All morning women came up to her, pressing into her hands slips of paper with their names and phone numbers, hoping she could find a solution to their problems. She listened to them all and then dashed off with an aide to hear concerns of workers at Textron Lycoming and to another meeting before eventually returning to her New Haven home with her husband, Stanley Greenberg, president of a research and polling firm and the father of three grown children. During the week they live in Washington but almost all weekends are spent in New Haven.

Luisa DeLauro would be there too, later, supplying dinner, which she does every Sunday—heaping plates of chicken, artichokes and macaroni. "They say to me, 'Let's go out to dinner' but not me, I like my own cooking," Luisa said.

Flo Consiglio, the owner of Sally's Apizza on Wooster Street, put it this way: "I think you could walk around Wooster Square and it would be hard to find anyone who didn't like them both, mother and daughter. Luisa would do anything for anybody. Years back when some of the boys in the neighborhood would get picked up by the cops, for loitering on the corner or something like that, they'd always call Luisa and she'd get down there and bond them out. She's a woman who worked hard and earned everyone's respect and now her daughter has followed in her footsteps and gone beyond."

Although the Representative's dark hair and deep brown eyes are in contrast to her mother's, there is no mistaking the mother-daughter bond. They fill in the blanks in each other's sentences; they laugh easily and often together.

"When I grew up, all of Wooster Street was a family place. We all knew everyone. There was the butcher and the man who sold chickens on the corner," the daughter and Representative said.

"Tony the chicken man," the mother and Alderman noted.

"Tony the chicken man," the Representative repeated with a smile.

"They are a pair," said Theresa Argento, the president of the St. Andrews Ladies Society. "They are each their own person and yet they are also very much alike. Luisa is beloved in this city because she's made a life out of helping people, anybody at all who calls on her, and Rosa is probably one of the warmest people I've ever met. What those two women together have done for politics in New Haven is unbelievable."

In the Beginning

Their story begins with Luisa who was born on Christmas Eve 1913, to Cesare and Luisa Canestri, who owned the Canestri Pastry Shop on Wooster Street. Luisa quit school at 14, as soon as she reached the legal age to work. She met her husband, Ted, who had come from Italy and left school in the seventh grade after classmates made fun of his broken English. They married, and he sold insurance door to door.

"He used to come to my house to sell insurance and he would sit down with my father and talk to every one of us," said Ruby Proto of the Santa Maria society. "My father would send him home with some of our wine. They were a wonderful, hard-working family."

Rosa, born in 1943, was an only child who grew up amid cousins, cakes and cannoli at the bustling Canestri Pastry Shop. "It was day care, family care, a great network of family and friends," Ms. DeLauro said.

Luisa DeLauro went to work in a New Haven dress shop, a sweatshop, and Rosa would have to meet her there after school. "I still have the images of all of these women working over their machines," Representative DeLauro said, "the half-eaten oranges, the brown paper bags that held their lunches. They never got up from their seats because they were paid by the piece and they wanted to do as much work as they could." At night, Luisa DeLauro took in sewing, patching the trousers and jackets of Yale students.

Although Luisa said Rosa never liked the noise of the machines in the sweatshop, Rosa said waiting after school there was a valuable lesson. "My mother was trying to show me how important an education was," she said. "I never forgot that."

Instinctively, Rosa became a student. "She would go right up to her room and do her studies, that's just how she was," Luisa said. She took tap dance lessons, piano lessons. "She wanted to take Spanish lessons from nuns at a convent and I said to my husband 'How will we pay the rent?' and he said, 'Don't worry about the rent. Get her the lessons.' "

"She was always a special little girl," Luisa said. "Rosa never wanted to hurt anyone's feelings. Me, I might say something and not mean to hurt somebody but I would and Rosa would say, 'Ma, I don't think you should have said that.' "

Rosa DeLauro attended the London School of Economics in 1962 and 1963, graduated cum laude from Marymount College (Tarrytown, N.Y.) in 1964, and earned a master's degree in international politics from Columbia University in 1966.

She said it was no surprise to herself or others when she went into public service as one of the first community organizers in the War on Poverty program. She was the first woman to serve as executive assistant to the Mayor of New Haven, managed Frank Logue's mayoral campaign in 1978, and was chief of staff to United States Senator Christopher J. Dodd from 1981 to 1987.

It was during one of Senator Dodd's campaigns that Rosa DeLauro found out she had ovarian cancer. Her mother said: "I wanted to move right into her hospital room with her but her husband, Stanley, said there probably wouldn't be room for three. That man never left her side. And Rosa was herself right after. She had piles of papers all over her bed and had the phone right next to her."

After treatment, Ms. DeLauro decided she wanted to run for office. Nearing the end of her second Congressional term, she plans to seek another. She is at work on the crime bill and on health care. Like her mother, she is an of-the-people legislator. Her weekends in New Haven are taken up by drop-in office hours, in front of supermarkets, at senior centers, at local festivals and dinners and at town halls. Over and over, she said, people come to her with concerns about health care and about jobs. If she can't attend a function, her mother fills in.

"Rosa is completely accessible," said Vivian Ventura, an administrative aide for several oncologists who talked with the Representative about cancer patients who have no health insurance. "I've watched her go to work helping people out."

Representative DeLauro said she loves her work. "These aren't extraneous issues—education, crime, health care. They are real issues for people," she said.

Her mother forges on as well as an Alderman and works in New Haven's probate judge's office. Neither meddles too much in each other's politics although Luisa is known to send notes on her aldermanic letterhead asking her daughter to consider different legislative packages.

Late last year, when friends and colleagues threw an 80th birthday party for Luisa, 800 people showed up. "I could have sold another 200 tickets," said Mrs. Argento of the St. Andrews Ladies Society.

Rosa chuckled quietly over the woman holding court at her table, telling stories about how she made her way in politics. "My mother has always been able to make her presence known," she said.

As the Representative prepared to leave the communion breakfast, she took her mother's hand and told her she would see her that night. She was on her way to more public gatherings, her mother on her way to another party before going home to make sauce and bake chicken to take to her daughter's house.

Before she left, they reminisced for a moment about how they used to go shopping together in downtown New Haven when Rosa was a young girl.

"Every Saturday," Luisa said. And then they would go out for tea.

"They had those little date nut sandwiches," Rosa said. "Remember those?"

"I do," Luisa said. "Such fun."

Heat

Jameson Currier

She had tried to get Richard to finish the basement room years ago when Andy had claimed it as his haven, an escape from his older, rowdier brother Craig and his two nosy younger sisters, Lisa and Julie. She had convinced Richard that he could sheetrock over the gray concrete walls, put in a light switch and fixtures, a carpet on the cement floor, but other projects had always happened first: building the sun-room off the kitchen, replacing the gutters, repaving the driveway. Andy had not cared about the condition of the room, only that it was his sanctuary, stringing a hammock between two of the walls and setting up a stereo. This was the room she knew her son had used to discover many things: rock music, cigarettes, pot and sex.

She had come downstairs this afternoon to find the large straw hat she had once bought for Richard, her fingertips leading the way down the steep wooden staircase. She had forgotten almost instantly about the hat, struck instead by the sweet damp air of the basement. Outside, the August Georgia sun had baked the red clay soil for so many days that it no longer sweated; inside, the overused air-conditioner seemed to act only as a fan. She had sat on the bottom stair, drawing in the cool darkness about her, relieved to have found a refuge from the heat. It was then she noticed the door to the room, no bigger than a closet, actually, and she had thought again about Andy, missed him, really, and was pulled toward the door as if by a magnet.

The room was still as Andy had left it when he left for college twenty years ago, unpainted but with the hammock hooks still in the walls, a bare lightbulb and a string hanging in the center from a wire. The posters had long ago disappeared, but she couldn't remember if Andy had taken them with him or if they had fallen down. What had they been of, she tried to remember: Meatloaf, Joni Mitchell, a Broadway show—*Pippin*. Was there something she should have known then about her son, something that could have prevented his future? She stood by the wall where Andy had kept piles of paperback books and cassette tapes and spiral notebooks and record albums leaning against the cement blocks, wishing they were still there, to sort through now, to try to understand the path his life had taken. Andy had gone to Tulane for college and afterwards he had moved to San Francisco.

She and Richard had gone to New Orleans for Andy's graduation, had brought back a scrapbook of photographs and hurricane glasses from Pat O'Brien's. But they had never visited their son in California, had always waited instead for his infrequent trips home. Now she imagined she could still smell that cooped up odor of musty clothes and the young male body that had used to linger in the room, and it made her realize, vividly, how much of a mystery her son's adult life was to her; certainly the man who had died in the upstairs bedroom seemed not even related to the boy who had grown up in the basement.

The news of Andy's illness had arrived like a flash of fire: pneumonia, Ward 86, AZT, DDI, and AIDS. She had years ago come to accept Andy's homosexuality, even though she had relegated the concept of it as something she could not understand. She had accepted the friends and lovers who often answered his phone the mornings she called; accepted, too, Richard's refusal to talk to his son about anything beyond the weather. Andy had become a silent fact that they had carried around with them for years. When he arrived home for the last time, gaunt with a goatee, earrings, his eyes burning with desperation, she had moved him into the upstairs bedroom where he lived for two months before he died. Only the books and music seemed to connect the man with the boy she had known, the only recognizable source for her in a once-familiar bedroom transformed by oxygen tanks, IV poles, bedpans and towels. She had not imagined she would become a caretaker so soon again since her mother's battle with Alzheimer's only last year. The day she packed up Andy's belongings, Richard handed her each item—his jeans, his watch, the books—as if each were a bomb about to explode. Weeks later after they had moved everything up to the attic, they repainted the bedroom a different color, not so much to forget about Andy, but to keep the memories of him from haunting them.

The sound of the lawnmower approached the basement like an airplane, and she looked up at the small rectangle of a window near the ceiling and watched the cut grass smash against the window pane. Richard had become such a senseless man in his old age; they argued about everything now, simply as a way of talking to each other. This afternoon he insisted that he needed to mow the yard in spite of the heat wave. When she admonished him, warned him that he would have a stroke out in the sun, his face had flushed with indignation and he claimed the yard could not wait another day. She knew it was not so; he was only as restless as she was. He had to be somewhere, doing something. Grief was not something they could take to a restaurant or the mall, but instead needed to find sanctuaries and sweat. Now she noticed that Andy had placed the hammock hooks in the wall so that he could lie and look up at the bright green rectangle of grass. The lawnmower roared by again and she watched the grass this time merely tap against the window. Andy's friends were right, she knew, the effect of his death was at first numbing, then chilling, then anger.

She looked up at the window again and now imagined the heat scorching everything on the lawn, the grass and trees and ivy turning yellow and then brown and then bursting into a violent fire. Fire would burn across the grasses of the highways, into the brushes and the hills and the mountains. It would burn through the cemetery where Andy was buried, the marble cross reduced to ashes. She imagined waves of heat rising, the wind carrying the fire like a storm across the continent. It would burn everything in its path, destroying even the city and street and building and apartment and room where Andy had lived for so many years out of her sight.

Above her she heard the kitchen door open and slam, followed by a series of short clicks against the ceiling. A voice cried something unintelligible but she knew it was Lisa arriving with her children for a visit. She left the cool of the room as if being released from a cell. She could not let this happen again. She had to find something to do, someone else to fight.

Two Poems

Tom Baer

Watch
Thumbs
on hips,
fingers
on backs . . .

Mothers,
childbearers!
So
they

stand
their
tidal
watch.

These Dear Ones
Thong-bikinied,
at once at laughter,
swaying, dance,
at serious, grave
conversation as they march—
thus at seventeen.

At eighteen, mothers
(wee babes in cradle or arms
or on crazy march nearby;)
as often as otherwise
big-bellied once more,
they hover, lean, swoop about . . .
O, these dear ones,
these dear ones.

The Scorpion Wore Pink Shoes

Janice Levy

"*Despiértate,* wake up, Soledad!" Clara hissed.

Soledad groaned and rubbed her eyes.

"Come on, *ya se hace tarde,* it's getting late, and we have a lot to do."

Squinting through one eye, Soledad saw that Clara was already wearing her gray dress and white apron, the name, "Harrington Hotel" stitched over its top pocket. Crescents of sweat darkened the cotton uniform under her arms. Soledad stretched slowly, her aching legs sticking up under the white sheet of her cot. She coughed up the phlegm that stuck in her throat like lumps of glue. She felt like a leftover meal.

As Clara pushed her cleaning cart filled with disinfectants, toilet scrub brushes, and plastic bags out of the basement, she gestured with her nose at Soledad to hurry. The housekeeping staff lived in the basement of the Harrington Hotel in New Hampshire, with sheets hung across the ceiling to separate the cots. Soledad's bed was closest to the row of washing machines. She stared at the clothes spinning around and wondered how it would feel to be sucked up and tossed about until you became just a blur of color.

She threw off her blanket and walked stiffly to one of the dryers to take out some pillowcases and sheets. She rested her head on top of a whirring machine and imagined herself slow dancing, her body pressed against the warm chest of a handsome man. The deep, soothing noise of the machine reminded her of Geraldo's humming in the shower, while she lingered in bed and inhaled his scent from the sheets. But that was a long time ago, when she had been almost as young as her daughter, Gabriela, was now, and there was still a reason to linger.

When Clara's friend, Mr. Jones, came to Costa Rica looking for women to bring back to the States with him, Soledad left her job at the factory where her boss stood with a watch to make sure she scaled and gutted fifteen fish an hour. She asked her mother to take care of Gabriela. "You'll see, *Mamá,* I'll send you money so the doctors can take the veins out of your legs and Gabriela can go to the *Universidad* to study."

She told her daughter she would come back in a year. *"Te prometo,* I promise." Gabriela had stared at her with lizard eyes.

Mr. Jones wore a toupee that looked like a dead pigeon and his cheeks were the color of an emery board. He got Soledad a tourist visa and a social security card that changed her into "Maria Rivera," a Puerto Rican from New York. When she started working in the hotel, she sometimes leaned against the door of a room before knocking and strained to make sense of the words that shot out in English as fast as gun fire. But after six months, she could say little more than, "good morning," "sorry," and "room clean?"

Clara learned English because she cleaned Mr. Jones's house on her day off. Soledad saw her friend and Mr. Jones coming out of the service elevator together early one morning, Clara's face had been flushed and her hair messed up. Clara said you could make fifty dollars in four hours, but you had to be smart.

Every Sunday night, Soledad made a three-minute phone call to Costa Rica, covering one ear with her hand to block out the noise from the hallway. While waiting their turns on the long line that snaked down the hall, the maids passed around letters and pictures. Soledad's mother had sent her a picture of Gabriela, standing with Gabriela's father, Geraldo, in front of a neighbor's house. Gabriela was, at fourteen, as tall as Soledad and already wore her mother's shoes and clothes. In the photograph, she stood slumped forward, her fists rolled up under her chin, her head tilted away from her father. Geraldo had one hand on her shoulder. Soledad couldn't make out her daughter's face clearly, but she knew how her daughter was feeling. Gabriela didn't like to be touched. By anyone. Ever.

Geraldo faced the camera, mustachioed and heavy lidded, with his hips jutting forward. Soledad remembered how just touching his thigh lightly with her fingertips used to make her legs turn to jelly. In the six months Soledad had been in the United States, she had received one letter from Geraldo, the handwriting smeared and running up and down the page like crawling worms. Soledad heard he had remarried. She wondered if he hit his new wife in the face after yelling at her.

On the telephone, Gabriela spoke excitedly about her upcoming *quinceañera.* In another month she would be fifteen years old. Gabriela thanked Soledad for sending the money to buy fabric so *Abuelita* Rosa could make the dress for her big party. But now the problem was finding a pair of matching shoes.

"I've looked everywhere, in all the stores, and I can't find anything I like. They have to be perfect."

Soledad could picture her sullen daughter pacing up and down and frowning.

"I want shoes that a princess would wear; princess slippers, with high, high heels. And pink. They've got to be pink."

When Soledad asked if she had chosen an escort for her party, she heard Gabriela take a deep breath and she knew her daughter was tapping her foot up and down.

"Yes, *mami*, I asked Juan but don't worry because we're not *novios*, he's just my friend. But, so anyway, about the shoes, you won't forget to send the money for them, okay?"

Soledad wiped her eyes when her daughter used up the last moments of the phone call with kisses.

Soledad knocked on the door of the first room she had to clean. She opened the door with her key and pushed her cleaning cart into the center of the room. Holding her breath, she emptied the overflowing ashtrays. She put clean glasses with paper tops on the dresser, replaced the stationery in the drawers, and filled a little wicker basket in the bathroom with bottles of shampoo and conditioner. As Soledad filled a vase with water and added a red carnation, she thought of her mother's house, where she had returned after Geraldo had left her lying on the kitchen floor. The house was small, the color of tarnished silver. The roof was wooden; the balcony a slab of colored stones. On the front porch steps, Soledad had placed red flowers in brightly painted tin cans. She painted the cans herself, with images of fuschia-feathered roosters and scampering little black pigs, all the things she saw while she sat on the porch and waited for Geraldo to make it all good again.

When he did, it was always the same. He'd bring *Mamá* Rosa some flowers, swing Gabriela in the air, and toss his hat across the room for Soledad to catch. Soledad would cook his favorite dishes and wash his clothes. She'd stroke his face and lay her head on his chest. Once, Geraldo stayed for a few weeks and they took a trip to Poás, the volcano, outside the city of Alajuela. As the taxi huffed its way on the winding roads, through the green fields and small farms, Geraldo chewed on her ear and played with her hair. They walked, arms around each other, up the trail to the crater of the volcano. As they walked through the forest of clouds, Soledad matched her breathing to Geraldo's and thought his face looked like *un ángel del cielo*.

Soledad sighed and threw off the sheets and put them in her laundry bag. She remade the bed and put on fresh pillowcases. She hugged a pillow and closed her eyes. Those were the times to remember, she thought. Not the times when Geraldo paced the house and scratched himself like a dog in heat, went out at night and came back stumbling and falling against things. He'd come back later and later, until Soledad knew he was finally gone, because the only sounds in the house when the sun came up were the muffled sobs of Gabriela and the ticking of a clock.

Soledad pushed her cart down the hall to Suite 710, the best accommodations on the floor with a living room, a fireplace in the bedroom, and a telephone in the bathroom. She picked up the breakfast tray from the floor and put the leftover rolls and packets of orange marmalade in her pocket. Several bottles of perfume, all opened, sat on the bathroom sink, their tops lying nearby. A makeup case floated in the half-filled bathtub, forming lily pads of greasy rainbows on the water's surface. False eyelashes swirled like drowning spiders under the faucet. Soledad shut off the dripping water and walked into the living room. Three fur coats were rolled up on the couch— they looked like drunks holding their stomachs. A purple suede hat with a corkscrew stuck through its brim sat in a bucket of melted ice on the bar's countertop. Soledad looked at the wine stains on the bedsheets and the broken champagne glasses on the hearth. She suddenly felt tired and looked around for a clean place to sit down.

Flung over the back of a chair was a man's tuxedo and a pink gown with a neckline of white feathers. She ran her hand down the front of the dress, over a big orange stain, touching sequins and beads and pearls, some hanging by loose threads. A cigarette had burned a hole over the left shoulder.

As a bead from the gown fell into her hand, Soledad thought of her daughter's *quinceañera* dress. Gabriela wanted a traditional dress, down to the floor, tight on top and full at the bottom, with a skirt shaped like a wedding bell. She mailed a sketch of the dress to Soledad, along with a piece of material and for weeks, Soledad kept the swatch of pink satin with tiny white rosebuds on it in the pocket of her uniform. When she touched it, she could almost see *Padre* Vargas, the pastor at *la Iglesia de Cristo,* giving her daughter the blessing at the *quinceañera* mass, just as he had blessed her, sixteen years ago, making the sign of the cross as she knelt in front of him. Soledad remembered her own *quinceañera* and her tall, handsome escort, who danced a kind of waltz with her, weaving in and out among the other fourteen girls and their escorts, forming small and then big circles, like the ripples on a pond. She had stood with all the girls on the sidewalk outside the church, giggling when a car drove by and made a great *poof* that made their full dresses fly up. Soledad fingered the cross around her neck and thought of the *Iglesia de Cristo,* with its hard wood pews and a ceiling so high it made her neck hurt to see its top. The stained glass behind the altar glistened in the sunlight like multi-colored dewdrops. Soledad wondered if *Padre* Vargas still kept a pail hanging outside the side door of the church for the children to deposit their bubble gum in.

Soledad held the pink gown against her body and looked in the mirror. Her tall, dark escort, mustachioed and heavy lidded, had flirted and danced with all the girls, but he caught her eye with a look, quiet and still, like a gift held just out of reach. In back of the church, against a tree in the woods, he took her hair and tied it under her chin so it framed her face like a bonnet. He held her so close that she could feel his eyelashes on her cheeks.

"*Te necesito,* I need you, Soledad," he had pleaded.

Soledad had let him find his way past the bows and ties of her dress, under the satin slips. His face had looked like a wounded bird, so she had held him and stroked his head until he shivered and stopped.

After they were married, Soledad and Geraldo lived with his parents in Sarchi, northwest of San José, the capital. Geraldo worked with his father building ox carts that the farmers used to carry their coffee beans. *Turistas* liked to watch them work in the open sheds. Soledad painted geometric designs on the ox carts and listened to Geraldo practice his English with the men in baggy shorts and gold watches, men with cameras around their necks. Geraldo told them the wheels he carved made music as they turned.

He winked and smiled at the overdressed ladies in high heels and ropes of jewelry. He took them by the hand and sat them down in his handmade, wood rocking chairs. He took off his hat and fanned them, using a mixture of Spanish and English to describe their beauty. Almost always the men bought something, if only to get their wives out of the rocking chairs, because Soledad knew the *señoras* could sit there forever, giggling and running their fingers through their hair.

Once Geraldo caught a man with a big belly and baseball cap, wiping paint off Soledad's cheek with a handkerchief, then opening his wallet and pointing to her. Geraldo had grabbed Soledad by the back of her neck and dragged her behind the shed. He covered her mouth so she wouldn't frighten away the *turistas*. Many hours later, Geraldo pinned her against the bed and squeezed her wrists as if he were stapling her to the sheets. He pushed his weight against her again and again until he had felt the blood rush down her legs and then he fell asleep with his legs across her hips. Soledad rolled out from under him and walked outside to sit in the darkness. She wondered if the man with the big belly and baseball cap was showing his wallet to other women that night or if he made love gently and so quietly, that his wife wept. When she counted back, she knew that was the night Gabriela was conceived.

With a heavy sigh, Soledad began wiping the mirrors with glass cleaner. As she pulled down hard on the curtain cord to bring in more light from the high windows overlooking a little terrace, she tripped over a pair of shoes that lay behind the curtain.

The shoes were pink satin with tiny white rosebuds. The toes of the shoes were open except for a transparent lace covering that looked like a bridal veil. The inner side of the shoes curved toward the middle like the waistline of a young girl. Little silver chains of pearls were strung around the heels, which were several inches high. Soledad cradled the shoes in her hands and noted the soles looked clean and a piece of the price tag had not been scraped off one of them.

"Maybe he carried her all night," she said to herself. "Maybe in his arms like a *princesa.*" Soledad looked to find the size of the shoes. She slipped them on her feet and smiled. She held out her gray uniform and curtsied to the mirror. Soledad spun around the room, her arms moving like the waves of an ocean. As she arched her neck and pointed her toes, she pretended she was a rich lady, having returned to Costa Rica. She imagined she was making the eight-hour train ride with a lover, from San Jose to Puerto Limón, to vacation by the Caribbean Sea. They would dangle their hands out the windows and pass through the shoulders of huge mountains, into tangled jungles, along the Reventazón River with its rapids and high rocks. They would see white sand and blue seas and palm trees that looked like feather dusters as they swayed in the wind. Her lover would buy her peanuts and *papas calientes,* hot potatoes, from the small boys who jumped on the trains and sold them down the aisles. The barefooted ladies who wore aprons would call her *Doña Soledad* and stand before her selling yucca and hot fish. Her lover would snap his fingers in the air and a man would run over with a paper cone filled with bits of ice, berry red with fruit juice. Soledad and her lover would share one and lick their lips, melting the ice in each other's mouths with their tongues. She would put her feet in his lap and he'd take off her pink shoes with the white rosebuds and lightly kiss her ankles, never taking his eyes off her face.

Soledad caught sight of herself in the mirror, her hair messed and swirly. She untied the belt of her uniform and her stomach protruded forward. Soledad shook her head as she took off the shoes. *"Ay, Soledad, que tonta eres,* how silly you are," she said. She thought of her serious, amber-eyed daughter and wondered if Gabriela still believed in the magic of such things.

Soledad heard voices coming from the hall and quickly put the shoes behind the curtain, in the same corner where she had found them. She looked at the clock and realized she would have to work extra fast to finish cleaning all the rooms on the seventh floor. Soledad jumped as a man walked into the room, stumbling as if he had a third leg that kept bumping into the other two. A woman wearing a bathing suit and clumps of jewelry at her ears and throat pushed past him. Soledad thought she looked like a doll whose hair grew when you pressed her stomach, a doll that she had once bought for Gabriela. The woman looked at Soledad and scrunched up her eyes, nose, and lips. She shook her fingers in the air as if shooing away pigeons. She threw her purse on the floor, kicked her shoes off, and fell back on the bed. The man said something to Soledad and then repeated it louder. He opened his eyes so wide his eyelashes reached up to his eyebrows. He pointed around the room and spoke louder and louder, his earlobes turning as red as the rising mercury of a thermometer. Soledad bit her lip and said, "Good morning, sorry, clean room?" in one fast breath and quickly pushed her cleaning cart out of the room.

That night, Soledad dreamt of two scorpions mating. The male and female moved back and forth, front legs gripping front legs, mouthparts locked together. The male whipped his tail forward and stung the female again and again, dragging her thrashing body around a dance floor. The female wore pink shoes with white rosebuds. A band played a waltz; then the music switched to mariachi sounds and the female, heavy in her ruffled dress, bit off the male's head and kicked it with the point of her shoe.

Soledad woke up, sticky with sweat. She stood on tiptoe to look out the basement windows. A light snow was falling, the first snowfall Soledad had ever seen. The branches of the trees stiff under the flakes made her think of crinoline; the patches of frozen pond reminded her of icing on a cake.

As she watched the sun scratch away the night, Soledad covered her cheeks with her hands and tapped the sides of her head with her fingers. She pushed her tongue hard against the back of her front teeth. Soledad dressed quickly. As she pushed her cleaning cart out into the hall, she saw Mr. Jones walking towards her, waving a piece of paper. Bulky in his dark fur coat and hat, Soledad thought he looked like a circus bear.

"*Buenos dias,* good morning," he said. "Getting an early start today?" He spoke in broken Spanish. "There's been a change in one of your rooms. The people in Suite 710 had some kind of an emergency and they checked out late last night. I think they flew out to Canada. The new guests are checking in early, before noon. So start on the suite first."

Soledad nodded and Mr. Jones reached out and pushed a strand of her hair behind her ear. "I hear you've got a daughter who wants to go to college? If you're looking to make some extra money, let me know. Your friend Clara tells me you're real smart."

Soledad jerked her cleaning cart forward and bumped into a standing ashtray. She could hear Mr. Jones laughing as she reached the service elevator. Soledad took the elevator to the seventh floor. The hall was quiet, except for the sound of a baby crying. She ran to Suite 710. She saw the "Do Not Disturb" sign lying in a breakfast tray outside the door. Soledad pushed the door open. Wet towels stuck like leeches against the chairs. Orange juice from a pink rimmed glass dripped onto the pillows. The floor looked like the bottom of a hamster cage, with its piles of ripped up newspapers and bits of half-eaten food. Soledad quickly made her way across the room to the windows that overlooked the terrace. Biting her knuckles, she drew open the curtains and looked into the corner.

"*Soñadora,* dreamer," she said, spitting out the words. "What did you expect?"

Soledad straightened her shoulders and roughly tugged at her gray uniform. She thought of Mr. Jones and shivered. She looked at the top of the dresser for a tip and brushed aside some dirty tissues and empty cigarette packs until she found an envelope. Soledad put the three dollars in her pocket and walked toward the door to get her cleaning cart. She threw the empty envelope at the garbage pail, but it landed on the floor. She bent down and stuffed the envelope, hard this time, into the pail. It was then that she felt the blood pound in her ears as she pulled out the pair of shoes; princess slippers, pink with white rosebuds, and high, high heels.

Mommy Wars

Kim Hirsh

Since my daughter, a toddler, lately has decided there's nothing as thrilling as the smiles of other children, I've started taking her to a neighborhood "playgroup," which is just a formal name for a bunch of mothers who get their kids together each week at the same swingset.

Ours is an eclectic gathering according to the measure by which mothers today often judge themselves: Do you work outside the home or not? Among the half-dozen or so women who attend each week are some who stay home full time with their kids; some who, like me, work part time; and one mother who's a full-time attorney and dashes in and out of our back yards on her way to court.

We get together for our kids, but also for ourselves, since it's nice, especially when you're home a lot, to get out and enjoy adult conversation. When we walk away from the group each week, we spend the rest of the day in different contexts—in offices or in the kitchen or at the park. But when we're together, there are no such boundaries. It's just a lot of friendly conversation about the usual things: our kids, the neighborhood, vacations, and so on.

The playgroup always raises a question in my mind: If this kind of get-together is so easy and so natural, why can't women do this in a broader context? Why can't we end the "Mommy Wars"?

I'm referring to the not-so-subtle put-downs career women and stay-at-home moms frequently launch at each other, causing emotional damage on both sides.

I'm talking about working moms who let it be known that they don't think much of women who've chosen to stay home and (yes) bake cookies—if that's what the kids feel like doing—rather than climb the corporate ladder. I'm also talking about stay-at-home moms who wonder too loudly why working moms "abandon" their children in day care centers, as if they were dropping them on the moon.

I have grown a little sensitive to the umbrage felt on both sides because in the last year, I've found myself somewhere in the middle. Since I leave my daughter in someone else's care several days a week while I work as a writer, it always makes me furious to hear comments like: "Why did you have a child if you don't want to be with her?" Of course I want to be with her. But I want to do other things, too.

Since I'm also a stay-at-home mom for part of the week, and since I work out of my home instead of from a "real" office, I can also relate to the exasperation of overworked stay-at-home moms when people act as if they do nothing but paint their nails all day. When we are surrounded everyday with images of women in business suits—or police uniforms, construction hats, or doctor's white coats—it's difficult, sometimes, to convince yourself that taking care of children full-time is also a respectable vocation.

I think we all want to feel that the choices we make—or those that are forced on us by economic realities—are the right ones. The problem comes in when someone assumes that her lifestyle—because it works for her—is the right one for everyone. These are personal decisions that we make based on a whole range of factors, from whether we need the health insurance to how we perceive ourselves. What works for one person may be unworkable—or a disaster—for the next.

The signs are around us that working moms and stay-at-home moms are growing closer together. Greater numbers of career women (and, in some cases, men) are demanding more flexibility in their fields, to make it easier to spend more time at home. And more women who consider themselves full-time moms actually perform work other than child care. According to a recent story in *Working Woman* magazine, when the "Mothers at Home" newsletter surveyed its 15,000 subscribers, it found that 48 percent earn income from home based businesses.

So as these two spheres intertwine, perhaps there will be more respect for and understanding of the other side. I hope there's also a realization that though we may be making different choices, we're doing so for the same reasons: for our families—and for ourselves.

Real Enough

Alison McGhee

The baby's born dead and April, she sits in her old room at her parents' house in North Sterns, rocking. Frowning, April's mother lets Jimmy in the door. He slides on past her and goes upstairs.

Baby I brought you some ice cream. I made you black raspberry today.

He puts some on a little wooden spoon and slips it into her mouth. He's still wearing his blue Sof-Tee smock.

Babies don't die in North Sterns. They just get born, lots of them, crying already. They leak out of rusty-bottomed trailers like the one April's father bought them when they had to get married.

Baby how's that ice cream goin down?

I feel old, says April.

Well you're not old, honey, he says, you're just sixteen.

She's rocking, her hands on her stomach like they used to be when her belly was huge. Have some more ice cream, he says, and he drizzles a little into her mouth.

April fell in love waiting in line at the Sof-Tee, watching him sneaking free cones to the littlest kids. Don't tell, he said, winking at her. You want some? I made it myself.

I'm late, April said to him after a few months. Three weeks.

We'll get married, Jimmy said.

April looked at him, spread her hands over her stomach. Still flat. The stomach of a little girl.

Married? she said the word soft. Yeah, married, he said. They looked at each other and grinned. Just two more North Sterns kids with a bun in the oven.

Jimmy takes his hand-packed pints up to April's room where she's sitting and rocking and feeling old, older than sixteen.

Darlin I brought you two kinds today. Made it myself.

She opens her mouth like a baby bird. You know what they're sayin to me now, she says, Mama and Dad?

Have some, he says. I made this just for you.

They're sayin let it dissolve, she says. They're sayin don't try to hang on, just let it go.

Babies don't die in North Sterns, they just get born. They grow up, like corn that's dropped on a hard dirt road. Like rust. Like love.

Let what dissolve, he says. This ice cream? He spoons some more into her mouth, watches it melt on her tongue. There's real peaches in there, he says.

Us. You and me. April puts her hands on her empty gut that's flat again. They're sayin we haven't got reason to be married now. That it wasn't real love to begin with.

Try some of this, Jimmy says. It's chocolate peanut-butter, I made it myself.

He scoops some into her mouth. You got to use smooth, he says, not chunky. I had to throw my first batch out. She swallows and opens her mouth for more.

We got reason, Jimmy says. He spoons up more ice cream. You don't like this chocolate peanut-butter, he says, I'll make you some other kind.

Jimmy leans in close. We'll make another, he says. We'll make another one. There's chocolate on his breath. Smells real enough to April.

The Child Has Seen the Wind

John Grey

The child straddling the fallen oak now knows
the way winds can coke themselves up into
a roaring furnace, blast the guts out of a forest
that seemed as eternal as a mother's hand.

And each root ripped from the earth
is a slap across that smooth white face,
the bruises of a giddy, relentless night
when the squalls left everyone collapsed
behind their tears, shaking.

Light through gray clouds is not violent.
It rubs the body that remains
like a soft towel after a hot, steamy bath.
The child presses her fingers into the bark,
but even the bright yellow sprinkling
down its silty trunk cannot hide how
dead it is, how something is missing even
in this buoyant, laughing after-storm.

And her mother can never be the one whose
deer-hide body gave birth to her.
Each violent clap of thunder,
each kamikaze burst of bad weather,
pushes them further and further apart.
And the recriminations,
the sorry effort to stand that oak back
on its broken trunk,
can not shrink the distances.

Tito Fuentes, Topps #177, 1967

Frank Van Zant

*With her same water-gleam eyes, he is my mother's image caught
in Havana flesh of bronze and strength. Knowing I loved
his Giants, my mother, piano master of our little town,
would call the music of his name:
Teee-towww-Fooo-wennn-tase!
What did she know of baseball, that organ-loft old lady of mine?*

*But she was the one
lobbing softballs at me, teaching me
the music of a fat thud from heavy ash.
She was my role-model male etching out of our back yard
the basepaths of my childhood:*

> *run! the curved tree, that's FIRST!
> there! the kicked-out patch, the dirt! SECOND,
> the knot-bulge, the knot-bulge, THIRD, run
> run home come HOME
> my Tito Fuentes boy!*

Life Ain't Never Settled

LaVonne Dressinia McIver

Life wasn't always so bad for Cassie. At one time, some twenty years past she was Cassie, the homecoming queen; Cassie, the honor student; Cassie with the big legs and broad smile; Pretty Cassie.

But life ain't never settled when you think it is. You got to keep strivin; keep searchin for great things, lest you end up like Cassie with a whole lot of dreams deferred or worse, a heavy heart that aches even at rest while all else is still and the day seemingly peaceful.

Cassie never could pin-point where she went wrong. But I could. When we were in high school all she ever talked about was goin to college and becomin a teacher unless she found a husband first who opened his heart wide enough and long enough to let Cassie's dreams inside.

Never let no boys come near her until Trevor came along. They wanted to. Everybody loved Cassie. Teachers too!!

One day while we were eatin watermelon behind the old schoolyard where the sun was always right down on us and we were baskin in its glow, Cassie was talkin about all her big dreams. It seems Mr. Adams, our science teacher kissed her—on the cheek she said—but I knew better cause he tried the same thing with me and blive me when I tell you he wasn't aimin for no cheeks. I didn't tell Cassie cause afterwards he treated me different; same way he treated Cassie and that made me feel special.

Cassie musta shonuff loved Trevor. Only the Good Lawd knows why cause if Trevor loved Cassie he never showed it. Not that I could see anyhow and I had a pretty good view. I lived right cross the street from Trevor and Cassie for eleven years. Not a day went by when I didn't feel sorry for my friend Cassie.

She tried really hard to make Trevor happy but nothin she did was ever good enuff. He'd just beat her down at every turn; tell her that if she hadn't of gotten pregnant he wouldn't of had to marry her and get stuck in such a "small shit town" he called it. No man could ever love a women as stupid as Cassie he boasted in front of her and whoever else was around. And when Cassie tried to go back to school to get her teachers certificate Trevor insisted that no wife of his be outta the house all day.

Truth of the matter was Trevor wouldn't of left town anyway cause his mother was a paraplegic. He cared for her until she died. Did a good job too. He shonuff loved that mama (to death you might say). She wasn't always a paraplegic you know. No! No! No!

When Trevor was eleven years old that mama started spendin time with Mr. Shepard. He was tall and yellow. Came from the city, I think. Had a smile that could light up a long country road. A real ladies man. You know the type. Well…he took a special likin to Trevor's mama. I know cause I remember seeing them in church on first Sundays. All of the unattached women and some of the married ones too were jealous of that mama. I paid close attention to their whispers of "I don't know what he sees in that woman. She ain't nothin to look at." And the like.

They had a point, if you ask me. That mama was a great big woman. Was ugly too—had one of those crunched up faces that half smiled occasionally if you paid special attention to her.

At first, Trevor really liked Mr. Shepard. I used to see them around town doin things that men and boys like to do. Every Saturday morning they'd play catch on the front yard right before Mr. Shepard took that mama to get groceries. I can tell you that I never saw Trevor so happy. Mr. Shepard would throw that ball up as high as he could and Trevor would jump up with all his might—laughin all the way—and snatch the ball out of the sky.

The laughter stopped after Mr. Shepard asked that mama to marry him and soon after Mr. Shepard's proposal Trevor fell into a rage. Didn't want another man around permanently, I guess. Who knows about men anyhow??

Trevor jumped on top of Mr. Shepard and beat him down. Said "nobody gone marry my mama." That mama heard the two of them fightin and fell down two flights of stairs tryin to stop them from killin each other. She never did walk again. That was the end of Mr. Shepard too. I didn't see him for at least five years. Then one day out of the blue—there he was with a whole bunch of the prettiest flowers I'd ever seen. He didn't stay long though. But I bet that mama was happy to see him again.

Not long after that, while Trevor was at the mill for days work his house—the one he lived in all of his life and the one his mama crushed both her legs in—burned to ashes. The firemen said it was an electrical fire. Didn't matter much what kind of fire it was. That mama couldn't walk so she burned to death in that big empty house. I hope she still had those pretty flowers though.

Now you see what I mean when I say Trevor loved that mama to death. I always think that if Trevor hadda gone and let that mama marry Mr. Shepard, she woulda lived a long happy life. I bet Trevor blive the same way. That's probably why he lived his life so bitter. Couldn't forgive himself, I think.

Anyway…right before the fire Cassie found out she was pregnant. That poor chile tried to hide it from Trevor cause he had already dun told her that he wasn't gettin married. Said he wanted to leave town to get a better job and live life a little. Cassie knew he was lyin cause he would never leave that mama. Never. I guess after that mama died Trevor woulda left town but Cassie's father begged him to do right by his daughter. Trevor did have half a heart when it came to Cassie. Just half. He kept the other half locked for safekeeping somethin or someone known only to him.

Cassie and Trevor were married by the justice on a Friday. Cassie didn't want a big wedding cause she was already showin and didn't want everybody in town to think she was pushed to get married cause she was pregnant. My friend Cassie had a bustful of pride.

That baby never made it out of Cassie. Not the way Mother Nature intended anyhow. One day that summer. (I know it was summertime cause I was waitin for my mama's roses to blossom so that I could cut one and give it to Duke. He's my husband now. I gave him one of my mama's roses each of the three years we courted.)

Enuff about me. Lawd…Lawd…Lawd…. I get so wrapped up in these stories that sometimes I forget they ain't about me. Like this story—it's about Cassie—so let's get back to Cassie. My friend Cassie.

Well…on this one summer day, Cassie called me and said her morning sickness followed her into the afternoon and then into the evening. She didn't have the strength to make a big meal, biscuits and gravy was all Cassie could muster.

As Cassie's luck would have it, Trevor came home early that day with some guys from the mill to play cards (and drink a little whiskey). Cassie didn't tell me that part but some things you gotta figure for yourself. When Trevor realized Cassie hadn't made a proper dinner he insisted that she do her duty like "any women would." Cassie asked Trevor why his company couldn't go somewhere else and eat. She had a point too. Those men had wives who could cook just as good as Cassie. Trevor didn't say a word he just raised his fist and knocked Cassie to the floor. Can you blive that!!! Hit his pregnant wife right in front of those men and didn't think nothin of it. Told her to watch her manners in front of grown men.

Later that night Cassie's bottom felt heavy. She dragged her tired feet to the bathroom but before she could lift up her gown bits of her own flesh was all over Cassie. She couldn't move. Cassie just sat there in all that blood feeling sorry for herself. When Trevor woke up the next morning, she was still in the bathroom.

Now any decent man woulda held on to his wife and soothed her with kind words for a while at least. If Trevor hadda opened his heart a little, Cassie wouldn't of felt so badly. Not Trevor. He didn't have a kind word in him. Would you blive he actually scolded his wife for getting blood all over a clean floor. Said he didn't want no babies anyhow. Cassie sho was strong...had to be cause she just cleaned herself up and made that no good husband of hers a hot breakfast and sent him off to work with a smile.

That half-a-husband of hers abused Cassie in so many ways that I can't remember them all. Cassie was afraid to leave him cause Trevor said that if she did he would find her—wherever she was and bring her back cause she was his wife. Now ain't that something. His. Treated her like dirt but she was still his.

It took almost ten years but Cassie finally got tired of being tired. We were sitting down to tea. We had tea every Tuesday. We liked to call it "Tuesday's Tea." I don't know what got into Cassie this one Tuesday cause no matter what Trevor did she never had a bad word to say about him. Cassie always did have a passion for murder mystery stuff. She took to reading books on real-life crime. I guess you could call it research cause while I was makin tea Cassie asked me if I could keep a secret. What a strange question I thought. We'd been friends for over 20 years and had told each other lots of secrets. I said "of course I could keep a secret, chile. What you got in mind."

Cassie was readin about how this wife killed her husband in a fit of rage after he had dun tried to beat her to death. The good part about it was she didn't serve no time either. Judge said it was self-defense and let her go. Free!! Cassie had it in her mind to do the same thing to Trevor. Now, if I didn't know everything she had been through with that excuse for a husband of hers, I might of tried to stop her but I didn't. Forgive me.

Cassie didn't tell me exactly when she planned to do it. But I figured she'd try it on a Friday. Trevor always got drunk on Fridays. And I was right. That Friday Trevor came home in a drunken stupor. He started hittin on Cassie before he even made it to the door. They went inside and that was the last I saw of Trevor. Can't say I missed him either.

Cassie carried out her plan like she wanted to. She said Trevor never felt a thing. And I'm sure he didn't—alcohol numbs pain you know. Cassie stabbed him in the heart three times. Didn't want him to suffer much I guess. She picked a good spot as far as I'm concerned. What good is half a heart anyhow??

She later told me that while the blood made its way down Trevor's head it paused at the nape of his neck. Cassie couldn't forget his dying eyes. She watched and waited until she heard Trevor's last breath. Then she cried. Cassie knew things would never be the same.

She was right. The sounds of sirens woke me up the next morning. I knew somethin had gone wrong cause Duke said he saw the police taking Cassie out in handcuffs. "She done killed that no good husband of hers," he mused.

Things didn't work out quite like Cassie had planned. They never did.

They gave her a lawyer for free. He pushed Cassie to plead guilty to manslaughter so she wouldn't have to face a jury trial for murder. He said no jury would blive that Trevor beat up on Cassie so bad cause she never called the police or went to the hospital for treatment.

Life is funny. You got to let your husband beat up on you and if you're still alive call the police; then find your way to a hospital before you can say he's abusin you.

Anyway...Cassie took the lawyer's advice. He said she would only have to serve 3–5 years at best with the possibility of getting out earlier for good behavior.

The Good Lawd sho works in mysterious ways. Cassie found out she was pregnant a few days before her sentencing so the judge sent her to a women's work center. Cassie said it wasn't like no real jail. The women there were really nice to her. They made little things for the baby and tried to comfort Cassie every way they could. They couldn't do much of course but at least they tried.

At one of our Tuesday Teas Cassie asked if Duke and me would take care of the baby until she was released from the center. I said "yes" of course.

A young social worker came to our house before my next visit to the center. When she saw how clean our house was and how well me and Duke got along, she said we'd make perfect foster parents.

We were so excited! We never had a baby of our own. When I was six I had a bout with the mumps. Doctors said it musta made me sterile. Duke never made no fuss over it. He said we had each other and that was all that counted. But I know he musta wondered what it would be like to have a little one around.

Cassie delivered in July. She was so proud. She insisted that we name her so I chose Rose, after the only other living thing I'd ever given Duke.

The day I came home with our Rose, Duke had dun went over to mama's and cut up one of her bushes. That man had roses all over the house!! He said "a rose for a rose, baby." Well, those roses from that bush been dead for nearly two years already. But we're still carin for our Rose. July is a special month for us now. Duke got this bright idea to celebrate Rose's birthday every day of the month. Silliest thing I ever heard. But you can't tell him nothin when it comes to his Rose. She calls him Dadda and his face just lights up every time.

She don't call me mama but that's O.K. cause she knows who her mama is. And everybody ought to know their mama. On Tuesdays she comes with me to see Cassie. God couldn't of painted a prettier picture. The two of them together is somethin to see. Duke bought our Rose this white dress with little red roses all over it. I swear that little Rose wants to wear it every time we visit her mama. Have a fit if you don't let her put that dress on. I told Cassie people gone think we never buy that chile no clothes. Cassie just laughed and said, "It's clean ain't it. That's all that matters, chile."

My friend Cassie sho is somethin special.

She looks like a new women now. Her hair is long and shiny like it was in high school. That smile dun found its way back to the center of her face. She's takin college courses through this program at the center and when Cassie gets out she's goin to the community college to get her teacher's certificate. She dun gained weight too. Got those big legs again, chile. That girl sho is looking good all over. So good that Jimmy, a security guard at the center dun fell in love with her!!! Say he gone marry her when she gets out.

Maybe he will and maybe he won't. Don't much matter if you ask me cause Cassie's busy lovin herself now and that's what counts. My friend Cassie's still chasin those big dreams too. That's fine with me. Gives us somethin to talk about on Tuesdays.

Conception

Galway Kinnell

Having crowed the seed
of the child of his heart
into the egg of the child
of her heart in the dark middle
of the night, as cocks
sometimes cry out to a light
not yet visible to the rest,
and lying there with cock
shrugging its way out of her,
and rising back through phases
of identity, he hears
her say, "Yes, I am two now,
and with you, three."

Giving Birth

Margaret Atwood

But who gives it? And to whom is it given? Certainly it doesn't feel like giving, which implies a flow, a gentle handing over, no coercion. But there is scant gentleness here, it's too strenuous, the belly like a knotted fist, squeezing, the heavy trudge of the heart, every muscle in the body tight and moving, as in a slow motion shot of a high-jump, the faceless body sailing up, turning, hanging for a moment in the air, and then—back to real time again—the plunge, the rush down, the result. Maybe the phrase was made by someone viewing the result only: in this case, the rows of babies to whom birth has occurred lying like neat packages in their expertly wrapped blankets, pink or blue, with their labels scotch-taped to their clear plastic cots, behind the plate-glass window.

No one ever says *giving death,* although they are in some ways the same, events, not things. And *delivering,* that act the doctor is generally believed to perform: who delivers what? Is it the mother who is delivered, like a prisoner being released? Surely not; nor is the child delivered to the mother like a letter through a slot. How can you be both the sender and the receiver at once? Was someone in bondage, is someone made free? Thus language, muttering in its archaic tongues of something, yet one more thing, that needs to be re-named.

It won't be by me, though. These are the only words I have, I'm stuck with them, stuck in them. (That image of the tar sands, old tableau in the Royal Ontario Museum, second floor north, how persistent it is. Will I break free, or will I be sucked down, fossilized, a sabre-toothed tiger or lumbering brontosaurus who ventured out too far? Words ripple at my feet, black, sluggish, lethal. Let me try once more, before the sun gets me, before I starve or drown, while I can. It's only a tableau after all, it's only a metaphor. See, I can speak, I am not trapped, and you on your part can understand. So we will go ahead as if there were no problem about language.)

This story about giving birth is not about me. In order to convince you of that I should tell you what I did this morning, before I sat down at this desk—a door on top of two filing cabinets, radio to the left, calendar to the right, these devices by which I place myself in time. I got up at twenty-to-seven, and halfway down the stairs, met my daughter, who was ascending, autonomously she thought, actually in the arms of her father. We greeted each other with hugs and smiles; we then played with the alarm clock and the hot water bottle, a ritual we go through only on the days her father has to leave the house early to drive into the city. This ritual exists to give me the illusion that I am sleeping in. When she finally decided it was time for me to get up, she began pulling my hair. I got dressed while she explored the bathroom scale and the mysterious white altar of the toilet. I took her downstairs and we had the usual struggle over her clothes. Already she is wearing miniature jeans, miniature T-shirts. After this she fed herself: orange, banana, muffin, porridge.

We then went out to the sunporch, where we recognized anew, and by their names, the dog, the cats and the birds, bluejays and goldfinches at this time of year, which is winter. She puts her fingers on my lips as I pronounce these words; she hasn't yet learned the secret of making them. I am waiting for her first word: surely it will be miraculous, something that has never yet been said. But if so, perhaps she's already said it and I, in my entrapment, my addiction to the usual, have not heard it.

In her playpen I discovered the first alarming thing of the day. It was a small naked woman, made of that soft plastic from which jiggly spiders and lizards and the other things people hang in their car windows are also made. She was given to my daughter by a friend, a woman who does props for movies, she was supposed to have been a prop but she wasn't used. The baby loved her and would crawl around the floor holding her in her mouth like a dog carrying a bone, with the head sticking out one side and the feet out the other. She seemed chewy and harmless, but the other day I noticed that the baby had managed to make a tear in the body with her new teeth. I put the woman into the cardboard box I use for toy storage.

But this morning she was back in the playpen and the feet were gone. The baby must have eaten them, and I worried about whether or not the plastic would dissolve in her stomach, whether it was toxic. Sooner or later, in the contents of her diaper, which I examine with the usual amount of maternal brooding, I knew I would find two small pink plastic feet. I removed the doll and later, while she was still singing to the dog outside the window, dropped it into the garbage. I am not up to finding tiny female arms, breasts, a head, in my daughter's disposable diapers, partially covered by undigested carrots and the husks of raisins, like the relics of some gruesome and demented murder.

Now she's having her nap and I am writing this story. From what I have said, you can see that my life (despite these occasional surprises, reminders of another world) is calm and orderly, suffused with that warm, reddish light, those well-placed blue highlights and reflecting surfaces (mirrors, plates, oblong window panes) you think of as belonging to Dutch genre paintings; and like them it is realistic in detail and slightly sentimental. Or at least it has an aura of sentiment. (Already I'm having moments of muted grief over those of my daughter's baby clothes which are too small for her to wear any more. I will be a keeper of hair, I will store things in trunks, I will weep over photos.) But above all it's solid, everything here has solidity. No more of those washes of light, those shifts, nebulous effects of cloud, Turner sunsets, vague fears, the impalpables Jeannie used to concern herself with.

I call this woman Jeannie after the song. I can't remember any more of the song, only the title. The point (for in language there are always these "points," these reflections; this is what makes it so rich and sticky, this is why so many have disappeared beneath its dark and shining surface, why you should never try to see your own reflection in it; you will lean over too far, a strand of your hair will fall in and come out gold, and, thinking it is gold all the way down, you yourself will follow, sliding into those outstretched arms, towards the mouth you think is opening to pronounce your name but instead, just before your ears fill with pure sound, will form a word you have never heard before . . .).

The point, for me, is in the hair. My own hair is not light brown, but Jeannie's was. This is one difference between us. The other point is the dreaming, for Jeannie isn't real in the same way that I am real. But by now, and I mean your time, both of us will have the same degree of reality, we will be equal: wraiths, echoes, reverberations in your own brain. At the moment though Jeannie is to me as I will some day be to you. So she is real enough.

Jeannie is on her way to the hospital, to give birth, to be delivered. She is not quibbling over these terms. She's sitting in the back seat of the car, with her eyes closed and her coat spread over her like a blanket. She is doing her breathing exercises and timing her contractions with a stopwatch. She has been up since two-thirty in the morning, when she took a bath and ate some lime Jell-O, and it's now almost ten. She has learned to count, during the slow breathing, in numbers (from one to ten while breathing in, from ten to one while breathing out) which she can actually see while she is silently pronouncing them. Each number is a different colour and, if she's concentrating very hard, a different typeface. They range from plain Roman to ornamented circus numbers, red with gold filigree and dots. This is a refinement not mentioned in any of the numerous books she's read on the subject. Jeannie is a devotee of handbooks. She has at least two shelves of books that cover everything from building kitchen cabinets to auto repairs to smoking your own hams. She doesn't do many of these things, but she does some of them, and in her suitcase, along with a washcloth, a package of lemon Lifesavers, a pair of glasses, a hot water bottle, some talcum powder and paper bag, is the book that suggested she take along all of these things.

(By this time you may be thinking that I've invented Jeannie in order to distance myself from these experiences. Nothing could be further from the truth. I am, in fact, trying to bring myself closer to something that time has already made distant. As for Jeannie, my intention is simple: I am bringing her back to life.)

There are two other people in the car with Jeannie. One is a man, whom I will call A., for convenience. A. is driving. When Jeannie opens her eyes, at the end of every contraction, she can see the back of his slightly bald head and his reassuring shoulders. A. drives well and not too quickly. From time to time he asks her how she is, and she tells him how long the contractions are lasting and how long there is between them. When they stop for gas he buys them each a Styrofoam container of coffee. For months he has helped her with the breathing exercises, pressing on her knee as recommended by the book, and he will be present at the delivery. (Perhaps it's to him that the birth will be given, in the same sense that one gives a performance.) Together they have toured the hospital maternity ward, in company with a small group of other pairs like them: one thin solicitous person, one slow bulbous person. They have been shown the rooms, shared and private, the sitz-baths, the delivery room itself, which gave the impression of being white. The nurse was light-brown, with limber hips and elbows; she laughed a lot as she answered questions.

"First they'll give you an enema. You know what it is? They take a tube of water and put it up your behind. Now, the gentlemen must put on this—and these, over your shoes. And these hats, this one for those with long hair, this for those with short hair."

"What about those with no hair?" says A.

The nurse looks up at his head and laughs. "Oh, you still have some," she said. "If you have a question, do not be afraid to ask."

They have also seen the film made by the hospital, a full-colour film of a woman giving birth to, can it be a baby? "Not all babies will be this large at birth," the Australian nurse who introduces the movie says. Still, the audience, half of which is pregnant, doesn't look very relaxed when the lights go on. ("If you don't like the visuals," a friend of Jeannie's has told her, "you can always close your eyes.") It isn't the blood so much as the brownish-red disinfectant that bothers her. "I've decided to call this whole thing off," she says to A., smiling to show it's a joke. He gives her a hug and says, "Everything's going to be fine."

And she knows it is. Everything will be fine. But there is another woman in the car. She's sitting in the front seat, and she hasn't turned or acknowledged Jeannie in any way. She, like Jeannie, is going to the hospital. She too is pregnant. She is not going to the hospital to give birth, however, because the word, the words, are too alien to her experience, the experience she is about to have, to be used about it at all. She's wearing a cloth coat with checks in maroon and brown, and she has a kerchief tied over her hair. Jeannie has seen her before, but she knows little about her except that she is a woman who did not wish to become pregnant, who did not choose to divide herself like this, who did not choose any of these ordeals, these initiations. It would be no use telling her that everything is going to be fine. The word in English for unwanted intercourse is rape, but there is no word in the language for what is about to happen to this woman.

Jeannie has seen this woman from time to time, throughout her pregnancy, always in the same coat, always with the same kerchief. Naturally, being pregnant herself has made her more aware of other pregnant women, and she has watched them, examined them covertly, every time she has seen one. But not every other pregnant woman is this woman. She did not, for instance, attend Jeannie's pre-natal classes at the hospital, where the women were all young, younger than Jeannie.

"How many will be breast-feeding?" asks the Australian nurse with the hefty shoulders.

All hands but one shoot up. A modern group, the new generation, and the one lone bottle-feeder, who might have (who knows?) something wrong with her breasts, is ashamed of herself. The others look politely away from her. What they want most to discuss, it seems, are the differences between one kind of disposable diaper and another. Sometimes they lie on mats and squeeze each other's hands, simulating contractions and counting breaths. It's all very hopeful. The Australian nurse tells them not to get in and out of the bathtub by themselves. At the end of an hour they are each given a glass of apple juice.

There is only one woman in the class who has already given birth. She's there, she says, to make sure they give her a shot this time. They delayed it last time and she went through hell. The others look at her with mild disapproval. *They* are not clamoring for shots, they do not intend to go through hell. Hell comes from the wrong attitude, they feel. The books talk about *discomfort.*

"It's not discomfort, it's pain, baby," the woman says.

The others smile uneasily and the conversation slides back to disposable diapers.

Vitaminized, conscientious, well-read Jeannie, who has managed to avoid morning sickness, varicose veins, stretch marks, toxemia and depression, who has had no aberrations of appetite, no blurrings of vision—why is she followed, then, by this other? At first it was only a glimpse now and then, at the infants' clothing section in Simpson's Basement, in the supermarket lineup, on streetcorners as she herself slid by in A.'s car: the haggard face, the bloated torso, the kerchief holding back the too-sparse hair. In any case, it was Jeannie who saw her, not the other way around. If she knew she was following Jeannie she gave no sign.

As Jeannie has come closer and closer to this day, the unknown day on which she will give birth, as time has thickened around her so that it has become something she must propel herself through, a kind of slush, wet earth underfoot, she has seen this woman more and more often, though always from a distance. Depending on the light, she has appeared by turns as a young girl of perhaps twenty to an older woman of forty or forty-five, but there was never any doubt in Jeannie's mind that it was the same woman. In fact it did not occur to her that the woman was not real in the usual sense (and perhaps she was, originally, on the first or second sighting, as the voice that causes an echo is real), until A. stopped for a red light during this drive to the hospital and the woman, who had been standing on the corner with a brown paper bag in her arms, simply opened the front door of the car and got in. A. didn't react, and Jeannie knows better than to say anything to him. She is aware that the woman is not really there: Jeannie is not crazy. She could even make the woman disappear by opening her eyes wider, by staring, but it is only the shape that would go away, not the feeling. Jeannie isn't exactly afraid of this woman. She is afraid for her.

When they reach the hospital, the woman gets out of the car and is through the door by the time A. has come around to help Jeannie out of the back seat. In the lobby she is nowhere to be seen. Jeannie goes through Admission in the usual way, unshadowed.

There has been an epidemic of babies during the night and the maternity ward is overcrowded. Jeannie waits for her room behind a dividing screen. Nearby someone is screaming, screaming and mumbling between screams in what sounds like a foreign language. Portuguese, Jeannie thinks. She tells herself that for them it is different, you're supposed to scream, you're regarded as queer if you don't scream, it's a required part of giving birth. Nevertheless she knows that the woman screaming is the other woman and she is screaming from pain. Jeannie listens to the other voice, also a woman's, comforting, reassuring: her mother? A nurse?

A. arrives and they sit uneasily, listening to the screams. Finally Jeannie is sent for and she goes for her prep. *Prep school,* she thinks. She takes off her clothes—when will she see them again?—and puts on the hospital gown. She is examined, labelled around the wrist, and given an enema. She tells the nurse she can't take Demerol because she is allergic to it, and the nurse writes this down. Jeannie doesn't know whether this is true or not but she doesn't want Demerol, she has read the books. She intends to put up a struggle over her pubic hair—surely she will lose her strength if it is all shaved off—but it turns out the nurse doesn't have very strong feelings about it. She is told her contractions are not far enough along to be taken seriously, she can even have lunch. She puts on her dressing gown and rejoins A., in the freshly vacated room, eats some tomato soup and a veal cutlet, and decides to take a nap while A. goes out for supplies.

Jeannie wakes up when A. comes back. He has brought a paper, some detective novels for Jeannie, and a bottle of Scotch for himself. A. reads the paper and drinks Scotch, and Jeannie reads *Poirot's Early Cases*. There is no connection between Poirot and her labour, which is now intensifying, unless it is the egg-shape of Poirot's head and the vegetable marrows he is known to cultivate with strands of wet wool (placentae? umbilical cords?). She is glad the stories are short; she is walking around the room now, between contractions. Lunch was definitely a mistake.

"I think I have back labour," she says to A. They get out the handbook and look up the instructions for this. It's useful that everything has a name. Jeannie kneels on the bed and rests her forehead on her arms while A. rubs her back. A. pours himself another Scotch, in the hospital glass. The nurse, in pink, comes, looks, asks about the timing, and goes away again. Jeannie begins to sweat. She can only manage half a page or so of Poirot before she has to clamber back up on the bed again and begin breathing and running through the coloured numbers.

When the nurse comes back, she has a wheelchair. It's time to go down to the labour room, she says. Jeannie feels stupid sitting in the wheelchair. She tells herself about peasant women having babies in the fields, Indian women having them on portages with hardly a second thought. She feels effete. But the hospital wants her to ride, and considering the fact that the nurse is tiny, perhaps it's just as well. What if Jeannie were to collapse, after all? After all her courageous talk. An image of the tiny pink nurse, ant-like, trundling large Jeannie through the corridors, rolling her along like a heavy beachball.

As they go by the check-in desk a woman is wheeled past on a table, covered by a sheet. Her eyes are closed and there's a bottle feeding into her arm through a tube. Something is wrong. Jeannie looks back—she thinks it was the other woman—but the sheeted table is hidden now behind the counter.

In the dim labour room Jeannie takes off her dressing gown and is helped up onto the bed by the nurse. A. brings her suitcase, which is not a suitcase really but a small flight bag; the significance of this has not been lost on Jeannie, and in fact she now has some of the apprehensive feelings she associates with planes, including the fear of a crash. She takes out her Lifesavers, her glasses, her washcloth and the other things she thinks she will need. She removes her contact lenses and places them in their case, reminding A. that they must not be lost. Now she is purblind.

There is something else in her bag that she doesn't remove. It's a talisman, given to her several years ago as a souvenir by a traveling friend of hers. It's a rounded oblong of opaque blue glass, with four yellow and white eye shapes in it. In Turkey, her friend has told her, they hang them on mules to protect against the Evil Eye. Jeannie knows this talisman probably won't work for her, she is not Turkish and she isn't a mule, but it makes her feel safer to have it in the room with her. She had planned to hold it in her hand during the most difficult part of labour but somehow there is no longer any time for carrying out plans like this.

An old woman, a fat old woman dressed all in green, comes into the room and sits beside Jeannie. She says to A., who is sitting on the other side of Jeannie, "That is a good watch. They don't make watches like that any more." She is referring to his gold pocket watch, one of his few extravagances, which is on the night table. Then she places her hand on Jeannie's belly to feel the contraction. "This is good," she says; her accent is Swedish or German. "This, I call a contraction. Before, it was nothing." Jeannie can no longer remember having seen her before. "Good. Good."

"When will I have it?" Jeannie asks, when she can talk, when she is no longer counting.

The old woman laughs. Surely that laugh, those tribal hands, have presided over a thousand beds, a thousand kitchen tables…"A long time yet," she says. "Eight, ten hours."

"But I've been *doing* this for twelve hours already," Jeannie says.

"Not hard labour," the woman says. "Not good, like this."

Jeannie settles into herself for the long wait. At the moment she can't remember why she wanted to have a baby in the first place. That decision was made by someone else, whose motives are now unclear. She remembers the way women who had babies used to smile at one another, mysteriously, as if there was something they knew that she didn't, the way they would casually exclude her from their frame of reference. What was the knowledge, the mystery, or was having a baby really no more inexplicable than having a car accident or an orgasm? (But these too were indescribable, events of the body, all of them; why should the mind distress itself trying to find a language for them?) She has sworn she will never say that to any woman without children, engage in those passwords and exclusions. She's old enough, she's been put through enough years of it to find it tiresome and cruel.

But—and this is the part of Jeannie that goes with the talisman hidden in her bag, not with the part that longs to build kitchen cabinets and smoke hams—she is, secretly, hoping for a mystery. Something more than this, something else, a vision. After all she is risking her life, though it's not too likely she will die. Still, some women do. Internal bleeding, shock, heart failure, a mistake on the part of someone, a nurse, a doctor. She deserves a vision, she deserves to be allowed to bring something back with her from this dark place into which she is now rapidly descending.

She thinks momentarily about the other woman. Her motives, too, are unclear. Why doesn't she want to have a baby? Has she been raped, does she have ten other children, is she starving? Why hasn't she had an abortion? Jeannie doesn't know, and in fact it no longer matters why. *Uncross your fingers,* Jeannie thinks to her. Her face, distorted with pain and terror, floats briefly behind Jeannie's eyes before it too drifts away.

Jeannie tries to reach down to the baby, as she has many times before, sending waves of love, colour, music, down through her arteries to it, but she finds she can no longer do this. She can no longer feel the baby as a baby, its arms and legs poking, kicking, turning. It has collected itself together, it's a hard sphere, it does not have time right now to listen to her. She's grateful for this because she isn't sure anyway how good the message would be. She no longer has control of the numbers either, she can no longer see them, although she continues mechanically to count. She realizes she has practised for the wrong thing, A. squeezing her knee was nothing, she should have practised for this, whatever it is.

"Slow down," A. says. She's on her side now, he's holding her hand. "Slow it right down."

"I can't, I can't do it, I can't do this."

"Yes you can."

"Will I sound like that?"

"Like what?" A. says. Perhaps he can't hear it; it's the other woman, in the room next door or the room next door to that. She's screaming and crying, screaming and crying. While she cries she is saying, over and over, "It hurts. It hurts."

"No, you won't," he says. So there is someone, after all.

A doctor comes in, not her own doctor. They want her to turn over on her back.

"I can't," she says. "I don't like it that way." Sounds have receded, she has trouble hearing them. She turns over and the doctor gropes with her rubber-gloved hand. Something wet and hot flows over her thighs.

"It was just ready to break," the doctor says. "All I had to do was touch it. Four centimetres," she says to A.

"Only *four*?" Jeannie says. She feels cheated; they must be wrong. The doctor says her own doctor will be called in time. Jeannie is outraged at them. They have not understood, but it's too late to say this and she slips back into the dark place, which is not hell, which is more like being inside, trying to get out. *Out,* she says or thinks. Then she is floating, the numbers are gone, if anyone told her to get up, go out of the room, stand on her head, she would do it. From minute to minute she comes up again, grabs for air.

"You're hyperventilating," A. says. "Slow it down." He is rubbing her back now, hard, and she takes his hand and shoves it viciously farther down, to the right place, which is not the right place as soon as his hand is there. She remembers a story she read once, about the Nazis tying the legs of Jewish women together during labour. She never really understood before how that could kill you.

A nurse appears with a needle. "I don't want it," Jeannie says.

"Don't be hard on yourself," the nurse says. "You don't have to go through pain like that." *What pain?* Jeannie thinks. When there is no pain she feels nothing, when there is pain, she feels nothing because there is no *she.* This, finally, is the disappearance of language. *You don't remember afterwards,* she has been told by almost everyone.

Jeannie comes out of a contraction, gropes for control. "Will it hurt the baby?" she says.

"It's a mild analgesic," the doctor says. "We wouldn't allow anything that would hurt the baby." Jeannie doesn't believe this. Nevertheless she is jabbed and the doctor is right, it is very mild, because it doesn't seem to do a thing for Jeannie, though A. later tells her she has slept briefly between contractions.

Suddenly she sits bolt upright. She is wide awake and lucid. "You have to ring that bell right now," she says. "This baby is being born."

A. clearly doesn't believe her. "I can feel it, I can feel the head," she says. A. pushes the button for the call bell. A nurse appears and checks, and now everything is happening too soon, nobody is ready. They set off down the hall, the nurse wheeling. Jeannie feels fine. She watches the corridors, the edges of everything shadowy because she doesn't have her glasses on. She hopes A. will remember to bring them. They pass another doctor.

"Need me?" she asks.

"Oh no," the nurse answers breezily. "Natural childbirth."

Jeannie realizes that this woman must have been the anaesthetist. "What?" she says, but it's too late now, they are in the room itself, all those glossy surfaces, tubular strange apparatus like a science fiction movie, and the nurse is telling her to get onto the delivery table. No one else is in the room.

"You must be crazy," Jeannie says.

"Don't push," the nurse says.

"What do you mean?" Jeannie says. This is absurd. Why should she wait, why should the baby wait for them because they're late?

"Breathe through your mouth," the nurse says. "Pant," and Jeannie finally remembers how. When the contraction is over she uses the nurse's arm as a lever and hauls herself across onto the table.

From somewhere her own doctor materializes, in her doctor suit already, looking even more like Mary Poppins than usual, and Jeannie says, "Bet you weren't expecting to see me so soon!" The baby is being born when Jeannie said it would, though just three days ago the doctor said it would be at least another week, and this makes Jeannie feel jubilant and smug. Not that she knew, she'd believed the doctor.

She's being covered with a green tablecloth, they are taking far too long, she feels like pushing the baby out now, before they are ready. A. is there by her head, swathed in robes, hats, masks. He has forgotten her glasses. "Push now," the doctor says. Jeannie grips with her hands, grits her teeth, face, her whole body together, a snarl, a fierce smile, the baby is enormous, a stone, a boulder, her bones unlock, and once, twice, the third time, she opens like a birdcage turning slowly inside out.

A pause; a wet kitten slithers between her legs. "Why don't you look?" says the doctor, but Jeannie still has her eyes closed. No glasses, she couldn't have seen a thing anyway. "Why don't you look?" the doctor says again.

Jeannie opens her eyes. She can see the baby, who has been wheeled up beside her and is fading already from the alarming birth purple. *A good baby,* she thinks, meaning it as the old woman did: *a good watch,* well-made, substantial. The baby isn't crying; she squints in the new light. Birth isn't something that has been given to her, nor has she taken it. It was just something that has happened so they could greet each other like this. The nurse is stringing beads for her name. When the baby is bundled and tucked beside Jeannie, she goes to sleep.

As for the vision, there wasn't one. Jeannie is conscious of no special knowledge; already she's forgetting what it was like. She's tired and very cold; she is shaking, and asks for another blanket. A. comes back to the room with her; her clothes are still there. Everything is quiet, the other woman is no longer screaming. Something has happened to her, Jeannie knows. Is she dead? Is the baby dead? Perhaps she is one of those casualties (and how can Jeannie herself be sure, yet, that she will not be among them) who will go into postpartum depression and never come out. "You see, there was nothing to be afraid of," A. says before he leaves, but he was wrong.

The next morning Jeannie wakes up when it's light. She's been warned about getting out of bed the first time without the help of the nurse, but she decides to do it anyway (peasant in the field! Indian on the portage!). She's still running on adrenaline; she's also weaker than she thought, but she wants very much to look out the window. She feels she's been inside too long, she wants to see the sun come up. Being awake this early always makes her feel a little unreal, a little insubstantial, as if she's partly transparent, partly dead.

(It was to me, after all, that the birth was given, Jeannie gave it, I am the result. What would she make of me? Would she be pleased?)

The window is two panes with a venetian blind sandwiched between them; it turns by a knob at the side. Jeannie has never seen a window like this before. She closes and opens the blind several times. Then she leaves it open and looks.

All she can see from the window is a building. It's an old stone building, heavy and Victorian, with a copper roof oxidized to green. It's solid, hard, darkened by soot, dour, leaden. But as she looks at this building, so old and seemingly immutable, she sees that it's made of water. Water, and some tenuous jellylike substance. Light flows through it from behind (the sun is coming up), the building is so thin, so fragile, that it quivers in the slight dawn wind. Jeannie sees that if the building is this way (a touch could destroy it, a ripple of the earth, why has no one noticed, guarded it against accidents?) then the rest of the world must be like this too, the entire earth, the rocks, people, trees, everything needs to be protected, cared for, tended. The enormity of this task defeats her; she will never be up to it, and what will happen then?

Jeannie hears footsteps in the hall outside her door. She thinks it must be the other woman, in her brown and maroon checked coat, carrying her paper bag, leaving the hospital now that her job is done. She has seen Jeannie safely through, she must go now to hunt through the streets of the city for her next case. But the door opens, it's only a nurse, who is just in time to catch Jeannie as she sinks to the floor, holding on to the edge of the air-conditioning unit. The nurse scolds her for getting up too soon.

After that the baby is carried in, solid, substantial, packed together like an apple. Jeannie examines her, she is complete, and in the days that follow Jeannie herself becomes drifted over with new words, her hair slowly darkens, she ceases to be what she was and is replaced, gradually, by someone else.

Mother's Milk: A Dairy Tale

Gayle Brandeis

The breast pump stretches Ruth's nipple out so far, it looks like a hitchhiker's thumb. Ruth pushes the button that makes the pump "suck," nursing this plastic baby, its whirring mechanical hunger. No milk flows yet, and won't for awhile—it will take weeks of pumping, twenty minutes on each breast, each day, before the first drop peals from her body. Until then, Ruth ices her sore nipples at night, and wonders if they'll shrink back to their normal size. Her rose bud areolas are spreading into rounds of bologna, nearing sandwich proportions. The breast pump box says nothing about big nipples—then again, it is called "Gentle Expressions," and there is nothing gentle about the pump.

Ruth's sister, a working mother who pumped three times a day in the executive washroom, gave Ruth the pump "just in case." That "case" never came to be, and Ruth felt resigned to the fact that it never would. But one day, while getting a cavity filled, Ruth heard the dentist's radio over his drill. A story was featured about women who nurse their adopted babies. The women pump their breasts for months before the babies are due; the mechanical sucking stimulates lactation even in women who have never been pregnant. Ruth spit into the sink, her breasts suddenly feeling empty. After the filling set, she walked out of the dentist's office as if in a trance, forgetting her free toothbrush, her mouth still stuffed with cotton. Once home, Ruth pulled the pink breast pump from her closet, and quickly skimmed the instructions. She tore off her shirt and started pumping.

Now blue veins begin to snake their way across Ruth's breasts. Her bra size increases in both numbers and letters. She aches like she did when her breasts first began to bud in the seventh grade. She wonders what in the world she is doing.

The milk comes in slowly—thin, bluish, drops which Ruth licks from her fingers, amazed. In a couple more weeks, her breasts really begin to swell. Ruth feels as if they might burst—she can't pump the milk out fast enough. The milk! It has changed, become sweeter, richer, more bountiful. Ruth's horns of plenty drench her shirts, send sharp streams shooting across the shower. The face of a baby, or sometimes the cry of an animal, brings the milk prickling into her nipples. Due to her constant leaking, Ruth smells slightly sour, slightly spiced.

Ruth advertises herself as a wet nurse, and is soon feeding most of the babies on her block, as well as some of the men and two neighbor women. Although the men may stroke her other breast while they nurse, they do not make sexual advances. Many cry unlike they have in years. The women both fall asleep at her breast; Ruth lets them nap until they have to pick up their children at school.

Even with her steady flow of customers, Ruth finds she has more milk than she knows what to do with. She forms Mother's Milk Merchandising in her kitchen, and markets custards, muffins, and cheese under the MMM label. The cheese sells for $15 an ounce at the local deli.

To increase her output, Ruth hand expresses one breast while she pumps the other. She prefers the manual method—it feels more "right," more connected, to do it by hand. Dairy maid, dairy animal, Ruth luxuriates in her new calling. As her nipples toughen, stretch marks furrowing her breasts, Ruth's face opens like a baby's mouth, becomes as calm and radiant as her milk.

Aware of the antibacterial properties of breastmilk, Ruth creates drops for pink eye, as well as a healing skin balm. She fills milk baths at health spas, and bon bons at confectionaries. She donates to milk banks, sends cartons of breast milk to third world nations, and boycotts Nestlé, which pushes artifical infant formula there.

And while her neighbors dream their milky dreams, Ruth takes off her shirt in her back yard. She throws her arms out, her head back, and sprays the night sky with new constellations.

The Woman With the Wild-Grown Hair Keeps Her Vigil

Nita Penfold

*She tries to keep up with normalcy, folding the sun-drenched
laundry, banana bread filling the apartment with artificial warmth,
watching the tv with half an eye. It is October, the flaming trees
pulling their moisture in to preserve life until spring, drying leaves
dropping downward in death. The tv tells of nine-year-old Sarah
from Wayland who went for a woods/walk and never returned. Her
father appeals to the cameras, face stiff and drowning, trying to
keep from crying out the horror that his soft-faced child might
possibly be dead. The Woman concentrates on the empty swing beside
him, the way the wind blows the ropes, the worn board dipping and
reeling. Her own eleven-year-old Sarah is alive, but it is a
tentative thing. She wants to die, sits hunched over in a metal
wheelchair with invisible pain, doctors finding no damage from the
Tylenol she says she took, no diagnosis to explain why she cannot
stand straight. The Woman reels and rewinds her own film
clips of that morning she dreamed she was drowning in an upside-
down bathtub, struggling for breath. Then Sarah saying she
wanted to die, it hurt too much, and the Woman thinking for a
moment that she was still caught in the nightmare. Until the
sobbing child is warm in her arms. Then there are the hospitals,
therapists, relatives, friends, time standing still like a sepia
photograph bled of color, trying not to examine her daughter too
closely, aching to mend her like a broken doll with needle & thread,
feeling the guilt creep up her veins like a cold needle, knowing the
healing has to come from this child, this hurting child who she loves
so hard she has to restrain herself from engulfing her, as the
wanting, the needing came from this child, so too must the dredging*

up of anger, the letting go come from this child, and the Woman can
only love and wait, and throughout it all, she keeps watch for a
sign of that other Sarah, each report of a sighting a burst of
faith, trusting that if she can be found, there may be hope
left for them all.

Like Her Uterus Ripped Out

Lonna Lisa Williams

Jessica, now fourteen months old, emerges a young lady. She runs, her high-top shoes pattering across the linoleum floor. She still wrinkles her nose when she smiles, her eyes big as those sentimental paintings of children with little mouths and huge foreheads, done in pastel colors. I bathe her, touch the damp curls on her nape. What treasure could be greater than damp curls, alive with sparks when brushed, softer between my fingers than gold, transitory? I dress her in blue overalls and a blue-flowered turtleneck, pull on her lacy socks and high-top shoes, tying the laces into double bows.

That little boy's mother must have bathed him and dressed him that morning. Perhaps she rushed, thinking what an active boy he'd been the night before, getting into the cupboards and pulling out all the pots and pans.

As she reached for his blue shirt and buttoned it, she glanced at his crowded room, thought of all the things they'd collected for him: clothes and shoes (constantly exchanged for bigger ones), stuffed animals, miniature trucks, bed, dresser, books....As she touched his cheek, she must have thought of all the times before his birth that she and his father shopped and visited doctors and painted the room sky blue and waited and waited....She remembered what it was like to hold his unborn body in hers, feel it grow, nurtured by her own blood and later by her milk. She combed back his blondish curls as he squirmed and whined, ready to run into the day. She kissed him.

A shopping day at the mall, like any other. She pulled his puffy coat over his arms, arranged the hood, glanced into his blue eyes. In a hurry to meet her sister-in-law, she didn't think much about the soul that hid behind the two-year-old irises.

A happy day outside, people about, store windows full of things to see but not touch. The little boy tred beside his mother, she holding his hand, keeping him from the many temptations. At the butcher's shop the crowd pressed around the two of them. The mother turned to answer the butcher's question. The toddler saw his chance to explore, to be a big boy, to touch the forbidden. He squirmed his fingers out of his mother's. She, still talking to the butcher and clutching her handbag, did not notice at first the absence of one small hand in her palm.

When she turned around to look for him, he was gone.

How did she feel in those first hopeful, frantic moments? She searched the butcher's shop first, then out into the mall. Her sister-in-law helped, hampered by her own toddler. Was the mother embarrassed to ask a security guard for help, hoping to find her child soon anyway, feeling foolish for letting him go?

As she swept through the Mothercare maternity shop and the Boots pharmacy, scanning row after row of merchandise, did panic begin welling in her chest like the day she went into labor, not knowing what to expect, not knowing if he would be born whole and alive?

Did she know she would not see him alive again? Did she, somehow, know? Later that night, after searching the area thoroughly, police and friends alike, the mother and father appeared on television and pleaded for their son's return. Her long hair, curly at the ends, framed her puffy-eyed face. *He's only two,* she begged, *he needs his mother.*

And so he did. When the two ten-year-old boys, who planned ahead to catch a child, lay in wait outside the butcher shop, Jamie needed his mother. When they lured him away with promises of sweets and toys (and perhaps even that they'd take him to his mother), he needed her to rip their hands from him and carry him away.

But she couldn't come. She couldn't hear. The only ears that heard ignored and mocked the child's cries.

What did the two-year-old who had known only love and happiness and careful nestling in his mother's arms, beside her curved breast, in his father's sturdy hands, beside the firm chest, what did he see and feel those last hours of his life?

Who could have prepared him, made him understand why Mommy couldn't hear or come or stop the terror and the pain?

Where were the angels when the two bullies grabbed him roughly by his arms and swung him toward the rush-hour traffic and hit him on his forehead, causing a bruise that made several witnesses notice but not stop the abusive boys?

They dragged him to the canal to drown him, but Jamie, tenacious of life, wouldn't fall in. They dragged him toward their own run-down, overcrowded welfare neighborhood, where their dysfunctional, absent-father families huddled in neglect, abuse, molestation, whatever. By this time Jamie suffered several bruises on his face, and sobbed. Perhaps he wet his pants. Perhaps he wanted a drink of water. Most of all, he wanted to go home.

Two women accosted the trio and demanded what the boys were doing with Jamie. They said they had found him and were taking him to the police. Another woman, the last adult to see him alive, stood outside her flat with her seven-year-old daughter. The daughter knew what the boys intended. She saw it in their eyes. She grabbed Jamie away from them. Did he cling to her thin arms?

The mother, perhaps too busy to be bothered, with the roast cooking and the baby crying from inside, believed the boys' story and gave Jamie back to them.

What did her daughter do? She watched him being dragged away, her eyes still like deep water.

The kidnappers forced him through an alley near their own homes, to the railroad track. There, for fifteen minutes of torture few adults ever suffered in this world's long history, the two boys threw housebricks at Jamie's face and head. Jamie kept getting back up. He wouldn't stay down. Perhaps he knew, if he did, he would never see his mother again, not in this world.

How could the boys rip open the soft white skin of a baby? How could they let the innocent blood spatter on their trousers and shoes? How could they keep hitting him, until finally, grown impatient, one picked up a heavy metal rod and shattered James Bulger's tiny skull?

And what did Jamie know those last few moments? Did he feel, instead of cold bricks under his bare feet, his father's leather shoe he used to tromp around the house in, trying to be big? Did he dream, half conscious, of his mother's smell (sweet, like milk), hear her heartbeat, as when they laid him, newborn, on her stomach to nurse? Did he taste her milk instead of blood in his mouth? Did he see her eyes, the first eyes he saw that moment after birth, instead of the murderers', blurry and dark?

I imagine angels there, toward the end, when Jamie must have swooned from too much pain and fear and too long crying with no answer. I imagine them waiting nearby, their invisible wings folded, otherworldly, silent. When at last Jamie fled from his captors, when at last they could hurt him no more, the angels must have gathered his soul from the violated body, like a mother scoops milk from a fractured earthen cup.

They whisked him away to where we all hope the clouds and the sky and the sun and the stars sing together, beyond time and pain. This the angels did while the murderers placed the half-nude body on the railroad tracks, where a passing train sliced it in two.

Someone reported, after the long, agonizing, sleepless mother's night, a body found by the railroad tracks. Police gathered there. They erected a shield, like a giant white balloon, over the cracked remains. No one could see, then, the abomination, the small symbol of where we as humans have arrived.

Jamie was buried in a white casket with brass rings and handles. The entire English town, in black, mourned him, especially the witnesses who might have rescued him: the tentative onlookers at the mall, the scores of pedestrians and commuters, the neighbors, the seven-year-old girl and her mother. People cried in the streets and placed bouquets of flowers beside the railroad tracks. And Jamie's mother mourned too, feeling the great loss like her uterus ripped out, remembering again the tiny web of tissues that once grew inside her body and her dreams about the child to be and his long, happy life, and how she would nurse and feed and bathe and dress and hold and kiss him when he fell and hit his head.

The police found the boys. The boys confessed. Mobs screamed outside the courthouse during the trial. The boys were found guilty. Then the world paused: people in churches, supermarkets, schools, living rooms, bars, streetcorners—even Presidents shook their heads and commented on the crime.

Jamie's mother will have another baby in a few weeks. Does Jamie's room wait for the new child? Did his mother keep the bears, the trucks, the building blocks, the bed and bedspread, the clothes and shoes and books? Will she paint the room a different color—green, perhaps, or pink? Whatever she does, she won't make that one forgivable and understandable and every-parent's-worst-fear mistake again, that let the murderers scoop Jamie away.

I took Jesse to the mall last night. She wore her green coat over her overalls, and over that the pink harness with its embroidered bear, Velcro ties, and leash connected firmly to my wrist. Her chubby legs propelled her past the Christmas-decorated windows. She looked up at the lights until she nearly fell backwards, her mouth one rounded "AAAH!" People almost bumped into her. People stared at the harness, perhaps thinking it cruel. One elderly lady remarked to another, "She's got the right idea."

I walked past two ten-year-old boys in baseball caps and Dodgers jackets, who sat on a bench outside a department store. I looked into their eyes and wondered.

The Fault

Sondra Zeidenstein

for Laura and Susan

These two women, lovers,
mothers of newborn
Julian
split the earth
along its fault:

those who trust
that love
surely
as the rush
of milk
will nourish;

and those who'd
narrow
to the sanctioned
jet of semen
who would be allowed
to bear a child.

These two women lovers
drive a canyon
deep as Susan
witching her love

when labor slowed
in the terrible night
with tales
of how the moon

draws down the tides
draws down;

wide as Laura
on her hands and knees
opening.

These two women
draw the line

firm as the memory
of curls
in Laura's sweated hair

unambiguous
as Julian's
crimson cry

sure as the fit
of lips to nipple.

Let skeptics
wriggle
in discomfort—

the blessed
hold up a flower
and smile.

Small Things

Sarah Willis

She thinks without ever hearing the words. They go directly into muscle and motion and she would deny the thoughts if challenged. She stops taking the pill because the box gets thrown into the garbage, buried under wet Kleenex. The apartment is quiet and no one is there to say, Didn't you forget? The apartment needs a baby anyway. There are only so many furniture arrangements to be made to change the mood. Something drastic is needed. The pills in the garbage get carried out and put on the curb Sunday night. She is twenty-four and the bag is not heavy as she walks down the three flights of metal steps.

She sleeps with a man she met two months ago at the beauty shop. A salon for men and women. She cut his curly black hair and they just took up. They go dancing at the Euclid Tavern, see some movies. He doesn't seem too serious, but the sex is good, and he keeps calling. Recently she has gotten edgy when he leaves, always before midnight. She wishes he would stay the night, but the words aren't there and she doesn't ask.

She is pregnant. She imagines the baby shower at the shop. She has never really had a party given for her since she was six and she thinks about this a lot. The way she will smile and acknowledge each gift. She pictures them wrapped like candy with pink rattles attached to bright bows. She smiles and thinks it will be fun. She has not told anyone yet. It is too early.

A weak indigestion troubles her and she burps, dismissing the uneasy feeling with a loud belch. She wants to feel the baby move. At fourteen weeks she gets impatient, reading a book that states: "The feeling of movement may begin at the end of the first trimester." She feels a contact with the written word when they prove right, soon after, and she reads more. With a fascination that distorts time, she studies the pictures of a fetus growing, its enormous head, the development of arms and legs from the tadpole shape of a curled alien. She can't take her eyes off the translucent skin, the pale beginnings of eyes, nose, mouth. Emotion gets stuck in her throat and she blinks back the feeling of being overwhelmed by something she can't name, something she doesn't quite understand.

She doesn't tell the father of the baby until her stomach starts to protrude, until all discussions of whether to have the baby or not would be useless. Not that she wants to trick him, but that having the knowledge that she's pregnant; no one else knowing, feels so fine, like a prize. A light smile never leaves her face. She is silent also because she is afraid, somewhere, lurking inside, is the idea that something might go wrong. To mention her pregnancy might jinx the baby. The books mention how many things might go wrong. Those parts, that she reads without wanting to, are the thoughts she goes to sleep with. But in the day, in the light, she places her palm on her stomach and smiles.

When she tells him, in bed, just before midnight, he gets mad, flustered, hops out of bed and gets dressed; as if protecting himself. He paces, slapping the top of her bureau to add emphasis to his words. "How could you?" Thump. "What were you thinking?" Thump. "God, I'm sorry, but . . ." Thump. "I gotta go now. I gotta think." Thump.

She shakes her head to keep the tears back. Her teeth tighten against each other until her jaw aches. Then she thinks, this is just how men react. They're afraid of small things, delicate things. He'll come back. And she'll tell him she'll take care of the baby. She wants to. Not to worry. Men are too afraid to think about the future. As she drifts off into sleep, a thought slips by, has she thought about the future? She dreams of kittens, they are soft, small, climbing over each other while a mother kitten lies on her side. One by one people come into the room, a pink, brightly decorated bedroom, and take the kittens until there are none left. She can't see herself in the dream, but she can hear sobs and she wakes crying.

The father of the baby says he is not sure what to do. She calls him often. She doesn't bring up marriage, but suggests his moving in. Or her moving in with him. It will save money, she says. His place is nicer, more modern, with large windows. She thinks about what she could do with all that space. But he never commits, just listens silently, visits less often. Sometimes they argue over whether to go out for a pizza or call in; how stupid a movie was that she liked; a cut she got at the salon he thinks makes her face look wide. Often they don't talk at all. They watch TV. They have sex. He leaves by midnight. Still, she is sure when he sees the baby he will change. She turns off worries like an alarm clock, setting it for another time.

She is six months pregnant and loves the attention she gets at work. It is exactly as she expected. She buys some new clothes. People tell her labor stories and give her recipes for homemade baby foods. She reads about bottle versus breast-feeding and settles on bottles. All of a sudden she notices other women who have round stomachs, healthy skin. She thinks they notice her too.

Her mother and father give her advice, yell, then take her to dinner and press twenties into her hand. In the past they have left her pretty much alone, it is a large family, nine other children, and they believe in living your own life, suffering your consequences. Her mother gives her an ad for cribs and tells her this is a sale she cannot afford to miss. The apartment fills up with new and used baby items. Disney takes over and Mickey smiles from pictures on the walls, a Donald Duck lamp she found at the thrift shop plays some unknown tune.

The shower is held on the small parched lawn in back of the beauty shop. They sit on a patchwork quilt the owner has brought in, with a basket of geraniums in the middle. It is a beautiful June day and the sky couldn't be bluer. She feels blessed, a feeling of rightness, a feeling of being special. The girls she works with rub her stomach for good luck, amazed at the hardness. She imagines dressing the baby, sure that it's a girl. Sometimes the baby kicks her pelvic bone and she thinks it must be ready. Every now and then she gets queasy and food looks alive. It's not at all like the light nausea of the first three months; it's hard and definite and she can't turn it off.

The boy, for he really wasn't a man yet, decides to go back to college in Denver, a long way from Cleveland. His parents live out west. She never learned where. He gives her five hundred dollars and leaves no forwarding address. He says he will stay in touch but just can't be responsible.

She goes into labor and the girls at work get jumpy and excited. The labor starts off very slow and she thinks it's not too bad. She finishes the hair cut she is giving, not rushing, proud she can do this. She will be the talk of the shop for finishing this cut. The client gives her an extra big tip, tells her to tell her husband he is one lucky guy. After eighteen hours she is in the hospital attached to a monitor, a blood pressure cuff, an epidural in her spine, her feet in stirrups. She feels like Christ on the cross, her sweat the blood from the thorns. Her screams have a meanness she hasn't felt in a long time. She pushes for over two hours and swears at the nurse, God damn it, get it out of me!

The baby is a boy, seven pounds, eight ounces, and everyone looks at him and smiles. She is exhausted and faints when the baby is placed on her chest after being washed and wrapped. They make her leave the hospital the next day, she only has insurance for forty-eight hours. She wants to stay.

Everyone visits her at her apartment. Her parents can't put the baby down. The girls from work giggle. She finds it all very annoying the way they all talk as if she weren't there at all, as if the baby glowed. The place feels crowded and too busy, but she can't ask them to leave. This is what she had wanted, this attention, and she should have it. When she is alone the baby cries and she tries to get the nipple of the bottle in his mouth at the right angle so he can really clamp onto it. Drink, she thinks, drink a lot and then take a nap. She thinks about going back to work.

She goes on welfare. It's a hassle, especially taking the baby with her, filling out forms, standing in line. And then there's food stamps. Another place to go. But it is the only way she can make it right now. It's temporary and she needs it. She'll go back to work as soon as she can. Right now, just going to the laundromat is a big trip. But when she gets there, people always talk to her, to the baby. It's not so bad.

When the baby is a little over two months old she sees this *is* like a job, but more so. She's responsible day and night, over and over again, deciding herself what must be done. A satisfaction comes in the walking, the burping, the dressing, the feeding, the bathing, the murmuring. His lashes are so long and thick and innocent. She sees herself reflected in the shine of his eyes and wills her reflection to be confident, sure. Sometimes she is afraid this new found picture of herself is only a fragile mask, a false mask. Other times, even the trying times when a bath won't soothe his cries, she believes hard enough and he smiles. Still, some days the apartment feels like a trap and he is her foot.

In December, right before Christmas, he rolls over and falls off the couch. She wasn't watching, but she hears a thud. There is silence, a time no one breathes, and then a shriek and a wail. It was such a short fall, she thinks. Nothing could be wrong. But with these thoughts comes a deadness in her stomach, a knowledge of the fact she could never eat again if he is hurt. She doesn't run to the couch, her body moves slow, allowing her time to think. She picks him up and smiles. "Sorry, Honey, it's OK. You're fine." But he yells louder. She rubs her hands down his head, there are no bumps.

She rubs his arms. When she touches his left arm, the scream is louder and her heart stops. There is a small voice in her that is mad at him, sees this as unfair, the weather is terrible, she hates the hospital, but the louder voice is thinking; I can't put a coat on him, I'd have to move his arm, I'll wrap him in some blankets, Please God, let him be fine.

She walks down the frozen steps like a two year old, both feet firmly planted before the next step. Her mind replays the last fifteen minutes with an intensity she can't control. She drives carefully, but misses the emergency entrance and wants to cry. Finally she is inside and notices the baby has fallen asleep. She tells the receptionists her story, begging them with her eyes to move quickly. They tell her to sit down and wait and then she does cry, very quietly. She looks at his forehead, almost all that is showing through the blue blanket, and whispers. "Everything will be fine." In the end, she is told he has dislocated his shoulder, a common problem, easily taken care of, really no problem. "You just have to watch them very closely, when they start moving around, all sorts of things can happen." She starts to cry again, her eyes filling. I'm scared, she thinks.

The baby is five months old and her parents have gone to Florida for the winter. The girls come sometimes on Mondays when the shop closes at three. Sometimes they say the streets are too icy.

She plays bicycle with his legs and sit-up games she has read about in a baby book. She talks to him, hearing her own words, telling him things he can't possible understand, but that finally, she can. She tells him how much she loves him, but he's a lot of work; how they are stuck together, but that's good too. She tells him when Grandma and Grampa come back she might ask them to watch him. Maybe she could go back to college. Maybe just back to work. She lives with the words she hears and they stick in her head and go around and around, building, shaping. A thought will keep her up at night.

As she goes to bed, she remembers to put a pot of water on the stove, so heating up the bottle won't take so long in the cold of the night. She thinks about waking up, how she will bring the baby into her bed for the warmth and comfort of his body. She decides they will get all wrapped up tomorrow and go out.

The Christmas Ritual

Susan Clayton-Goldner

Alone at the grave, she wipes
leafy snow from her son's name,
pulls a pine along the birch-lined path
to a wooden stand planted in snow.
She leans forward touching these ornaments—
winter scenes worn smooth
from outdoor hangings,
reindeer without legs,
and a smudged-eyed Santa with half a beard.

Under the green, weighted branches
in a place more quiet than breath,
her first child
looks into whatever he was before life.

The snow falls
on the back of her hand.
She closes her pliers
tightens each wire's grip,
studies the globes,
one by one, holds them
in the palms of her hands
like a baby's face
the face of another son
waiting at the window
for his mother to be born or
like her own face,
the face of my sister,
now very far from herself,
held briefly in shadow
against the white birch.

from 7 Folk Songs with Refrains

Vainis Alexsa

2.
the woman bites
down but it is said she
doesn't. it is said
she sounds like wolves
and the men see it's true.
      the men see it's true.

3.
one night there will
be lights in the trees
and the wolves will sound
like babies.
a manchild
will be born
without pain.
the news will travel
west in stories, east
in figurines, south down
through the amber routes,
a drab and mean-
spirited people have
become the sanctuary
of new
grace
          the sanctuary
of new
grace

7.
the midwife shuts
the window. men
tonight you lose
a mother or a manchild.
the woman hears
a wolf, *a* vilkas,
a welq.
apollo
takes it
as a tribute
to his mom singing,
"if this boy
lives, he will rise
above the squalor
of the town
bringing peace.
but if he dies
it's no skin off
my teeth."
so he takes
the manchild
to heaven
and in return
relieves
the woman's burden.
the rites of birth
are left intact
and the child born
is not a manchild
but a child nevertheless
wiped
and laid upon
the woman's breast.
hush
the woman says
to echo leto's
wolf*howl,*

hush

Black Bear Eating Salmon

George Keithley

Every morning for twelve days the huge black bear has plodded this same path down to the river. It's her path, made by her coming and going each day with the three cubs trailing behind her. All along her route you can see where the leafy brush has been broken by her shuffling bulk, and where overhanging leaves and the tender bark have been stripped from the low trees and the long grasses have been flattened underfoot.

Again this morning she stops. She rises on her broad hind-legs and with her forepaws she strips leaves from the scrub trees beside her path. She eats a few of the leaves, then lets others fall to the ground where her cubs chew them, drop them, pad around as they search to find them, and at last discover the mashed leaves in the grass where their paws have trampled them. Their mother, meantime, has been eating more leaves, dropping more. She lurches on and the cubs amble after her, roaming into the high grass but quickly returning, falling into place behind her. She stops abruptly. She rises up to rake the trunk of a tree, shredding its bark, and the cubs bound around her feet, gathering the tender scraps into their mouths.

Now the great sow breaks into a purposeful, jogging pace while the cubs scramble along. Finally, where the path of the bears reaches the river-bank, the ground has been drubbed into mud by the mother's previous visits and sedge grass lies matted in the embankment.

She wades into the river, the cubs tumbling in behind her. They make no effort to conceal their entry into the river from the salmon or the smaller fish; the bears clamber into the current, splashing, roiling the water. While her cubs flop in the shallows the mother nudges herself upstream. The long blue river flows steadily down from the mountains, and the salmon, which have swum up to spawn, hang in the water now, lethargic, exhausted by their effort. The sow spoons a salmon up to the surface and presses it to her chest, but as she rises the fish slips free. She falls back into the current, sways a little to one side, and swoops up a second salmon nearly as large as the first one. For a moment it floats motionless on the surface. She paws at it, then with her mouth she plucks the fish from the water. Quickly she rises, and her paws press its tail to her chest as her mouth closes over the salmon's head. As she eats, bits of the fish fall into the current, where they're swept along, but the cubs show no interest in these scraps.

She gnaws the fish, rakes it with her claws, shoves it farther into her mouth. The cubs claw back up the slick bank and browse through the grass and brush, snapping at leaves, until they reach the base of the nearest tree, where they begin to rake the trunk with their claws. It's a tree they've worked before, their slash marks are on the trunk, below their mother's, and they quickly nibble what nourishment they can tear loose from the bark. The huge mother stands in the shallows, watching her cubs, while her mouth works over the last of the salmon still lodged between her jaws, as pale shreds of the fish fall into the water.

The river sweeps through a meadow flanked by steep slopes covered with pines, and eleven miles farther it passes under an old steel trestle. Parents who've pulled their trucks and vans off the road stand along the river-bank, casting their lines into the current. Smoking his pipe, a man reels in his line to cast again. A woman kneels to stub out her cigarette in the bare bank. Their children climb the roadbed and walk out on the bridge to peer at the salmon that have slipped this far downstream, the large fish lying sluggish in the water below. Over the trestle the narrow mountain road swings southwest until it joins the highway, which runs a winding route for another twenty miles, dropping down into Weaverville, with its bait stores, coffee shop, tavern, bakery, and an authentic Western museum.

Child Has No Say

Ellen Goodman

It's just about over now. The legal moving papers are in order. The change of parental address has been determined. The child has been told.

The very last ditch effort to delay the process that will turn Jessica DeBoer into Anna Schmidt was referred Wednesday to the full Supreme Court by Justice Blackmun after a dramatic appeal claiming that she would suffer "unimaginable harm." But if that fails, the only thing left will be the packing.

By Monday in all likelihood, a two-year-old girl will be transferred from her adoptive family to her biological family, from the people who raised her to the people who conceived her, from those she loves to those she doesn't even know. She'll be moved from Michigan to Iowa like a piece of furniture awarded in a property dispute. Only furniture doesn't feel loss or confusion.

For all the emotion surrounding it, this never was an easy case. In February 1991, an unmarried woman and the man she claimed to be the father gave a baby up for adoption. Weeks later, this despairing and regretful Cara Clausen told the biological father, Dan Schmidt, the truth. He decided to go after the girl and the adoptive parents decided to fight back.

The human story behind the case forced many to think about nature and nurture, about the rights of parents and the best interests of children. In the end, many were shocked at how little the child's view counted in the eyes of blind justice.

When Jessica DeBoer becomes Anna Schmidt, the people most deeply affected will be the host of maybe, would-be, might-be adoptive parents all over the country. They will be touched by another fear about adopting children they want to call their own.

What this case raises, after all, is the specter that in some places, in some circumstances, any biological parent who hasn't given up his rights can come in from the cold to claim a child.

In a most bizarre Florida case, two biological parents have pursued their daughter who was switched at birth. Since discovering the switch five years ago, a distraught Regina and Ernest Twigg, who raised the other child until her death, have virtually stalked Kimberly Mays. Now the 14-year-old is going to court to try and "divorce" the Twiggs on the very same day Jessica becomes Anna.

But the much more common, everyday, garden-variety fear is of the unknown father. After all, most birth mothers who give children up for adoption either don't know or won't tell who the father is.

She may not want him to know; he may not want to know. Dan Schmidt himself had fathered two earlier children. One he'd abandoned, one he'd never seen. Though he worked with Cara all through her pregnancy, he never asked if the child was his.

In real life rather than courtroom dramas, unwed or unknown fathers are rarely anxious for custody or even for identification. Paternity suits are, on the whole, filed by women pursuing men.

But in the law these days, equal rights have sometimes streaked ahead of equal responsibility. We share a powerful cultural desire to promote fatherhood, to nurture the nurturing men. In some places, the law has become too willing to distribute the full rights of fatherhood, even to men who contributed only genes and the labor of lovemaking.

The appearance of a man like Schmidt to stop an adoption and reclaim a child is rare indeed. But there is the real risk that his victory could become another barrier to would-be adoptive parents, to adoption itself.

In the wake of this case, clusters of proposals are being considered for a new and uniform law that would strike a balance between the rights of fathers and the needs of children to be placed in caring, permanent homes as soon as possible.

In some, a known father's rights would hinge on how early he came forward and how willing he was to raise a child, not just to prevent adoption. In others, the rights of unknown, even unknowing fathers, would be terminated at some point—perhaps 30 days—so a child could become part of a family.

With luck we may yet learn from this terrible story. We may learn that the current law cares too much about biological ties and not enough about caring relationships. That it cares too much about parents' rights and not enough about children. That childhood is painfully short and the law is brutally sluggish.

But for the moment we only know this: Two years ago, an infant went before the courts; now the law has sent a toddler packing. They call this justice. I wonder what Jessica—or, should I say, Anna—will call it.

After-Shock

J. B. Bernstein

The five year old girl/child remembers when she was born, remembers when the doctor scooped her out of her mama's slippery, bloody, oozing sac after cutting through layers and layers of muscle, elastic, shiny like a pink balloon, slicing away until her little body rose from all the fluid and popped into the icy cold white air waiting to be protected from her future. She remembers being early, fighting to stay inside, ensconced in warmth and softness like floating in the midst of a cumulus cloud, listening to muffled symphonies. Then her surroundings began to thunder and shove her with the force of Thor, shove her from side to side until her home for eight months slit open and she was snatched and poked and pulled and wiped and dried and wrapped and finally she felt warm again in the glass rectangled manger, snow white clean, warmed by lamps from heaven, the glow seeping through, too bright for her mucous layered eyes.

But the storm wasn't over, as she had thought. It had just begun. Soon, something strange attacked her four pound body and no matter how she tried, she couldn't stop it. She wanted something so badly that it made her want to kill for it. She began to shake and sweat and beat her little hands against the sheets until someone came and eyedropped paregoric on her tongue and she sighed and smiled to herself and finally went to sleep. And the next day it was the same and the next day it was the same and the next day it was the same. For weeks it was the same. Less each day, but still the same. And the girl/baby wanted her mama to stop it. And it finally stopped. And she went home with her mama who tried, really tried to be a good mama, changed her diapers, fed her when she was hungry, rocked her when she cried, but all the time, a voice kept calling her mama: come back, come back to freedom, to never-never land where there is no ache no pain no love no hate no work no give no take no trial no error no think no feel. And her mama couldn't stop the voice, gave into the voice, at first just a little, a few drinks here, a few drinks there, a pill here, a pill there, then a needle here a needle there, and the girl/baby grew into a girl/child while her mama didn't grow at all.

As time went by, the girl/child found out more and more about her mama, found out that Mama was sick, sick enough to die, that's what Mama said, she said: I have AIDS and I am going to die and I want you to know this and we are going to talk about this a lot so that you won't be surprised so you will be prepared so there will be no secrets between us and I will always tell you the truth the whole truth nothing but the truth so help me God. And the girl/child remembers, after this shot of truth serum, that her mama never let up, shot the truth into the girl/child as often as she could. And soon the mama decided it was time for *her* mother to fess up, deliver her from evil because her mother had trespassed against her and she did not forgive those who trespassed against her. And so the mama began writing letters to *her* mother. And the girl/child remembers when she would walk into the room and find her mama writing voraciously, devouring the paper with her pen, feeding her ravenous appetite like a petulant child anchored in a thick black liquid of sublime intention:

I was doing some thinking today and some talking and something came up that may help you understand what I am saying about communication or lack of it, that if you choose not to communicate with me, how can you possibly do my child justice when she wants communication and don't you think this child will have questions why you chose not to see her, see her mama for five years, so what will you say to that, will it be: never mind, girl/child, let's take it from here...or will it be your famous response: your mama used drugs, stuck needles in her arms, legs, face, neck...well, I hope you've let that one go, I woke up to that one five years ago, this is not the place to discuss this but I was drug-free for four years before the girl/child was born and two years after that, well, except for my daily dose of methadone, and fiorinal for my headaches, and pot sometimes to relax, and once in a while some other stuff at parties, and oh yes, that time I got drunk and the cops called you to take the child home so she wouldn't be sent to the State Home, so I just believe that until you can talk about what is, or was, really, I wonder if you really know within your own self, and until you do, how can I trust you with my own child and I don't know your real whys, why you shut me out, why you shut my child out, this all needs talk, I want to sit you down and tell you how you ruined my life how you stifled me when you finally said *no* how everything you did hurt me how you never *really* cared how unmotherly you were how you always always, never never, I need to have you sit before me so I can let you have it so I can feel better, if you will not open this up to me, then I see that I can't trust you to do this with my child when she needs it, yes, I needed it all my life and never got it, you abandoned me and never returned, I don't know who lives in your world, I don't know you, you don't want to deal with the past but you can't dismiss it anymore and you can't say anymore that you want us to start with today or you can't deal with me anymore when I use drugs, do you realize how easy it would have been for me to have forgiven you, forgiven you for being human, forgiven you for making mistakes, forgiven you for trying too hard, forgiven you for giving me my way, forgiven you for not saying no, forgiven you if you had only asked, so that's the way it is, if you do this to me, you do it to my child and I know how it feels, it feels awful. NO. You owe me the respect to talk. Otherwise—good-bye.

The girl/child remembers her mama seemed relieved after writing letters. Mama wrote letters to everybody: her brother, her brother's wife, her step-father, letters about her mother and how bad her mother was and how the only thing she wanted was to have her mother sit quiet and defend herself and communicate. But when her mama received letters, it was different. Mama didn't like *getting* letters from her mother: I remember when you were two years old I took you to a birthday party and you waved frantically to the hostess saying you wanted to sing a song, and I remember taking you to the zoo and out for Chinese food and reading stories every night before bedtime, and when you were older laughing raucously over something silly at the kitchen table, tears streaming down our faces, I remember seeing you at 7:30 AM combing your hair in front of the mirror before going off to school, and seeing you at 7:40 AM toppling off the kitchen chair, I remember chasing you around the house to keep you from stepping into the danger zone and you with the strength of Wonder Woman flinging the dining room table at my feet, and I remember getting a call from a hospital that you had overdosed on Metro North and some doctor had breathed you all the way to St. Vincent's, I remember you coming home after weeks on the streets and deciding to go to nursing school and you did, and going to your graduation praying this would be a new beginning, but it wasn't, and I remember wishing hoping wanting you to have everything I didn't have, but knowing I had gone about it all wrong, and I remember painting your new apartment white, the whitest white I'd ever seen, the white of angels' wings, hoping you would overdose on its purity, and I will never forget sitting at a huge oval oak table festooned with nursing commandants begging them to save your soul because I had screwed up fucked up given up grown up too late too late and I remember eight years ago I said a simple no and meant it, really meant it and wondered what I had to do to redeem myself and decided that if you could not stop blaming me for your entire universe, I needed to get out, and you wrote me that if only I had asked you to forgive me, forgive me for not saving you forgive me for not knowing how to be a good mother as my mother did not know how to be a good mother as her mother did not know how to be a good mother.

The girl/child is almost six years old. Sometimes, her blue eyes are wild, remembering the roller coaster ride, the carousel, wisps of fine hair blowing in the icicled air like the mane of a pony in full stride, her jaw slightly jutted. Sometimes she looks as though she can't find a comfortable place to sit, darting from one place to another, laughing to herself, moving moving moving like a puppy weaned too soon searching for its mama's teat. And sometimes, when no one is looking, the girl/child spreads her translucent wings, steps off the merry-go-round and flies away, and for the first time, feels free.

Breast Feeding

Neil Carpathios

Honey scent of his wife's nipple
her nostrils zero in on
like a hound's. Her tiny mouth
clamps on and gulps.
But it is the eyes,
the way they meet,
mother's, daughter's,
dancing to music only they
can hear. He spies,
looking up from a book,
jealous, for he can never have
what's theirs. She grunts a little,
swallowing too much.
His wife whispers something tender.
He pretends to read.

Sweet milk taste,
silent music.

Father, *he thinks to himself,* Father,
he tries out the word. As if
he were the child. Learning a new sound
for the first time.

The Last Wild Horses in Tennessee

Vivien Shipley

In separateness only does love learn definition
                    —Robert Penn Warren, "Revelation"

We stand at the crossing, children
circle us looking steady and hard
but all were mothered by women.
I want to shrink a pasture for Eric
who has less meat and hair than others.
Without immunity into January mornings
so cold the milk jug freezes
and cracks on the doorstep,
I will force his snowsuited body out,
boots scaling snow to track his map.
If there were a message or sign to send
but no one knows anything.

He strains to see beyond the point
of the corner. I pull him back.
Perhaps he will not ride the whole road.
Boarding the bus, he turns
on the landing and I reach
out to touch his shoulder.
Still, I stand remembering his hands
hanging limp as morning wet grass,
green, a color I had forgotten.
My finger ends dead, tighten over
me at six years: cowbarn,
outhouse, backdoor, cornbread,
woodpile, chickenhouse. I had

a plow horse to ride, no big
yellow bus. Before I rode
away, my father told me about
the last wild horses in Tennessee.
Scoured out of hills, they
were roped, tied down, nostrils
shut with clamps. Veins
in their necks pulsed like salmon
jumping upstream. The mares
all aborted; I know beyond
that word. Blinded, I bow my head,
cup my stomach and give him up,
willing that he wake small again
and again at each stop.

The Envelope

Maxine Kumin

It is true, Martin Heidegger, as you have written,
I fear to cease, *even knowing that at the hour*
of my death my daughters will absorb me, even
knowing they will carry me about forever
inside them, an arrested fetus, even as I carry
the ghost of my mother under my navel, a nervy
little androgynous person, a miracle
folded in lotus position.

Like those old pear-shaped Russian dolls that open
at the middle to reveal another and another, down
to the pea-sized, irreducible minim,
may we carry our mothers forth in our bellies.
May we, borne onward by our daughters, ride
in the Envelope of Almost-Infinity,
that chain letter good for the next twenty-five
thousand days of their lives.

About the Editors and Contributors

Vainis Alexsa of Chicago is parenting two children, teaching freshman English, and writing her dissertation on the little magazine.

Maya Angelou is the Reynolds Professor at Wake Forest University. She has published five poetry collections. She read her poem "On the Pulse of the Morning" for President Clinton's inauguration.

Margaret Atwood has published over twenty books, including novels, short story collections, poetry, and literary criticism. She lives in Toronto with Graeme Gibson and their daughter, Jess.

Tom Baer of Florida is a poet/playwright whose series of four theater pieces, "Trojan Horse and other Conundrums" was produced in Denver. His poem "$54 t'Atlanta" has been made into a broadside.

T. J. Banks of Avon, Conn., is the editor of the Animal Friends of Connecticut newsletter. Her work has been published and anthologized extensively.

J. B. Bernstein's work appears in many journals, including *Kalliope, A Journal of Women's Art, Furious Fictions,* and *Negative Capability.* She teaches part time at a community college in New Haven, Conn.

Robert Bly is a poet, storyteller, translator, and worldwide lecturer. His poetry has won many awards, including the National Book Award. He lives with his wife, Ruth, on a lake in Minnesota.

Gayle Brandeis of Riverside, Calif., is collecting writing and art from children around the world on the subject of liberty for an upcoming anthology.

Harry Brody is a poet/lawyer from Sarasota, Fla. A 1993 Robert Frost Fellow at the Bread Loaf Writer's Conference, his most recent book is *For We Are Constructing The Dwelling of Feeling.*

Gwendolyn Brooks was awarded a Pulitzer Prize for her second book of poems and two Guggenheim Fellowships. In 1969, she was named Poet Laureate of Illinois.

Neil Carpathios teaches high school English in Ohio. His book of essays and poems on fatherhood and child-raising is entitled *I The Father*.

Em Case was born in Newfoundland and worked as a nurse in Greenland and the U.S. Always interested in her roots, her art and poetry focus on her Newfoundland heritage.

Susan Clayton-Goldner of Williams, Oreg., has been writing novels for the last two years, but poetry remains her first love.

Elayne Clift of Potomac, Md., has published an essay collection, *Telling It Like It Is: Reflections of A Frustrated Feminist*. Her short story collection-in-progress is called *Croning Tales*.

Elizabeth Cohen, whose first book of poems is *Impossible Furniture*, is moving to New Mexico to write a non-fiction book about the first Navajo surgeon.

Esther Cohen lives in Cornwallville, N.Y., with her husband and adopted son, Noah. She teaches writing at Parsons School of Design and is working on her second novel, *Harbinger's Revenge*.

Leo Connellan is poet-in-residence at Connecticut State University. He has published twelve books of poetry, was awarded the Shelley Memorial Award and was nominated for a Pulitzer Prize.

Carol Corda is a native of Connecticut whose multi-disciplined lifestyle inspires her poetry. Her work draws deeply from family and environment and has appeared in several poetry journals.

Robert Creeley is David Gray Professor of Poetry and Letters at the State University of New York at Buffalo. He has published numerous books of poetry, essays, and criticism, including *Windows*.

Jameson Currier of New York City has recently published a collection of short stories, *Dancing on the Moon: Short Stories About AIDS*.

Toi Derricotte is Associate Professor of English at the University of Pittsburgh. Her poetry has been published in *American Poetry Review, Ploughshares*, and *Iowa Review,* among others.

Peter Desy is professor emeritus of English, Ohio University. His poetry collection is entitled *Driving from Columbus*.

Judy Doenges has been writer-in-residence at the Headlands Center for the Arts in Sausalito, Calif. She has published fiction in *Permafrost, Nimrod,* and *Green Mountain Review*.

Karen J. Donnelly lives in Bethany, Conn. Her work has been published in *Earth's Daughters, Women's Work, The World & I,* and others. She is working on a biography of Mary Jane Colter.

Franz Douskey has been published in *The New Yorker, The Nation*, and *Rolling Stone*. His third book of poetry is called *Rolling Across the Dark*. He lives in Hamden, Conn., with his wife and son, Max.

Rita Dove, poet laureate of the United States and professor of English at the University of Virginia, was awarded the Pulitzer Prize in 1987. Her books include *Thomas and Beulah*, and *Grace Notes*.

Hilda Downer of Sugar Grove, N.C., is a psychiatric nurse and teaches English at Appalachian State. Her book of poetry is called *Bandanna Creek*.

Judith A. Downey writes in North Wales, Penna. Her feminist fantasy has been included in *Unrealities, Gotta Write, Up Against the Wall, Mother*, and others.

Andrea Dworkin is a full-time writer and political activist from Brooklyn, N.Y. Her books include *Pornography, Intercourse, Ice & Fire*, and *Letters from a War Zone*.

Jonah Martin Edelman is the son of Marian Wright Edelman, founder and president of the Children's Defense Fund.

Elizabeth Engstrom teaches novel writing at Lane Community College in Oregon. Her upcoming fifth novel is called *Lizard Wine*.

Jackie Fitzpatrick is a staff writer for the *New York Times*.

Jan Frazier was a semi-finalist in the Massachusetts Artists Fellowship competition for poetry. She has work forthcoming in *Calyx, Yankee, Minnesota Review, Negative Capability*, and others.

Margaret Fulton is a psychologist/poet who teaches psychology at St. Mary's College in Minneapolis.

Lisa Gayle, a science teacher from Detroit, is working on a novel about women in auto plants. She and her husband adopted their son, Jacob, when he was two months old.

Ellen Goodman is a widely published syndicated columnist.

John Grey, Australian-born poet/playwright from Providence, R.I., was recently published in the *Wisconsin Review* and *Sequoia*. His plays have been produced in New York and Los Angeles.

Delisa Heiman is a professional artist who owns "Collage Gallery" in San Francisco. She majored in art and literature at University of California–Santa Cruz and wrote and illustrated a children's book.

Kim Hirsh is a freelance writer specializing in women's issues whose work has appeared in the *Chicago Tribune,* the *New York Times, MS.,* and other publications.

Ruth Harriet Jacobs is a continuing Research Scholar at Wellesley College Center for Research on Women. She is the editor of *We Speak for Peace*, a poetry anthology.

Marael Johnson, a travel writer and poet from California, was twice nominated for a Pushcart Prize. Her poetry collections include *Mad Woman On The Loose* and *Mad Woman, Bad Reputation*.

George Keithley lives in Chico, Calif. His sixth book of poetry is called *Earth's Eye*. An epic poem, "The Donner Party," has been adapted as a stage play and an opera.

Maxine Hong Kingston lives in Honolulu with her husband, Earl, and their son Joseph. Her books include *The Woman Warrior* and *China Men*.

Galway Kinnell is State Poet of Vermont and Samuel F. B. Morse Professor of Arts and Science of New York University. His *Selected Poems* won the National Book Award and the Pulitzer Prize in 1982.

Carolyn Kizer has written seven books of poems, including Pulitzer Prize winner, *YIN*. She lives in Sonoma and Paris with her husband John M. Woodbridge.

Maxine Kumin is a Pulitzer Prize winning poet, novelist, and critic. Her books include *In Deep, Halfway, Up Country: Poems of New England*, and *Through Dooms of Love*.

Marisa Labozzetta teaches Italian-American Studies at UMass. Her work has been included in the *Florida Review* and *When I Am An Old Woman I Shall Wear Purple*.

Janice Levy of Merrick, N.Y., has published poetry, short fiction, and juvenile fiction in anthologies and magazines. She was nominated for the 1993 Pushcart Prize.

Alison McGhee teaches writing in Minneapolis. She is currently at work on her third novel.

LaVonne Dressinia McIver of East Orange, N.J., is pursuing an M.A. in public relations at Glassboro State College and compiling *Boundaries*, her first collection of short stories.

Nancy B. Miller is the founder and director of Arts Workshop for Children in North Reading, Mass. Her poetry has appeared in two anthologies.

Judith Minty of New Era, Mich., recently directed the Creative Writing Program at Humboldt State Univ., Arcata, Calif. She has published five books of poetry and received many awards, fellowships, and grants.

Felicia Mitchell teaches Creative Writing and English at Emory & Henry College in Virginia. Her poems have appeared in *Spoon River Quarterly, Galley Sail Review,* and others.

Eliza Monroe is enrolled in the Creative Writing Program at Antioch University. Her stories and novel excerpts have appeared in *Amelia* and *The Widener Review*.

Sarah Morgan lives in Kansas City, Mo. In addition to short stories, she has published poems, book reviews, textbooks, and other non-fiction.

Meg Mott lives in Halifax, Vt., with two other women and a preponderance of animals.

Sharon Olds teaches poetry workshops in the Graduate Creative Writing Program at NYU and at Goldwater Hospital on Roosevelt Island. She won the National Book Critics Circle Award.

Alicia Ostriker, a poet/critic and Professor of English at Rutgers University, has published seven volumes of poetry. Her feminist criticism includes *Writing Like a Woman.*

Gus Pelletier teaches English at SUNY in Delhi, N.Y. His work has appeared in *The Kentucky Poetry Review, Maryland Review,* and *Poet & Critic.*

Nita Penfold has weathered the storms of motherhood with her two daughters and is now playing a young "Nana" to her granddaughters. Her work appears in *Cries of the Spirits* and *Love's Shadow.*

Marge Piercy is the author of ten books of poetry and ten novels. She has also published essays, reviews, and interviews. She and her husband, Ira Wood, live in Wellfleet, Mass.

Sylvia Plath's books include *The Bell Jar, Colossus,* and *Ariel.* Her collected poems, edited by her husband, Ted Hughes, after her death, won a Pulitzer Prize.

Anna Quindlen of New Jersey won a Pulitzer Prize in 1992. Her commentary has been collected in *Living Out Loud* and *Thinking Out Loud.* Her newest novel is called *One True Thing.*

Mary Connor Ralph of West Springfield, Mass., is working on a collection of short stories titled, *Some of the Things That Matter.*

Evelyn Roehl of Seattle is the author of *Whole Food Facts* and former managing editor of the *North Country Anvil* magazine.

Larry Rubin teaches English at Georgia Tech in Atlanta and has published three books of poetry.

C. D. Runyon is currently working on performance projects with Red Sky Poetry Theatre in Seattle. Her poetry manuscript is called *The Houdini of Housewives.*

Larry Schug of Avon, Minn., has published two books of poems, *Scales Out of Balance* and *Caution: Thin Ice,* both with North Star Press.

Joanne Lewis Sears of South Laguna, Calif., is a freelance writer, storyteller, professor of children's literature, film critic, and cookbook reviewer.

Meryl Shader, a freelance writer from Sacramento, Calif., has published numerous articles for a variety of local and national newspapers and a short story in *Kalliope.*

Vivien Shipley is a Professor of English at Southern Connecticut State University. Her latest book of poems is called *Poems out of Harlen County.*

Deborah Shouse of Leawood, Kans., is the co-author of *A Woman's Survival Guide to Business Communications.* Her story, "Diner" was recorded for NPR.

Dusty Sklar of Teaneck, N.J., is the author of *Gods and Beasts: The Nazis and the Occult.*

Rawdon Tomlinson has been published in *Sewanee Review* and *Kansas Quarterly*. The University of Central Florida will publish his first book of poetry. He lives in Denver, Colo.

Frank Van Zant teaches English and coaches three sports in Rockville Centre, N.Y. His work has appeared in *Yankee, Fan Baseball Magazine,* and others. He received a 1993 NEH fellowship.

Linda Vernon is a freelance writer from Newark, Calif. Her essays, which are often about family life, have appeared in *The San Diego Union Tribune, The Fremont Argus,* and others.

Anne Waldman ran the St. Marks Poetry Project in New York for over a decade. She currently directs the Master of Fine Arts Program in Writing and Poetics at the Naropa Institutes in Boulder, Colo.

Sue Walker is a poet and editor of *Negative Capabilities.*

Lonna Lisa Williams teaches English at Mount San Jacinto College in Menifee, Calif. She is married to a fellow college English teacher and writer (who helped her edit her essay).

Sarah Willis of Cleveland, Ohio, is a founding member of the East Side Writer's Group. Her work has been published in *Whiskey Island, No Roses Review,* and *Rockford Review.*

Sondra Zeidenstein operates Chicory Blue Press, a one-woman press. She is currently publishing a series of chapbooks by women past sixty years of age. Her work has appeared in *Taos Review, Embers,* and others.